EGYPT IN AFRICA

EGYPT IN AFRICA

Theodore Celenko, Editor

Indianapolis Museum of Art
in cooperation with
Indiana University Press

First edition

5 4 3 2 1

Library of Congress Cataloging-in-Publication Data

Egypt in Africa / Theodore Celenko, editor.
p. cm.
Includes bibliographical references.
ISBN 0-936260-64-5 (paper)
1. Egypt—Civilization—To 332 B.C.
2. Egypt—Civilization—African influences.
3. Africa—Civilization. I. Celenko, Theodore.
DT61.E328 1996 96-30847
932—dc20

ISBN 0-253-33269-9 (cloth)

Published by the Indianapolis Museum of Art, 1200 West 38th Street, Indianapolis, Indiana 46208. Distributed by Indiana University Press, 601 North Morton Street, Bloomington, Indiana 47404-3797.

Photography of objects from the Indianapolis Museum of Art, private collections, and the CRAFT Research Center by John Geiser and Hadley Fruits.

Designed by Image Concepts Incorporated, Indianapolis, Indiana

Printed by Hilltop Press, Indianapolis, Indiana

On the cover:

(top)
ancient Egyptian people
Saqqara
Egypt (Northeastern Africa)

Pharaoh Pepy II and mother figure
alabaster; h. 15 7/16 in.
Old Kingdom, 6th Dynasty
about 2410-2250 B.C.

Lent by The Brooklyn Museum
Charles Edwin Wilbour Fund
39.119

(bottom)
Nana Osei Bonsu (carver)
Asante people
Ghana (Western Africa)

royal mother and child figure
wood, pigment, gold leaf; h. 17 11/16 in.
1930s

Lent by The Seattle Art Museum
Gift of Katherine White and The Boeing Company
81.17.323

This project is dedicated to Harrison Eiteljorg. For over three decades he has collected sub-Saharan African art and fostered an appreciation of African culture in Indiana by sponsoring exhibitions and publications and by donating works of African art to several of the state's museums and universities. Foremost among his contributions is the major gift of African art that he and Mrs. Eiteljorg gave to the Indianapolis Museum of Art in 1989. He continues to support a greater understanding of Africa through his partial funding of this publication. His efforts have and will continue to enrich the lives of the people of Indiana. This is his legacy.

— *T. C.*

CONTENTS

CONTENTS

CONTENTS

CONTENTS

FOREWORD

Media debate has raged in recent years around a cluster of issues usually lumped together under the convenient but misleading label of "Afrocentrism." One of the issues about which this debate has swirled involves the culture and peoples of ancient Egypt. For Americans of African descent, this has long been a matter of special concern.

Tangible evidence of the enduring importance of ancient Egypt to African Americans is woven into the very fabric of the Walker Theatre in Indianapolis. Built in 1928 as the legacy of African American entrepreneur Madame C. J. Walker, the theater features African design motifs throughout—on exterior walls, interior moldings and cornices, floor tiles, and stair rails. This constellation of pan-African design elements reaches its apogee in the theater's proscenium arch, a rainbow of geometric motifs firmly anchored at either end by a pair of Egyptian sphinxes whose human heads surmounting leonine bodies have dark-skinned faces with Nubian features. The significance of this proud assertion was not lost on generations of black theater patrons who frequented the Walker: Egypt is African!

By contrast, the traditional teaching of world history in this country has wrenched ancient Egypt from its African context and treated it generally as a prologue to the glories of Greece, Rome, and Western Civilization. A glance at almost any college history textbook from the first six or seven decades of this century makes the bias of that approach abundantly clear. The 1969 revised and enlarged edition of H. W. Janson's ***History of Art***, the most widely used introductory text in its field, is a case in point. Sub-Saharan African art is treated summarily (and incongruously) by Janson in a chapter called "Magic and Ritual—The Art of Prehistoric Man." Here, after a breathless sprint from the caves of Altamira to Stonehenge, in a section called "Primitive Art," the reader is introduced to "a few human groups for whom the Old Stone Age lasted until the present day." Among these are "the so-called primitive societies of tropical Africa, the islands of the South Pacific, and the Americas." Egypt, on the other hand, is given its own separate, lengthy chapter. While repeating Plato's canard that "Egyptian art had not changed in 10,000 years," the author states admiringly, "Some of its great achievements had a decisive influence on Greek and Roman art, and thus we can still feel ourselves linked to the Egypt of 5,000 years ago by a continuous, living tradition." Janson's chapter on Greek art, reached after an excursion through "The Ancient Near East" and the Aegean cultures, is introduced with these words:

> *The works of art we have come to know so far are like fascinating strangers: we approach them fully aware of their alien background and of the "language difficulties" they present. If it turns out that, after all, we can understand something of what they have to say, we are surprised and grateful. As soon as we reach the Greeks, our attitude undergoes a change: they are not strangers but relatives, we feel, older members of our own family whom we recognize immediately.*

How, one wonders, would these words strike the audiences who at countless Saturday matinees imbibed the concrete lessons of the Walker Theatre, who perhaps secretly identified with the proud, lion-bodied rulers of ancient Egypt whose imposing, dark-skinned likenesses flanked the theater's great stage?

We at the Indianapolis Museum of Art do not have to look so far afield as Janson's influential text to find evidence of the same historical paradigm at work. "Why," we were asked by members of the advisory group convened to help plan programming for the exhibition this publication accompanies, "does the Indianapolis Museum of Art exhibit its few pieces of ancient Egyptian art only in the small gallery dominated by Greek vases and Roman sculpture? And why does the map of Africa at the entrance to the gallery housing the museum's extensive collection of African art exclude from consideration all the countries north of the Sahara?" For that matter, why do the duties of the IMA curator responsible for African art also include the arts of the South Pacific and Precolumbian America, the same geographically and temporally disparate cultures grouped by Janson under the heading "Primitive Art"? Good questions, all.

When the museum's ancient Egyptian holdings are reinstalled following the closure of the current exhibition, some of them will be incorporated into the African galleries. The map of Africa will be revised to show the continent in its entirety. While it would be absurd to present the diverse peoples and cultures of that vast land mass as an undifferentiated whole, we will eschew the equal absurdity of depicting ancient Giza as a picturesque suburb of Athens and Rome!

FOREWORD

As Theodore Celenko, the originator and primary organizer of *Egypt in Africa*, recognizes in the acknowledgments that follow, this exhibition is likely—indeed, almost certain—to be controversial. We have not embarked upon this project for the purpose of generating controversy, but neither have we been deterred by the prospect. The subject is too important to allow timidity to prevent serious discussion of issues that resonate deeply with many Americans. I join Ted Celenko in thanking the many lenders to the exhibition, the many scholars with divergent views who have contributed to the dialogue, and all the members of the staff of this museum who have worked diligently to make Ted's vision a reality.

We owe a particular debt of gratitude to the members of our community advisory group who politely but firmly pointed out the beam in our own institutional eye that makes it difficult to cast the mote out of our brother's. But most of all I wish to thank and acknowledge the unremitting efforts of our curator Theodore Celenko, whose mote-free vision informs every aspect of this publication and the exhibition it accompanies. I join with Ted in hoping that this enterprise will make a positive and lasting contributicn to the dialogue by means of which we explore the past in order to illuminate the present.

Bret Waller
Director
Indianapolis Museum of Art

ACKNOWLEDGMENTS

I thank the Indianapolis Museum of Art for approving and supporting a project so laden with controversy. The director, Bret Waller; the chief curator, Ellen Lee; and the exhibitions coordinator, Sue Ellen Paxson, have allowed me the latitude and intellectual freedom to pursue my curatorial vision. This exhibition and publication would not have been possible without the support of the Alliance of the Indianapolis Museum of Art; Harrison Eiteljorg; PSI Energy, a Cinergy Company; the Lila Wallace-Reader's Digest Fund Museum Collections Accessibility Initiative; the Institute of Museum Services; the Arts Council of Indianapolis and the City of Indianapolis; the Indiana Arts Commission, and the National Endowment for the Arts.

Numerous scholars have been supportive with ideas and data; twenty-seven of them are represented in this publication. I am grateful to the institutions, individuals, and publishers who have lent objects and provided photographic images for the exhibition and accompanying publication.

Frank Yurco, S.O.Y. Keita, Jim Romano, Timothy Kendall, and Roy Sieber, the five consultants for the project, offered their criticisms and suggestions for improvement that were essential for the evolution of the project. Two of these consultants deserve special mention. Frank Yurco, my ongoing Egyptologist consultant, was encouraging in spirit and supportive in facts and contacts from almost the beginning of the endeavor in 1993. He also served as content editor for portions of this publication. S.O.Y. Keita has been a font of information and ideas concerning this exhibition. His broad-based, multidisciplinary knowledge was critical in shaping aspects of the Early African Cultures and Faces of Egypt sections. Any shortcomings in the concepts or data of the exhibition and this publication are mine.

The museum staff has worked to make the exhibition and publication a reality. In particular, I acknowledge the skill and fortitude of the copy editor, Jane Graham, for managing to work with twenty-eight authors from different disciplines. I am grateful for the services of Rebecca Green, Susan Bailey, and Dorothy Nicholson, curatorial assistants; Anna Bennett and Becky Palmer, administrative assistants; interns Erika Kellar, Kimberly Gray, and Sheila Applewhite, and volunteer Emma Mickel. Susan Bailey researched and prepared drafts of maps, which were made by John Hollingsworth, cartographer, Department of Geography, Indiana University.

–T. C.

ill. 1

Africa

map of some African peoples, traditional states, and sites

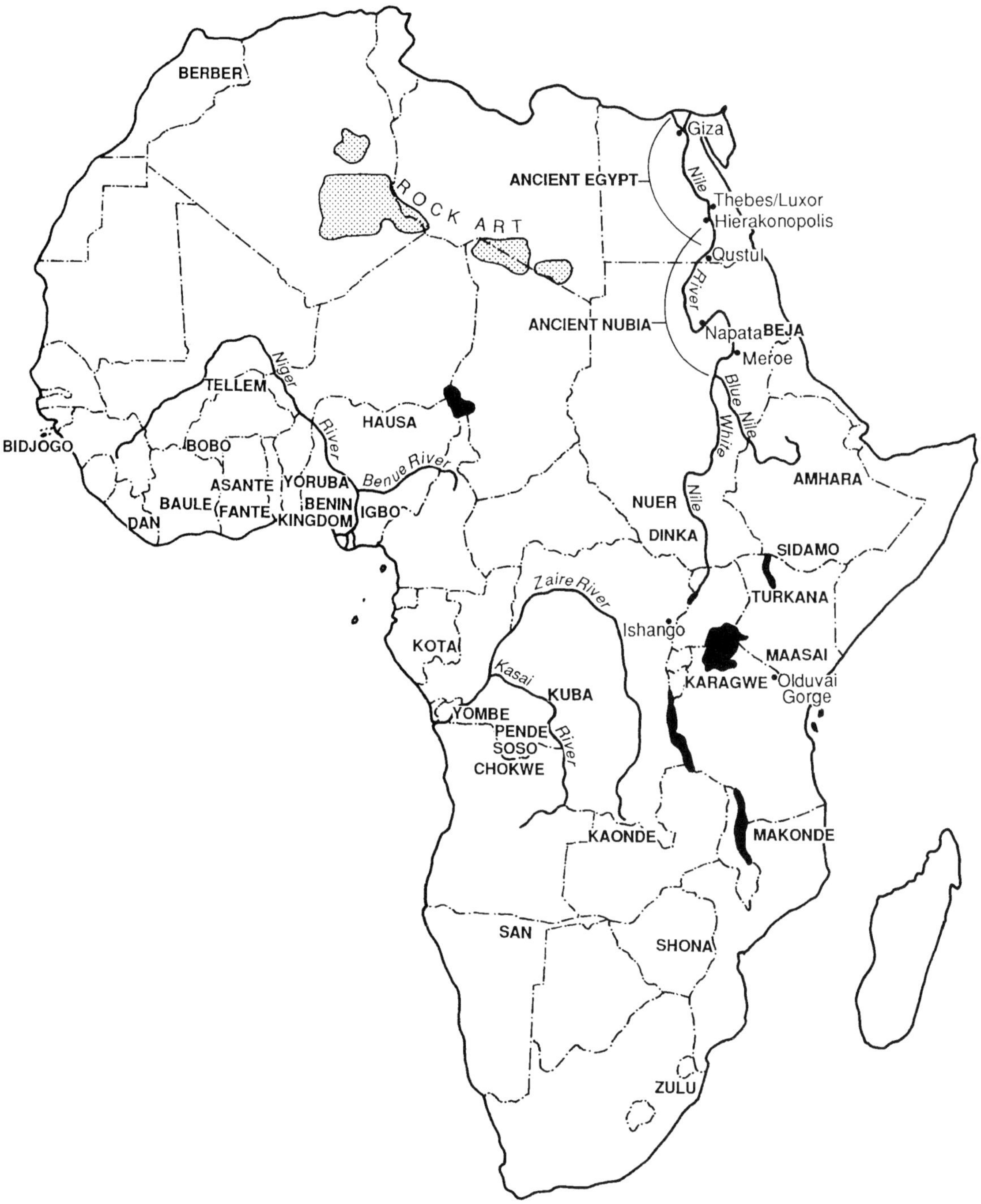

INTRODUCTION

Theodore Celenko
Curator of African, South Pacific, and Precolumbian Art
Indianapolis Museum of Art

This publication and the exhibition it accompanies examine the centuries-old topics of the African origin and African nature of ancient Egypt. There are thirty-two concise articles about specific topics, all of them original contributions by twenty-eight authors. A significant feature of this publication is its inclusion of diverse and sometimes opposing viewpoints. Indeed, this collection of focused writings is the first of its kind concerning this topic in that it provides perspectives from a wide range of fields, including archaeology, art history, physical anthropology, African studies, Egyptology, Afrocentric studies, and Classical studies. This inclusivity represents different cognitive orientations and methodological approaches. Another special feature of the exhibition is the range and rarity of the objects, for example, a 1.7-million-year-old stone tool (ill. 3, Early African Cultures section) and the first ancient Egyptian true mask to travel to America (ill. 62, Masking section). The nature of this exhibition and publication is selective rather than comprehensive, exploratory rather than definitive. This project is an attempt to advance a greater understanding of a multifaceted, complex subject.

Egypt in Africa places ancient Egyptians in an African context, in contrast to the tendency of universities, museums, and the popular media to view ancient Egypt from Mediterranean, Middle Eastern, and European perspectives. Almost all university courses about ancient Egypt are not in African studies curricula, but rather are found in departments of ancient Near Eastern studies, Classical Mediterranean archaeology, or Egyptology. Likewise, art and natural history museums in North America, Europe, and Africa, with few exceptions, display ancient Egyptian objects in a location apart from other African material. An unheralded and notable exception is a display about relationships between ancient Egypt and other parts of Africa at the American Museum of Natural History in New York. It was created by the late Colin M. Turnbull in 1969 and is still intact today. The exhibition *Africa: The Art of a Continent*, which opened at the Royal Academy of Arts, London, in 1995 (see acompanying publication, Phillips 1995), is the most comprehensive African art exhibition to date and includes *all* regions of the continent. However, even this recent endeavor fails to relate different regions of the continent to each other and does little to advance our understanding of possible connections within Africa.

Popular culture also contributes to the mindset that Egypt is not part of Africa. For example, the widely viewed movie *The Ten Commandments* (Cecil B. DeMille, 1956) has an "Egyptian" cast made up of Europeans and European-Americans, while the only dark-skinned characters are some of the servants and a visiting delegation from Nubia. Until recent decades, this lack of inclusion of Egypt in Africa was, and still is to some extent, due to the following factors:

1. There has been much ignorance about Africa and its cultures, particularly in America. For example, only since World War II has there been broad scholarly study of Africa. Even today most Americans would be hard-pressed to name five African nations or three of the continent's hundreds of ethnic groups. Also, most of what we know about the history and culture of Africa was learned decades after the establishment of Egyptology as a discipline.

2. The insular attitudes of many Egyptologists in the past, and even today, have contributed to a separation of ancient Egypt from the rest of Africa. A current example of the insularity of Egyptologists is the important traveling exhibition *The American Discovery of Ancient Egypt* (1995-1996) and its accompanying publications (Thomas 1995; 1996), co-organized by the Los Angeles County Museum of Art and the American Research Center in Egypt, the prestigious association of American Egyptologists. This exhibition, a significant effort reflecting current Egyptologist scholarship, focuses on the contributions of American scholars and institutions. Although the concern of this project is American Egyptology, it is yet another Egyptian exhibition that does not relate the ancient Egyptian civilization to a broader African context. Also, despite the inclusion of significant material from Nubia, the organization of the exhibition and its title do not sufficiently acknowledge this African civilization.

Rare examples of Egyptologists and their associates in other disciplines acknowledging

Egypt's connection to Africa are Gertrude Caton-Thompson's 1928 work "The Badarian Civilization," which acknowledged the influence of Saharan cultures on the Predynastic Period, and Henri Frankfort's 1948 *Kingship and the Gods*, which documented relationships between Egyptian cultural features and an African substratum. The Brooklyn Museum's 1978 traveling exhibition and accompanying publication *Africa in Antiquity: The Arts of Ancient Nubia and the Sudan* significantly advanced our understanding of Nubia and its relationship to Egypt and other African regions.

3. Associated closely with isolationist tendencies of some Egyptologists are the divergent histories of Egyptology and African studies. The latter, to a very large extent, focuses on Africa south of the Sahara, particularly with regard to the disciplines of archaeology and art history. When African studies burgeoned in the 1960s, Egyptology had been an established discipline for a century and a half. Thus, there was a tendency to focus on sub-Saharan or "black" Africa, leaving the ancient Nile Valley to Egyptologists. Conversely, Egyptologists have always thought of ancient Egypt as a separate and unique civilization, while acknowledging very minimal interaction with "inner" Africa. Contributing to the insularity of Egyptologists is the fact that it was not until the early decades of this century that much was understood about Egypt's Predynastic Period and about Nubian civilization. This understanding revealed African roots of Egyptian civilization. The tendency of scholarship to emanate from the perspective of Islamic, Biblical, Middle Eastern, or Near Eastern studies has also separated Egypt from the rest of the continent.

4. Scholastic racism has also been a factor in this view of ancient Egypt as separate from African culture. Beginning in the eighteenth century, Europeans and European-Americans detached ancient Egypt from Africa. The Hamitic hypothesis, which evolved in the nineteenth century and was in full authority in the early decades of this century, posited that an intrusive non-African population was responsible for ancient Egyptian civilization and other North and East African civilizations. It attributed any advanced cultural development in Egypt, and Africa as a whole, to European or Western Asian people, and usually to light-skinned rather than to more dark-skinned Africans. It was unthinkable to most Egyptologists of the time that ancient Egypt was African, originating from the same or related biological and cultural stock found elsewhere in Africa. Early in this century, a British anatomist, comparing Nubians and Egyptians, exemplified academic thinking when he wrote, "[T]he smallest infusion of Negro-blood immediately manifests itself in a dulling of initiative and a 'drag' on the further development of the arts of civilization" (Smith 1909:25). The Hamitic hypothesis was synthesized in Flinders Petrie's 1920 *Prehistoric Egypt* and in C. G. Seligman's 1930 *Races of Africa*.

Ancient Greek writers such as Herodotus, who visited Egypt in 448 B.C., viewed Egypt as a great African civilization. Europeans writing as late as the eighteenth century, for example, the Frenchman Constantin F. C. Volney (1787:74-77), acknowledged the "Africaness" of the great civilization. The new mindset about the relationship of Egypt and the rest of Africa had its beginnings at the end of the Atlantic slave trade and its consummation during the period of European colonization of Africa. This revisionism, which still lingers today, was racism at both the scholarly and popular level. This is a well-documented story not detailed here. Martin Bernal (*Black Athena*, vol. 1, 1987), Basil Davidson (*The Ancient World and Africa: Whose Roots?* 1989), and St. Clair Drake (*Black Folk Here and There* 1987; 1990) are scholars who elucidate this topic. (See Keita, Hilliard, and Asante in the last section of this publication.)

The foremost impetus for this project has been the persistent and often sensible voices of individuals whose base is in black or African American studies, mostly African Americans, and many of whom can be termed Afrocentrists. These voices are expressed through scholarly writings and in popular culture. Afrocentrists view the world from an African perspective, consider ancient Egypt an African culture, and the first great civilization of the world, and consider ancient Egyptians black people. They tend to avoid the term "Egypt," which is derived from Greek, but rather use the terms "Kmt" or "Kemet," literally, "black land," one of a number of names ancient Egyptians called their land. While most Afrocentrists are African-American, the father of the modern movement is Cheikh Anta Diop (1923-1986), a Senegalese whose major work is perhaps *The African Origin of Civilization: Myth or Reality* (1974, first published in French in 1955). However, the claim of African Americans that ancient Egypt was African and that ancient Egyptians were black people predates the relatively recent Afrocentric school and goes back to David Walker in 1829 and Frederick Douglass in 1854. Early in this century, W. E. B. Du Bois (1915) was among many who were vocal on this subject.

This publication includes all of the exhibition sections listed on the contents page, except for an Africa in Maps section. More than half of the ninety-eight exhibition objects and seventy-seven exhibition photomurals, line drawings, videos, and maps are illustrated. See Exhibition Components at the end of the publication.

The first section of *Egypt in Africa* focuses on early African cultures, establishes the great antiquity of humankind and culture in Africa, and describes the setting from which one of the world's great early civilizations emerged. It is during the formative phases of Egyptian civilization that an African imprint is most clearly discernible, for example, in stone tools and cattle pastoralism.

This publication, as well as the exhibition from which it emanates, focuses on a number of cultural features, or Africanisms, some of which may have survived from ancient times: maternity images, headrests, an African manner of depicting humans in works of art, ancestor worship and divine kingship, animal deities and symbols, masking, body art, and circumcision and male initiation. These features were chosen, in part, because they could be presented by objects in a museum installation. For example, headrests and masks were chosen rather than purely philosophical, religious, or social features, which do not easily allow for a presentation with objects. Beyond this limitation, there are many topics potentially connecting ancient Egypt and other parts of Africa that, for lack of resources and space, are not included. Among these subjects are staffs, beds, plows, harps, dance, and coiffure styles, as well as an investigation of possible ancient Nile Valley objects found in sub-Saharan Africa.

It is acknowledged that all of these features are found in other parts of the world. However, they are considered Africanisms because the oldest evidence of them is from Africa— circumcision, for example—or because of their widespread distribution and their similar forms or functions—headrests and maternity images, for example.

Some of the Africanisms included here, as well as others, have been noted earlier (for example, Diop 1974[1955]; Willett 1971:109-114; Davidson 1971:33-35; Noguera 1975; Zayed 1981). The outdated diffusionist notion that objects, concepts, and ways of life held in common by the "High Civilization" of Egypt, a "Mother Culture" for Africa, and the "backward" cultures of the rest of Africa must emanate from ancient Egypt is not valid (see Shaw 1978: 9-12 for a review of the literature on this subject). Indeed, this exhibition in some instances proves and in other instances speculates that ancient Egypt had African roots and was continually influenced by African cultures.

The purpose of the various sections focusing on proposed "Africanisms" is to present similarities among cultures and to suggest past interactions, however indirect, remote, and unprovable some of them may be. Furthermore, these "Africanisms" force us to see ancient Egypt within a broader African context without adhering to the concept of a unified African culture. The fact that the first evidence of circumcision comes from the continent and is documented in ancient Egypt and in more recent African cultures; the fact that body art occurred in African rock art depictions that predate ancient Egypt, as well as in ancient Egypt, and still exists in Africa today; and the fact that the veneration of ancestors as intermediaries between the living and forces in the supernatural world has been important throughout the continent—all help us to think of Egypt as African.

The significance of similar or related cultural features between various peoples is, in many instances, speculative. For example, there is no proof of direct historical connection between a Shona headrest (ill. 25, Headrest section) from Southern Africa and an ancient Egyptian headrest (ill. 26, Headrest section), removed by thousands of miles and years. The indirect cultural interaction between various cultural groups throughout past millennia is a matter of conjecture. It is reasonable to think in terms of influence in either direction between ancient peoples of present-day Sudan and ancient Egypt (compare ills. 31, 26, Headrest section). Perhaps a less speculative association is the "block" headrests from Middle and New Kingdom Egypt (ill. 29, Headrest section) that resemble twentieth-century examples from the Horn of Africa (ill. 30, Headrest section). It is well established that from the Old Kingdom through New Kingdom there were Egyptian relations with "Punt" in the Horn region.

The final section of this publication and the exhibition comes to terms with the physical appearance of ancient

Egyptians. It illustrates the broad diversity of the continent's indigenous populations. It disproves simplistic notions of how an "African" looks. There is no "typical" African from a scientific point of view. Social factors have created a stereotype. Natural selection and other evolutionary factors have produced this diversity.

Although the early Egyptians were biologically African, the terms "white" and "black," particularly as viewed though an American social lens, are not appropriate labels to describe ancient Egyptian populations. It is probable that there was significant diversity among indigenous Egyptians, with variation, for example, in skin color, nose width, and hair type. An enlightened view establishes that ancient Egyptians were not Europeans or Asians, and they certainly did not look like the Europeans or European-Americans who are presented as Egyptians in manifestations of popular culture, for example, the above-cited 1956 movie *The Ten Commandments*.

Ancient Egyptians, most notably during early periods, were biological Africans; that is, their ancestors originated within Africa. However, there are complexities to the population makeup of Egypt because of influxes of non-African populations, such as Western Asians from earliest times; Hyksos people from Western Asia in the seventeenth and sixteenth centuries B.C.; Greeks and Romans, from the fourth century B.C. to the fourth century A.D.; Arabs and others, accompanied by the spread of Islam, beginning in the seventh century, and later, beginning in the sixteenth century, Ottoman Turks. The settlement of Nubians in Egypt from earliest times is another factor. There is no data to determine the precise impact of these non-Egyptians on the gene pool of ancient and present-day Egyptian populations, but there was surely some alteration of the original population. The impact of foreigners, such as Greeks and Arabs, was more likely to be a factor in northern Egypt, although the entire population would have been affected over time. These foreigners became biologically and culturally assimilated into this African population.

Some of the contributors to the Early African Cultures and Faces of Egypt sections present viewpoints on this subject using various types of evidence available from physical anthropology, ancient writings, works of art, and other sources.

We may never know with full certainty what the ancient Egyptians looked like. The five contributors to the final section present viewpoints on this subject using various types of evidence available from physical anthropology, ancient writings, works of art, and other sources.

During the past half-century, the story of Africa's cultural contributions to the world has been told by many people from different perspectives. Some view ancient Egypt as the jewel in Africa's crown. Others regard this singular focus as a diminishment of the achievements of other cultures throughout the continent. The sophisticated Ifa divination system of the Yoruba people of Nigeria, the exquisite wood-carved ancestor figures of the Luba people of Zaire, and the complex political and military organization of the Zulu people of South Africa are to many, and should be to many more, cultural accomplishments comparable to the temples and hieroglyphs of ancient Egypt.

REFERENCES CITED

Bernal, Martin
1987 *Black Athena: The Afroasiatic Roots of Classical Civilization.* vol. 1. New Brunswick, New Jersey: Rutgers University Press.

Brooklyn Museum, The
1978 *Africa in Antiquity: The Arts of Ancient Nubia and the Sudan.* n.p. The Brooklyn Museum.

Caton-Thompson, Gertrude
1928 The Badarian Civilisation. In *Badarian Civilisation and Prehistoric Remains near Badari.* Guy Bruntun and Gertrude Caton-Thompson, eds. pp. 69-116. London: British School of Archaeology in Egypt and Bernard Quaritch.

Davidson, Basil
1971 *African Kingdoms.* Alexandria, Virginia: Time-Life Books.

1989 The Ancient World and Africa: Whose Roots? In *Egypt Revisited.* Ivan Van Sertima, ed. pp. 39-52. 2nd ed. New Brunswick, New Jersey, and London: Journal of African Civilizations, Transaction Publishers.

Diop, Cheikh Anta
1974 [1955] *The African Origin of Civilization: Myth or Reality.* Translated and edited by Mercer Cook. Chicago: Lawrence Hill & Co. (Antériorité des Civilisations Negre: Mythe ou Vérité Historique? 1955. Paris: Présence Africaine).

Douglass, Frederick
1854 The Claims of the Negro Ethnologically Considered, address delivered at Western Reserve College, July 12, 1854. In *The Life and Writings of Frederick Douglass,* vol. 2. pp. 289-309. New York: International Publishers, 1950.

Drake, St. Clair
1987,1990 *Black Folk Here and There: An Essay in History and Anthropology.* 2 vols. (1987, 1990). Los Angeles: Center for Afro-American Studies, University of California.

Du Bois, W. E. B.
1915 *The Negro.* New York: Henry Holt and Company.

Frankfort, Henri
1948 *Kingship and the Gods.* Chicago and London: The University of Chicago Press.

Noguera, Anthony
1976 *How African Was Egypt?* New York: Vantage Press, Inc.

Petrie, W. M. Flinders
1920 *Prehistoric Egypt.* London: British School of Archaeology.

Phillips, Tom, ed.
1995 *Africa: The Art of a Continent.* Munich and New York: Prestel Verlag.

Seligman, C. G.
1930 *Races of Africa.* London: Butterworth, Ltd.

Shaw, Thurston
1978 *Nigeria: Its Archaeology and Early History.* London: Thames and Hudson.

Smith, Grafton Elliot
1909 Anatomical Report (A). *Archeological Survey of Nubia Bulletin* 3: 21-27. Cairo: National Printing Department.

Thomas, Nancy
1995 *The American Discovery of Ancient Egypt.* Los Angeles: Los Angeles County Museum of Art.

1996 *The American Discovery of Ancient Egypt: Essays.* Nancy Thomas, ed. Los Angeles: Los Angeles County Museum of Art.

Volney, Constantine François Chassebuf
1787 *Voyages en Syrie et en Égypte pendant les années* 1783, 1784 et 1785. Paris.

Walker, David
1984 [1829] *Walker's Appeal to the Colored Citizens of the World . . .* Reprint Edition. Salem, New Hampshire: AYER Company, Publishers, Inc.

Willett, Frank
1971 *African Art.* New York and Washington: Praeger Publishers.

Zayed, A. Hamid
1981 Egypt's relation with the rest of Africa, with the collaboration of J. Devisse. In *General History of Africa,* vol. 2. *Ancient Civilizations of Africa.* pp. 136-154. Paris: United Nations Educational, Scientific and Cultural Organization.

EARLY AFRICAN CULTURES

African Prehistory and Human Evolution

Kathy D. Schick
Associate Professor of Anthropology
Indiana University

Nicholas Toth
Professor of Anthropology
Indiana University

Pliny once observed: *"Ex Africa semper aliquid novi"* (Out of Africa there is always something new). Indeed, Africa, often referred to as the "cradle of humankind," provides the longest record of human evolution and prehistory. Human evolution has entailed dramatic changes in anatomy and behavior throughout several million years. Especially prominent are changes in human locomotion, brain size and complexity, and dependence upon culture and technology. A wealth of prehistoric evidence, including fossils and archaeological remains, indicates that crucial early stages of this evolution occurred in Africa. Furthermore, evolutionary changes and cultural developments in Africa continued to play an important role in our evolution during the spread of our ancestors out of Africa into other areas and the ultimate emergence of modern forms of humans.

ill. 2
map of human evolution in Africa
4,000,000 years ago to modern man

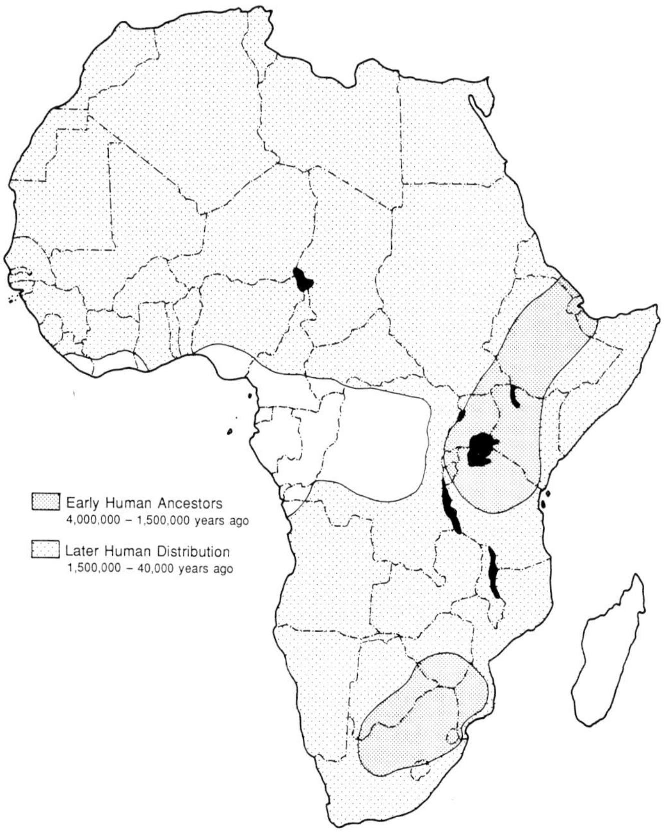

Early Primate Evolution

After the emergence of early primates—the order of mammals that includes monkeys, apes, and humans—about 65 million years ago, diverse primate lineages evolved and radiated into new and changing environments in a world being torn apart by continental drift. Thirty million years ago, primate forms that appear to be ancestral to both apes and Old World monkeys lived in Africa, as evidenced by the rich fossil deposits of the Fayum Depression in Egypt.

A variety of early apes subsequently emerged in Africa, Europe, and Asia between 20 million and 5 million years ago. A few million years ago, however, some of the apes in Africa began to undergo evolutionary changes that mark a distinctive, proto-human lineage (ill. 2). These include anatomical changes that facilitated upright or bipedal walking (by four million years ago), the advent of stone tool-making traditions (by at least two and a half million years ago), and a rapid expansion in brain size (beginning at least two million years ago). All of the evidence for these early evolutionary changes, so pivotal for the emergence of the human species, comes from Africa.

Emergence in Africa of Bipedal Walking, Brain Expansion, and Stone Tools

One of the earliest of the bipedal ancestors, all of which have been found in Eastern Africa, is *Australopithecus afarensis* (for example, the famous partial skeleton of "Lucy" found in Ethiopia). Different but related australopithecines have been found in South African cave deposits dating from approximately three million years ago. During the latter phases of their evolution, australopithecines evolved into forms referred to as "robust australopithecines," with very large chewing muscles and teeth. The first appeared in East Africa about two and a half million years ago and others were present in both Eastern and Southern

ill. 3
genus Homo (early ancestral humans)
Olduvai Gorge
Tanzania (Eastern Africa)

chopping tool or tool core
stone; l. 3⅜ in.
the time of early Homo and of Australopithecines
about 1,700,000 years ago

Lent by the CRAFT Research Center
Indiana University
TR 8481

Africa from about two million years ago until they became extinct approximately one million years ago.

Starting at least two million years ago, however, other bipedal protohumans were also present in Africa. These new forms tended to have smaller teeth than their contemporaries, the robust australopithecines, and an enlarged brain, another change distinctive of the human lineage. Thus, they are put in our genus, *Homo*, which evolved by 1.8 million years ago into a species often called *Homo erectus* and which shows a dramatic increase in brain and body size over time.

Another crucial evolutionary change, the emergence of stone-tool traditions, also occurred in Africa. The earliest evidence for this comes from deposits dated to 2.6 million years ago on the site of Gona in the Hadar region of Ethiopia. A great many sites with stone tools dating from at least two million years ago have been found in Eastern and Southern Africa. These tools, often called "Oldowan" technology (named after the famous site of Olduvai Gorge in Tanzania), consist of simple but deliberately fractured pieces of rock (ill. 3).

Starting about 1.5 million years ago in Africa, new technologies appeared that, in addition to simple Oldowan artifacts, also included large, carefully made cutting tools called hand axes (ill. 4) and cleavers, referred to as "Acheulean." Ancestral human populations *Homo erectus* or closely related forms using such tools spread out of Africa starting more than one million years ago and gradually expanded into much of Europe and Asia.

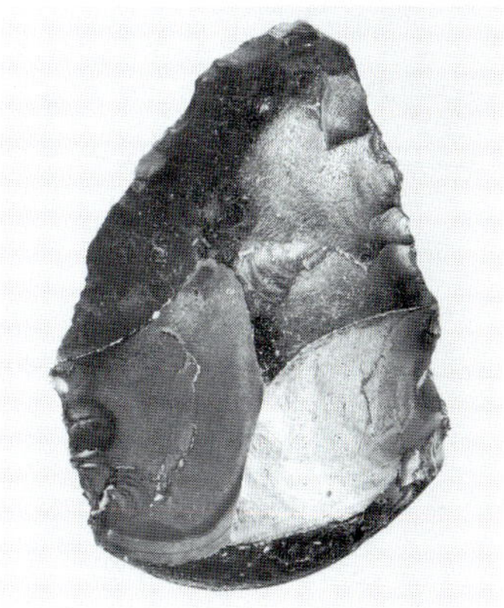

ill. 4
Homo erectus (human ancestor)
Thebes-Luxor
Nile Valley (Northeastern Africa)

hand axe
stone; l. 5⅛ in.
Paleolithic Period
300,000-100,000 years ago

Lent by The Metropolitan Museum of Art
Gift of C.T. Currelly, 1906
06.322.2

The Emergence of *Homo sapiens*

The fossil records in Africa, Europe, and Asia from several hundred thousand years ago show the emergence of early forms of humans (sometimes called "archaic" *Homo sapiens*). These have brains nearly the size of the brain of modern humans, but also retain many primitive features, particularly in the face and other parts of the skull. Starting a couple of hundred thousand years ago, Acheulean technologies in Africa began to disappear and were replaced by tool traditions consisting of flakes deliberately shaped into various tools, such as points or scrapers (a period known as "Middle Stone Age" or, in Northern Africa, the "Middle Palaeolithic").

The origin of modern humans (*Homo sapiens sapiens*) is currently a topic of much debate and research interest. Many researchers have recognized early modern forms in Africa and Western Asia dating back 100,000 years or more. Some genetic evidence also points to a common origin for all human populations, possibly within the past 50,000 to 200,000 years, that may be the result of a major population dispersal, perhaps from Africa.

Between 20,000 to 50,000 years ago, populations of anatomically modern humans became widespread in Africa as well as in Europe and Asia. Many cultural patterns

ill. 5
ancient Egyptian people
Fayum
Egypt (Northeastern Africa)

hollow-based arrow head
flint; l. 4 1/16 in.
early Predynastic Period,
Fayum A
6100-4000 B.C.

Lent by The Metropolitan Museum of Art
Gift of Herbert E. Winlock, 1926
26.10.68

became more modern as well. Tool kits of the African Later Stone Age show a great deal of geographic variability (perhaps partially reflecting ethnicity) and stylistic change over time, artwork and self-adornment emerged, and more systematic hunting and gathering patterns are evident (e.g., use of the bow and arrow). Thus, the Stone Age in Africa laid critical foundations both biologically and behaviorally for major cultural developments that ensued there and elsewhere in the next 10,000 years. The critical transition to the production of food (a period sometimes called the "Neolithic" or "New Stone Age," as stone tools such as sickles and arrow points (ill. 5) continued to be used) then laid the groundwork for the ultimate emergence of complex societies, metallurgy, and sophisticated art forms in many parts of Africa.

SUGGESTED READING

Clark, J. Desmond
1970 *The Prehistory of Africa.* London: Thames and Hudson.

Clark, J. Desmond, ed.
1982 *The Cambridge History of Africa,* vol. 1: From the earliest times to c. 500 B.C. Cambridge: Cambridge University Press.

Klein, Richard G.
1989 *The Human Career: Human biological and cultural origins.* Chicago: University of Chicago Press.

Phillipson, David W.
1993 *African Archaeology.* Second Edition. Cambridge: Cambridge University Press.

Schick, Kathy D., and Nicholas Toth
1993 *Making Silent Stones Speak: Human Evolution and the Dawn of Technology.* New York: Simon and Schuster.

The Geographical Origins and Population Relationships of Early Ancient Egyptians

S. O. Y. Keita
Department of
Biological Anthropology
Oxford University

A. J. Boyce
University Reader in
Human Population Biology
Oxford University

What was the primary geographical source for the peopling of the Egyptian Nile Valley? Were the creators of the fundamental culture of southern predynastic Egypt—which led to the dynastic culture—migrants and colonists from Europe or the Near East? Or were they predominantly African variant populations?

These questions can be addressed using data from studies of biology and culture, and evolutionary interpretive models. Archaeological and linguistic data indicate an origin in Africa (see Hassan and Ehret in this section). Biological data from living Egyptians and from skeletons of ancient Egyptians may also shed light on these questions. It is important to keep in mind the long presence of humans in Africa, and that there should be a great range of biological variation in indigenous "authentic" Africans.

Scientists have been studying remains from the Egyptian Nile Valley for years. Analysis of crania is the traditional approach to assessing ancient population origins, relationships, and diversity. In studies based on anatomical traits and measurements of crania, similarities have been found between Nile Valley crania from 30,000, 20,000 and 12,000 years ago and various African remains from more recent times (see Thoma 1984; Bräuer and Rimbach 1990; Angel and Kelley 1986; Keita 1993). Studies of crania from southern predynastic Egypt, from the formative period (4000-3100 B.C.), show them usually to be more similar to the crania of ancient Nubians, Kushites, Saharans, or modern groups from the Horn of Africa than to those of dynastic northern Egyptians or ancient or modern southern Europeans.

Another source of skeletal data is limb proportions, which generally vary with different climatic belts. In general, the early Nile Valley remains have the proportions of more tropical populations, which is noteworthy since Egypt is not in the tropics. This suggests that the Egyptian Nile Valley was not primarily settled by cold-adapted peoples, such as Europeans.

Art objects[1] are not generally used by biological anthropologists. They are suspect as data and their interpretation highly dependent on stereotyped thinking. However, because art has often been used to comment on the physiognomies of ancient Egyptians, a few remarks are in order. A review of literature and the sculpture indicates characteristics that also can be found in the Horn of (East) Africa (see, e.g., Petrie 1939; Drake 1987; Keita 1993). Old and Middle Kingdom statuary shows a range of characteristics; many, if not most, individuals depicted in the art have variations on the narrow-nosed, narrow-faced morphology also seen in various East Africans. This East African anatomy, once seen as being the result of a mixture of different "races," is better understood as being part of the range of indigenous African variation.

1. The comments are limited to statuary. The stereotyped red-brown color for men and the yellow-light for women in the Old Kingdom may have had religious significance. It is not likely that such uniformity has ever existed.

The descriptions and terms of ancient Greek writers have sometimes been used to comment on Egyptian origins. This is problematic since the ancient writers were not doing population biology. However, we can examine one issue. The Greeks called all groups south of Egypt "Ethiopians." Were the Egyptians more related to any of these "Ethiopians" than to the Greeks? As noted, cranial and limb studies have indicated greater similarity to Somalis, Kushites and Nubians, all "Ethiopians" in ancient Greek terms.

There are few studies of ancient DNA from Egyptian remains and none so far of southern predynastic skeletons. A study of 12th Dynasty DNA shows that the remains evaluated had multiple lines of descent, including not surprisingly some from "sub-Saharan" Africa (Pääbo and Di Rienzo 1993). The other lineages were not identified, but may be African in origin. More work is needed. In the future, *early* remains from the Nile Valley and the rest of Africa will have to be studied in this manner in order to establish the early *baseline range of genetic variation of all Africa*. The data are important to avoid stereotyped ideas about the DNA of African peoples.

The information from the living Egyptian population may not be as useful because historical records indicate substantial immigration into Egypt over the last several millennia, and it seems to have been far greater from the Near East and Europe than from areas *far* south of Egypt. "Substantial immigration" can actually mean a relatively small number of people in terms of population genetics theory. It has been determined that an average migration rate of one percent per generation into a region could result in a great change of the original gene frequencies in only several thousand years. (This assumes that all migrants marry natives and that all native-migrant offspring remain in the region.) It is obvious then that an ethnic group or nationality can change in average gene frequencies or physiognomy by intermarriage, unless social rules exclude the products of "mixed" unions from membership in the receiving group. More abstractly this means that geographically defined populations can undergo significant genetic change with a small percentage of steady assimilation of "foreign" genes. This is true even if natural selection does not favor the genes (and does not eliminate them).[2] This scenario is different from one in which a different population *replaces* another via colonization. Native Egyptians were variable. Foreigners added to this variability.

2. Examples of regions that have biologically absorbed genetically different immigrants are Sicily, Portugal, and Greece, where the frequencies of various genetic markers (and historical records) indicate sub-Saharan and supra-Saharan African migrants.

The genetic data on the recent Egyptian population is fairly sparse. There has not been systematic research on large samples from the numerous regions of Egypt. Taken collectively, the results of various analyses suggest that modern Egyptians have ties with various African regions, as well as with Near Easterners and Europeans. Egyptian gene frequencies are between those of Europeans and some sub-Saharan Africans. This is not surprising. The studies have used various kinds of data: standard blood groups and proteins, mitochondrial DNA, and the Y chromosome. The gene frequencies and variants of the "original" population, or of one of early high density, cannot be deduced without a theoretical model based on archaeological and "historical" data, including the aforementioned DNA from ancient skeletons. (It must be noted that it is not yet clear how useful ancient DNA will be in most historical genetic research.) It is not clear to what degree certain genetic systems usually interpreted as non-African may in fact be native to Africa. Much depends on how "African" is defined and the model of interpretation.

The various genetic studies usually suffer from what is called categorical thinking, specifically, racial thinking. Many investigators still think of "African" in a stereotyped, nonscientific (nonevolutionary) fashion, not acknowledging a range of genetic variants or traits as equally African. The definition of "African" that would be most appropriate should encompass variants that arose in Africa. Given that this is not the orientation of many scholars, who work from outmoded racial perspectives, the presence of "stereotypical" African genes so far from the "African heartland" is noteworthy. These genes have always been in the valley in any reasonable interpretation of the data. As a team of Egyptian geneticists stated recently, "During this long history and besides these Asiatic influences, Egypt maintained its African identity..." (Mahmoud et al. 1987). This statement is even more true in a wider evolutionary interpretation, since some of the "Asian" genes may be African in origin. Modern data and improved theoretical approaches extend and validate this conclusion.

In summary, various kinds of data and the evolutionary approach indicate that the Nile Valley populations had greater ties with other African populations in the early ancient period. Early Nile Valley populations were primarily coextensive with indigenous African populations. Linguistic and archaeological data provide key supporting evidence for a primarily African origin.

REFERENCES CITED

Angel, J. L., and J. O. Kelley
1986 Description and comparison of the skeleton. In *The Wadi Kubbaniya Skeleton: A Late Paleolithic Burial from Southern Egypt*. F. Wendorf and R. Schild. pp. 53-70. Dallas: Southern Methodist University Press.

Bräuer, G., and K. Rimbach
1990 Late archaic and modern *Homo sapiens* from Europe, Africa, and Southwest Asia: Craniometric comparisons and phylogenetic implications. *Journal of Human Evolution* 19:789-807.

Drake, St. C.
1987 *Black Folk Here and There*. vol 1. Los Angeles: University of California.

Keita, S. O. Y.
1993 Studies and comments on ancient Egyptian biological relationships. *History in Africa* 20:129-154.

Mahmoud, L., et al.
1987 Human blood groups in Dakhlaya, Egypt. *Annals of Human Biology* 14(6):487-493.

Pääbo, S., and A. Di Rienzo
1993 A molecular approach to the study of Egyptian history. In *Biological Anthropology and the Study of Ancient Egypt*. V. Davies and R. Walker, eds. pp. 86-90. London: British Museum Press.

Petrie, W. M. F.
1939 *The Making of Egypt*. London: Sheldon Press.

Thoma, A.
1984 Morphology and affinities of the Nazlet Khater man. *Journal of Human Evolution* 13:287-296.

Ancient Egyptian as an African Language, Egypt as an African Culture

Christopher Ehret
Professor of History, African Studies Chair
University of California at Los Angeles

Ancient Egyptian civilization was, in ways and to an extent usually not recognized, fundamentally African. The evidence of both language and culture reveals these African roots.

The origins of Egyptian ethnicity lay in the areas south of Egypt. The ancient Egyptian language belonged to the Afrasian family (also called Afroasiatic or, formerly, Hamito-Semitic). The speakers of the earliest Afrasian languages, according to recent studies, were a set of peoples whose lands between 15,000 and 13,000 B.C. stretched from Nubia in the west to far northern Somalia in the east (ill.6). They supported themselves by gathering wild grains. The first elements of Egyptian culture were laid down two thousand years later, between 12,000 and 10,000 B.C., when some of these Afrasian communities expanded northward into Egypt, bringing with them a language directly ancestral to ancient Egyptian. They also introduced to Egypt the idea of using wild grains as food (Ehret 1995; Ehret forthcoming).

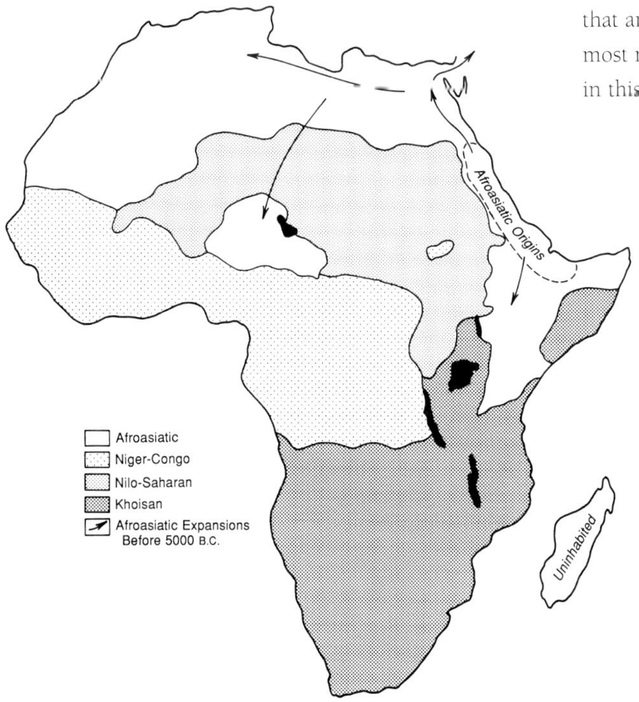

ill. 6
map of African language families
3,000-1,000 B. C.

Courtesy of Christopher Ehret

A new religion came with them as well. Its central tenet explains the often localized origins of later Egyptian gods: the earliest Afrasians were, properly speaking, neither monotheistic nor polytheistic. Instead, each local community, comprising a clan or a group of related clans, had its own distinct deity and centered its religious observances on that deity. This belief system persists today among several Afrasian peoples of far southwest Ethiopia. And as Biblical scholars have shown, Yahweh, god of the ancient Hebrews, an Afrasian people of the Semitic group, was originally also such a deity. The connection of many of Egypt's predynastic gods to particular localities is surely a modified version of this early Afrasian belief. Political unification in the late fourth millennium brought the Egyptian deities together in a new polytheistic system. But their local origins remain amply apparent in the records that have come down to us.

During the long era between about 10,000 and 6000 B.C., new kinds of southern influences diffused into Egypt. During these millennia, the Sahara had a wetter climate than it has today, with grassland or steppes in many areas that are now almost absolute desert. New wild animals, most notably the cow, spread widely in the eastern Sahara in this period.

One of the exciting archeological events of the past twenty years was the discovery that the peoples of the steppes and grasslands to the immediate south of Egypt domesticated these cattle, as early as 9000 to 8000 B.C. The societies involved in this momentous development included Afrasians and neighboring peoples whose languages belonged to a second major African language family, Nilo-Saharan (Wendorf, Schild, Close 1984; Wendorf, et al. 1982). The earliest domestic cattle came to Egypt apparently from these southern neighbors, probably before 6000 B.C., *not*, as we used to think, from the Middle East.

One major technological advance, pottery-making, was also initiated as early as 9000 B.C. by the Nilo-Saharans and Afrasians who lived to the south of Egypt. Soon thereafter, pots spread to Egyptian sites, almost 2,000 years *before* the first pottery was made in the Middle East.

Very late in the same span of time, the cultivating of crops began in Egypt. Since most of Egypt belonged then to the Mediterranean climatic zone, many of the new food plants came from areas of similar climate in the Middle East. Two domestic animals of Middle Eastern origin, the sheep and the goat, also entered northeastern Africa from the north during this era.

But several notable early Egyptian crops came from Sudanic agriculture, independently invented between 7500 and 6000 B.C. by the Nilo-Saharan peoples (Ehret 1993:104-125). One such cultivated crop was the edible gourd. The botanical evidence is confirmed in this case by linguistics: Egyptian *bdt,* or "bed of gourds" (Late Egyptian *bdt*, "gourd; cucumber"), is a borrowing of the Nilo-Saharan word **bud,* "edible gourd." Other early Egyptian crops of Sudanic origin included watermelons and castor beans. (To learn more on how historians use linguistic evidence, see note at end of this article.)

Between about 5000 and 3000 B.C. a new era of southern cultural influences took shape. Increasing aridity pushed more of the human population of the eastern Sahara into areas with good access to the waters of the Nile, and along the Nile the bottomlands were for the first time cleared and farmed. The Egyptian stretches of the river came to form the northern edge of a newly emergent Middle Nile Culture Area, which extended far south up the river, well into the middle of modern-day Sudan. Peoples speaking languages of the Eastern Sahelian branch of the Nilo-Saharan family inhabited the heartland of this region.

From the Middle Nile, Egypt gained new items of livelihood between 5000 and 3000 B.C. One of these was a kind of cattle pen: its Egyptian name, *s3* (earlier **sr*), can be derived from the Eastern Sahelian term **sar.* Egyptian *pg3*, "bowl," (presumably from earlier *pgr*), a borrowing of Nilo-Saharan **poKur,* "wooden bowl or trough," reveals still another adoption in material culture that most probably belongs to this era.

One key feature of classical Egyptian political culture, usually assumed to have begun in Egypt, also shows strong links to the southern influences of this period. We refer here to a particular kind of sacral chiefship that entailed, in its earliest versions, the sending of servants into the afterlife along with the deceased chief. The deep roots and wide occurrence of this custom among peoples who spoke Eastern Sahelian languages strongly imply that sacral chiefship began not as a specifically Egyptian invention, but instead as a widely shared development of the Middle Nile Culture Area.

After about 3500 B.C., however, Egypt would have started to take on a new role vis-a-vis the Middle Nile region, simply because of its greater concentration of population. Growing pressures on land and resources soon enhanced and transformed the political powers of sacral chiefs. Unification followed, and the local deities of predynastic times became gods in a new polytheism, while sacral chiefs gave way to a divine king. At the same time, Egypt passed from the wings to center stage in the unfolding human drama of northeastern Africa.

A Note on the Use of Linguistic Evidence for History

Languages provide a powerful set of tools for probing the cultural history of the peoples who spoke them. Determining the relationships between particular languages, such as the languages of the Afrasian or the Nilo-Saharan family, gives us an outline history of the societies that spoke those languages in the past. And because each word in a language has its own individual history, the vocabulary of every language forms a huge archive of documents. If we can trace a particular word back to the common ancestor language of a language family, then we know that the item of culture connoted by the word was known to the people who spoke the ancestral tongue. If the word underwent a meaning change between then and now, a corresponding change must have taken place in the cultural idea or practice referred to by the word. In contrast, if a word was borrowed from another language, it attests to a thing or development that passed from the one culture to the other. The English borrowing, for example, of *castle, duke, parliament*, and many other political and legal terms from Old Norman French are evidence of a Norman period of rule in England, a fact confirmed by documents.

REFERENCES CITED

Ehret, Christopher

1993 Nilo-Saharans and the Saharo-Sahelian Neolithic. In *African Archaeology: Food, Metals and Towns.* T. Shaw, P. Sinclair, B. Andah, and A. Okpoko, eds. pp. 104-125. London: Routledge.

1995 *Reconstructing Proto-Afroasiatic (Proto-Afrasian): Vowels, Tone Consonants, and Vocabulary.* Los Angeles: University of California Press, Berkeley.

forthcoming *The Historical Reconstruction of Nilo-Saharan: Phonology, Morphology, Subclassification, and Etymological Dictionary.*

Wendorf, F., et al.

1982 Saharan Exploitation of Plants 8000 Years B.P. *Nature* 359:721-724.

Wendorf, F., R. Schild, and A. Close, eds.

1984 *Cattle-Keepers of the Eastern Sahara.* Dallas: Southern Methodist University, Department of Anthropology.

Saharan Rock Art

Mohamed Sahnouni
Assistant Professor, Institute of Archaeology
University of Algiers, Algeria

ill. 7
unidentified people
Tassili Plateau
Algeria (Northern Africa)
rock art pastoral scene
with humans
Neolithic Period
7000-2000 B.C.

Photograph from Michel Leiris and Jacqueline Delange, *African Art*, 1968, ill. 292

The Sahara, from the Atlas Mountains to the Niger River and from Nubia to Adrar (Algeria, Egypt, Libya, Mauritania, Morocco, Niger, and Sudan), is strewn with rock art. Besides other evidence, this rock art indicates that the Sahara, now desert, was substantially wetter and more populated during the Neolithic Period (10,000-2200 B.C.). Rivers and lakes throughout the region supported abundant plants and animals as well as thriving human populations. In beautiful rock paintings and engravings, various cultural activities are portrayed, including hunting, people dancing, sheep and cattle herders, tattooed bodies, and enigmatic scenes of possible deities. Such cultural features, as old as early Neolithic, have persisted in parts of Africa into much later times, demonstrating the great resilience of many elements of African culture.

Different styles and traditions of Saharan rock art emerged over several thousand years of development. Although the chronologies are uncertain, most scholars distinguish five styles and periods, ranging from roughly 8000 B.C. to about 300 A.D. These periods and styles, from the oldest to the youngest, are the Bubaline or Hunting Period, the Rounded-heads style, the Bovidian or Pastoral Period, the Horse Period, and the Camel Period (Lhote 1959).

1. The Bubaline or Hunting Period, from about 8000 to about 6000 B.C., is named after rock engravings depicting large buffalo of a species now extinct (Lhote 1984). Other wild animals also are depicted with remarkable naturalism, including elephants, rhinoceroses, hippopotamuses, antelopes, giraffes, lions, and ostriches. Some associated human figures are shown bearing animal-head masks and armed with sticks, bows, and clubs. This period has often been called the Hunting Period due to an absence of scenes depicting domesticated animals (Hugot 1974:248). However, Muzzolini (1986; 1993:235) notes that some "Bubaline" rock engravings show apparent domestic animals and a milking scene, and thus regards this as a development contemporary with the later Bovidian Period.

2. The Round-Heads style, dating probably from about 6000 to about 4500 B.C., primarily is known in Tassili, in southern Algeria. Thousands of polychrome rock paintings portray human figures with spherical, featureless heads. Varying from schematic to naturalistic style, these forms range from small to giant-size. The significance of the faceless heads and rigid attitudes of the human figures is uncertain; some images may express divinities. Animal figures are rare and tend to be linked to scenes involving humans.

3. Rock art (ill. 7) from the Bovidian or Pastoral Period, from about 4500 to about 1500 B.C., depicts, in remarkably naturalistic style and with out overt symbolism, scenes of domesticated sheep and cattle and their keepers. The human figures usually are shown nude or wearing loin garments or other dress of fiber. Wild animals still are depicted, but buffaloes and hippopota muses are missing, suggesting growing aridity.

4. The Horse Period, from 1500 B.C. to 500 B.C., indicates the arrival of the horse and chariot in the Sahara, presumably introduced from Egypt. The style is highly schematic and geometric. Portrayed in both paintings and engravings, the human figures are stereotyped, tending to be rather elongated. Heads no longer are detailed, but rather are reduced to mere lines. Pastoral scenes are rare, suggesting intensified aridity, and are depicted in coarser style. War themes predominate, and the art displays files of warriors, horsemen, and war-chariots in "flying gallop."

5. The Camel Period, probably from about 500 B.C., coincides with the arrival of the camel, better adapted to the desert conditions then prevailing in the Sahara. Cattle no longer are depicted, and wild animals are rare. In terms of style, these paintings appear to have been hastily produced, and the engravings pecked out, indicating the decline of Saharan rock art.

People were depicted with a range of skin colors, from light to dark, and appear to represent groups with different cultures. Many cultural traditions expressed in the Saharan rock art are still found in other parts of Africa. These include the use of masks and body art, and pastoralism. Several mask types shown in the Tassili rock art (ills. 59-60, Masking section) resemble nineteenth- and twentieth-century examples documented from West and Central Africa. Body art depicted in Saharan rock art is also present in Africa today. A striking example is a painting of a woman from Aouanrhet (Tassili, southern Algeria). Three parallel dotted lines decorate her breast (ill. 66, Body Art section). The pastoral adaptation, portrayed in Saharan art during the verdant times of the Neolithic (ill. 7), persisted into much later times elsewhere in the African continent. The beginning of the desiccation of the Sahara, starting around 4000 B.C. and climaxing about 2000 B.C., caused large-scale movements of pastoralists out of the Libyan Desert into the Nile Valley (Clark 1980) as well as southward into the Sahel zones of West Africa (Smith 1980:498). In the Nile Valley, Tjemeh nomads appeared in Sudan around 2300 B.C. (Clark 1980:568). Later, in Egypt's New Kingdom, Libyan peoples, known as Libu and Meshwesh, were involved in the campaign against Egypt led by the "Sea-Peoples" (O'Connor 1982:900). Among present-day pastoralists in West Africa are the Peul (or Fulani), who are believed by Lhote (1976:145) to resemble the light-complexioned Africans depicted in the Bovidian Period paintings. These people live near River Niger and appear to have a life-style similar to the Saharan Neolithic pastoralists. According to an account of a Peul individual, the painting known as "kneeling cattle" illustrates the litori ceremony practiced today, in which cattle are made to kneel in a ritual observing the Peul belief in their aquatic origin (Lhote 1976:146).

There were probable influences between Saharan people and ancient Egypt. For example, engravings assigned to the Bubaline Period representing rams with spheres on their heads might be linked to the symbol of the god Amun of the Nile Valley (Gillon 1984:55), which appeared in much later times around 3000 B.C. Similarities between tailed garments portrayed in the rock art and that of Egyptian kings (ills. 8-9) suggest that the ancient Nile Valley population included immigrants from the Sahara as it began to become a desert.

ill. 8
unidentified people
Libya (Northern Africa)

scene with tailed garment similar to that of Egyptian kings
rock art
Neolithic Period
5000-1000 B.C.

Photograph from Palazzo Di Venezia, *Arte Preistorica del Sahara Libico,* 1960, ill. 9

ill. 9
ancient Egyptian people
Hierakonpolis (Nekhen)
Egypt (Northeastern Africa)

detail of King Narmer with tailed garment
(from Palette of Narmer)
Early Dynastic Period
about 3100 B.C.

Cairo Museum, Cairo, Egypt
Photograph from The Metropolitan Museum of Art
CG 14716

REFERENCES CITED

Clark, J.D.

1980 Human populations and cultural adaptations in the Sahara and Nile during prehistoric times. In *The Sahara and the Nile. Quaternary environments and prehistoric occupation in northern Africa.* Martin A. J. Williams and Hugues Faure, eds. pp. 527-582. Rotterdam: Balkema.

Gillon, W.

1984 *A short history of African art.* New York: Facts On File Publications.

Hugot, H. J.

1974 *Le Sahara avant le désert.* Paris: Editions des Espérides.

Lhote, H.

1959 *The search for the Tassili Frescoes.* London: Hutchinson.

1976 *Vers d'autres Tassilis. Nouvelles découvertes au Sahara.* Paris: Arthaud.

1984 Chronologie de l'art rupèstre nord-africain et saharien. *L'Anthropologie* 88:649-654.

Muzzolini, A.

1986 *L'art rupèstre préhistorique des massifs centraux sahariens.* Oxford: B.A.R. International series 318.

1993 The emergence of food-producing economy in the Sahara. In *The Archaeology of Africa. Food, Metals and Towns.* Thurstan Shaw, Paul Sinclair, Bassey Andah, and Alex Okpoko, eds. pp. 227-239. London: Routledge.

O'Connor, D.

1982 Egypt, 1552-664 B.C. In *Cambridge History of Africa.* vol. 1, *From the Earliest Times to c. 500 B.C.* J. Desmond Clark, ed. pp. 830-940. Cambridge: Cambridge University Press.

Smith, A. B.

1980 Domesticated cattle in the Sahara and their introduction into West Africa. In *The Sahara and the Nile. Quaternary environments and prehistoric occupation in northern Africa.* Martin A. J. Williams and Hugues Faure, eds. pp. 489-501. Rotterdam: Balkema.

The Predynastic of Egypt: Africa's Prelude to Civilization

Fekri A. Hassan
Petrie Professor
University of London

The Predynastic Period was a stage of political and economic transformation that culminated in the rise of a state society. The foundation for this profound transformation was the inception of farming in the Nile Valley and the Delta.

The earliest evidence of farming communities in the Nile Valley is dated to 4800 B.C. at Merimda Beni Salama in the Delta (Lower Egypt). Farming was introduced by pastoralists and cultivators from the Sahara and the Levant in the wake of severe droughts between 5000 and 4000 B.C. (ill. 7). In Upper Egypt (southern Egypt), the earliest farming communities appeared first in the Badari region about 4000 B.C. Sites in this region contain a ceramics suite referred to as the Badarian. In Upper Egypt, distinctive pottery types are also used to identify three successive phases: Naqada I (or Amratian), 3800 to 3500 B.C.; Naqada II (or Gerzean), 3500 to 3300 B.C., and Naqada III, 3300 to 3000 B.C., which is followed by the Early Dynastic Period. Pottery sequence and other archaeological remains document a continuous cultural development.

The political transformation from farming communities to a state society was primarily a result of the success of alliances between neighboring communities in combating the difficulties of early agriculture. Nile floods are highly erratic. The earliest farmers were faced with droughts, overflooding, and destruction of natural dikes. Initially, bonds of kinship and social ties provided a basis for intercommunity food exchange, to gain food security. Shrines and ceremonial centers emerged to enhance group solidarity. Subsequently, alliances led to the emergence of chiefdoms that were later consolidated and expanded to form kingdoms and principalities. This stage was achieved in Naqada II, as indicated by the tomb of a prominent chief or king at Hierakonpolis about 3500 B.C.

The emergence of kings and chiefs was linked to the development of a belief in cosmic forces responsible for the generation (birth) and regeneration of life (resurrection). Cow goddesses became a symbol of this belief. The iconography of deities on decorated Naqada II pottery (ill. 11, African Origins of Egyptian Writing section) prefigures that of the cow goddess at the top of the palette associated with Narmer (3000 B.C.), the founder of a unified Egypt (ill. 42, Ancestor Worship and Divine Kingship section). The cow symbolism was shared with Saharan pastoralists who lived west of the Nile at that time. Local political centers in the Nile Valley were, in addition, identified with local cult centers and totems. Many of these cult centers developed into towns with large cemeteries.

Both at Naqada and Hierakonpolis, the cemeteries initially included a few large, elaborate tombs with numerous grave objects (ill. 70, Body Art section), indicative of a powerful and wealthy elite. The elite then separated their burial grounds from the main cemeteries, and the largest tombs became progressively larger through time. This was a prelude to the building of monumental mastabas and pyramids that served as the tombs of the pharaohs during the Old Kingdom.

The production of religious and elite objects stimulated both trade and crafts. Maadi, a site at the apex of the Delta, was a station for overland trade with the Near East, while Buto handled sea trade. Hierakonpolis, in the south, was a center for trade with Nubia. Copper and gold jewelry, alabaster vases and other objects made from fine rocks and minerals, gemstones, and faience are common grave goods in the tombs of the elite.

By 3400 B.C., Naqada and Hierakonpolis were amalgamated in a single kingdom under rulers from the south. Later, they extended their power to Abydos, further north. Simultaneously, local Delta cultures were being replaced by elements from Upper Egypt during late Naqada II. This is well illustrated by burial customs and pottery at Minshat Abu Omar in the East Delta. Subsequently, by approximately 3200 B.C. the first steps toward a politically unified Egypt were undertaken, as shown by the tombs of great kings at Abydos. The unification, which led to a single nation-state under Narmer (3000 B.C.), was the culmination of political alliances and military confrontations (ill.42, Ancestor Worship and Divine Kingship section).

The development of kingship was closely linked with a religious ideology, which combined elements from different districts in Egypt. In historical times, every king was identified with the god Horus, represented by a falcon. Horus, the living king, was the son of a god, Osiris, who was considered the first king of Egypt. Horus was also affiliated with Isis, a goddess who retained the role of the Predynastic cow goddess as a nurturing and protective mother (ill. 20, Mother and Child Figures section).

The political and religious development of Predynastic Egypt is among Africa's great contributions to the world. Following the indigenous development of pastoralism in Sahara, settlers of the valley undertook a series of actions that culminated in the rise of dynastic Egyptian civilization. The developments in Egypt were also enriched by a continuation of cultural interactions between the Nile Valley and its neighbors. Many similarities between Egypt and other African societies are related to this common past, a common heritage of which Egypt is an integral part.

The cultural continuity with an African substratum and the strong historical cultural interactions between Egypt and other African societies clearly demonstrates that Africa was the cradle of Egyptian civilization.

Early African Cultures: An Afrocentric Perspective

Molefi Kete Asante
Chair and Professor,
Department of African American Studies
Temple University

Two sources have yielded the majority of information about the ancient African past: excavations and written texts. No ancient civilization left as much in terms of monumental or textual materials for later scholars to assess. The intellectual decline that led to the separation of the early African civilizations from the very people who created them has resulted in the need for the contemporary reassessment.

It is not problematic to find in the material evidence of the Nile Valley civilizations the imprint of Africa. Ancient Egypt was an African civilization; that is, it was geographically, materially, philosophically, and physically African.

The first *Homo sapiens* to decide how to cross streams, how to build shelter, how to farm, and what was edible were Africans. The earliest evidence of the origin of humans, whether biological, biochemical, or archaeological, points to the African continent.

It is not surprising, therefore, that along the Nile River, running wholly in the continent of Africa, we should discover the agency of African people. The idea that Africa is only South-of-the-Sahara was a recent invention to separate the ancient majesty and monumentality of Egypt from the rest of the continent. But the 4,100-mile length of the Nile, flowing from south to north, traverses only the continent of Africa. Cataracts aside, the ancient Nubians and Egyptians never considered the rocks in the river impregnable boundaries that prevented social, political, and military interactions and interventions.

The flora, fauna, and minerals of Egypt, as well as the pottery, houses, headrests, and ornaments for religious and social purposes were related to the rest of the continent. Indeed, Egyptian Queen Hatshepsut's famous expedition to present-day Somalia (Punt) has been noted—as one sees on her mortuary temple in Deir el-Bahari—for the goods brought back to Egypt by the leaders of the expedition. Of course, this was a remarkable expedition, but it was neither the first nor would it be the last to Punt. Djed Ka Re Isesi in the 5th Dynasty and Harkuf in the 6th Dynasty had made successful expeditions to Punt and even brought back Twa people. Thus, the gold, animals, trees, returned to Egypt by Hatshepsut's expedition, had been seen in Egypt prior to the 18th Dynasty.

Philosophically, the ideas of the ancient Egyptian civilization were connected to the rest of the African continent through interrelationships with the contiguous populations. Various studies have demonstrated the similarity of beliefs, kinship concepts, totemic ethics, age-grouping, burial practices, and passage ceremonies in ancient Egyptian and other African communities. Even more, the *mdw ntr*, the written text, came to represent the entire African universe. Each glyph was itself a small part of the universe, and thus writing as the materialization of thought was repeated throughout the African continent with sculpture as the making substance of thought.

Ancient Egyptians of the dynastic period were black people, probably much darker than the present population of African Americans. The fact that other Africans were also black, e.g., the Nubians, does not negate the blackness of the ancient Egyptians. Neither does the fact that the Egyptians and Nubians went to war with each other negate the fact of their blackness. Germans have fought with the French, Tutsi with Hutu, Chinese with Japanese, but such military action against other nations is not enough to say that the people are not the same complexion. But more important than the skin color of the ancient Egyptians is the fact that culturally their gifts to the world were African gifts. Thus, *Egypt in Africa* is an affirmation of what has always been the truth.

AFRICAN ORIGINS OF EGYPTIAN WRITING

The Origins and Development of Ancient Nile Valley Writing

Frank J. Yurco
Research Associate
Field Museum of Natural History

Egypto-Coptic, the language of ancient Egypt, is a member of the Afroasiatic language family, which has a North African subfamily and a Western Asian Semitic subfamily. Afroasiatic originated in North Africa (Blench 1993; Hodge 1980). Egyptian writing has roots in the early Predynastic age, Badarian to Naqada II, evidenced by decorated pottery of these eras (Hassan 1983; Arnett 1982). Some eighty signs found on the pottery later appear in dynastic writing and sign lists (Gardiner 1957; ill. 10). Several also occur on the Naqada II jar (ill. 11), including the standards atop the two ships (behind the rear cabins) on both sides of the jar. The signs are double fossil shells and three hills. These signs, known from later times, referred to the deities of the nomes (states), and so they were used already with such values in the Naqada II period. Min of Coptos, represented by two belemnites, is a very ancient deity, represented often in pharaonic times with an archaic round shrine behind him (Thomas 1995:218-221). Such round huts were common in Badarian-Naqada I, but were displaced by rectangular houses in Naqada II. Accordingly, Min dates back to Naqada I, if not earlier. The triple-hills sign seen on pottery, and also standards, represents Thebes, where the "three sisters," as the mountains are called now, still dominate the eastern horizon. The same style of buff-colored pottery still is made in the Abydos-Luxor area, though no longer painted. Also on the jar are pictures that represent a sail and wavy water signs, both later hieroglyphs.

ill. 10
Predynastic graphic images and hieroglyphs
Predynastic-Protodynastic Periods
3650-3100 B.C.

The period following is Naqada III, when elite chiefs first arose in Egypt. These elites began to use signs from pottery with phonetic values on larger versions of stone palettes, maceheads, ivory knife handles, and tusks (Davis 1993) to record their victories and other events. Late in the Naqada III Period, scenes and signs were organized in horizontal registers (ills. 12, 42, Ancestor Worship and Divine Kingship section). Likewise, pharaonic iconography started appearing as early as Naqada I: red and white crowns (Wainwright 1923; Yoyotte 1990:55, pl. 56, no. 359), Horus falcon, serekh (the palace gateway frame), and other signs, which, together with the victory scenes, have been called the Pharaonic Cycle (Williams and Logan 1987). Such depictions are concentrated in the Upper (southern) Egyptian Naqada culture and in A-Group (northern) Nubia.

ill. 11
ancient Egyptian people
Thebes/Luxor or Coptos
Egypt (Northeastern Africa)

vessel
ceramic; h. 8 in.
Predynastic Period, Naqada II
3650-3300 B.C.

Lent by the Indiana University Art Museum
Gift of Frederick Stafford
59.45

ill. 12
ancient Egyptian people

Hierakonpolis (Nekhen)
Egypt (Northeastern Africa)

tusk fragment with rows of animals in relief
elephant ivory; h. 7 11/16 in.
Protodynastic Period, Naqada III
3300-3100 B.C.

Lent by The University of Pennsylvania Museum of Archaeology and Anthropology
E4903

A-Group marked the divide between Egyptian and Sudanese culture, known as Khartoum Neolithic (Trigger 1976). Once the signs are depicted on the Naqada III material, they can be read in Egypto-Coptic hieroglyphic script, though already, on the Naqada II buff pottery, the signs on standards on boats are readable as hieroglyphic names of nome deities. Such standards topped with deity symbols also appear on Scorpion's and Narmer's palettes and mace heads, signifying the federated Upper Egyptian nomes (Davis 1993:162-163, fig. 38). It has been proposed by some scholars that Mesopotamian Uruk culture stimulated the adoption of writing by the Naqada III rulers (Ray 1986 and accompanying essay in this section).
The Mesopotamians in the Amuq region made contact with Egypt, but, as now documented, through the Nile Delta town Buto (Von der Way 1988, 1992; Moorey 1990). From this contact came cylinder seals, clay ceramic architectural cones, and perhaps certain other traits, but these were speedily absorbed and transformed by Egypt's Naqada culture. Neither cuneiform writing nor the idea of writing were adopted. When cylinder seals are decorated with script, it is Egypto-Coptic hieroglyphs. So, also, the hero-with-animals motif appears very much in Uruk-Mesopotamian style on the Gebel el-Araq ivory knife handle (Hoffman 1991:340-344, fig. 80, p. 341), but in the Hierakonpolis painted tomb the motif has been acculturated. This rapid absorption and the fact that the Naqada II painted buff pottery with the boat standards precedes the Mesopotamian contact—as do the red and white crowns—strongly indicate that Egyptian writing and culture were already well underway and rapidly adapted some Mesopotamian themes and iconography. Also, the fact that Egyptian writing arose in Naqadan Upper Egypt and A-Group Lower Nubia, and not in the Delta cultures, where the direct Western Asian contact was made, further vitiates the Mesopotamian-influence argument. It also negates the formerly proposed Wady Hammamat route for the Uruk traders. The Naqada II boat standards particularly are key, for they were adopted directly into the Naqada III-Early Dynastic decoration as symbols of the federated nomes of Upper Egypt, and also in the Late Predynastic shrine depictions of Naqada III. In Naqada II they symbolized the names of deities that were worshipped where the jars were manufactured, Abydos-Luxor, a restricted part of Upper Egypt. Such buff water jars—now undecorated—are still made for export all over Egypt. Once formalized, Egyptian hieroglyphs were a distinct blend of pictographs, phonograms, and determinatives, as seen on New Kingdom stelae (ill.13). In conclusion, Hassan (1983) and Arnett (1982) have the stronger argument.

Meroitic writing appeared in post-25th Dynasty Nubia-Sudan, in the Napatan culture. It probably derived ultimately from Egyptian hieroglyphs, which the early 25th Dynasty Kushite pharaohs had started using. Nubian languages appeared after the demise of A-Group. By C-Group times, 2350 B.C., Nubians were speaking a tongue foreign to Egyptians. When C-Group and Yam (Kerma) Nubians were recruited as mercenaries (Fischer 1961), those who commanded them had to be bilingual, and the specialized title "overseer of mercenaries" developed (Trigger 1976:56-57). Later, the 25th Dynasty spoke a Nubian language (a member of the Nilo-Saharan language family). When they shifted their capital to Meroe, from Napata, about 600 B.C., their script was made distinctive. That became Meroitic writing, such as seen on

ill. 13
ancient Egyptian people
Egypt (Northeastern Africa)

funerary relief (detail)
limestone; h. 16 5/16 in.
New Kingdom, early 18th Dynasty
1550-1389 B.C.

Lent by The Metropolitan Museum of Art
Gift of Mrs. S. W. Straus, 1925
25.184.3

ill. 14
ancient Nubian-Meroitic people
Meroe
Sudan (Northeastern Africa)

offering table
sandstone; h. 18 5/16 in.
Meroitic Period
593 B.C.-330 A.D.

Lent by the Museum of Fine Arts, Boston Harvard University-Museum of Fine Arts Expedition 23.1480

two objects in the exhibition, an altar (ill. 14), and the red slate plaque of King Tanyidamani and Apedemek, the Meroitic lion deity (ill. 56, Animal Deities and Symbols section) (Wenig 1978:300, no. 121).

REFERENCES CITED

Arnett, William
1982 *The Predynastic Origin of Egyptian Hieroglyphs.* Washington, D.C.: University Press of America.

Blench, Roger
1993 Recent developments in African language classification and their implications for prehistory. In *The Archaeology of Africa: Food, Metals and Towns.* Thurston Shaw, Paul Sinclair, Bassey Andah, and Alex Okpoho, eds. pp. 126-138. London, New York: Routledge.

Davis, John D.
1993 *Masking the Blow.* Berkeley, Los Angeles: University of California Press.

Fischer, Henry George
1961 The Nubian Mercenaries of Gebelein during the first Intermediate Period. *Kush* 9:44-80.

Gardiner, Alan H.
1957 *Egyptian Grammar.* 3rd ed. Oxford: Oxford University Press.

Hassan, Fekri A.
1983 The Roots of Egyptian Writing. *Quarterly Review of Archaeology* 4, no. 3(1):7-8.

Hodge, Carlton T.
1980 *Afroasiatic:* A Survey. The Hague: Mouton.

Hoffman, Michael A.
1991 *Egypt Before the Pharaohs.* 2nd ed. Austin: University of Texas.

Moorey, P. R. S.
1990 From Gulf to Delta in the Fourth Millennium B. C. E.: The Syrian Connection. *Eretz Israel: Archaeological, Historical, and Geographical Studies.* vol. 21. A. Eitan, R. Gophna, and M. Kochavi, eds. pp. 62-69. Jerusalem: Israel Exploration Society.

Ray, John D.
1986 The Emergence of Writing in Egypt. *World Archaeology* 17:307-316.

Thomas, Nancy
1995 *The American Discovery of Ancient Egypt.* Los Angeles: Los Angeles County Museum of Art.

Trigger, Bruce G.
1976 *Nubia Under the Pharaohs.* Boulder, Colorado: Westview Press.

Von der Way, Thomas
1988 Investigations concerning the early periods in the northern Delta of Egypt. *The Archaeology of the Nile Delta: Problems and Priorities.* E. C. M. Van den Brink, ed. pp. 244-249. Amsterdam: Netherlands Foundation for Archaeological Research in Egypt.

1992 Excavation at Tell El-Fara in Buto in 1987-1989. *The Nile Delta in Transition 4th-3rd Millennium B.C.* Edwin C. M. Van den Brink, ed. pp. 1-10. Tel Aviv: E. C. M. Van den Brink.

Wainwright, G. A.
1923 The Red Crown in Early Prehistoric Times. *Journal of Egyptian Archaeology* 9:26-33.

Wenig, Steffen
1978 *Africa in Antiquity,* Vol. II: The Arts of Nubia and the Sudan. Sylvia Hochfield and Elizabeth Riefstahl, eds. Brooklyn: Brooklyn Museum.

Williams, Bruce and Thomas J. Logan
1987 The Metropolitan Museum of Art Knife Handle and Aspects of Pharaonic Imagery Before Narmer. *Journal of Near Eastern Studies* 46, no. 4:245-285.

Yoyotte,Jean
1990 *L'Egypte des millenaries obscurs.* Paris: Hatier et Musées de Marseille.

The Mesopotamian Influence on Ancient Egyptian Writing

John Ray
Herbert Thompson Reader in Egyptology
University of Cambridge

It is well known that all writing systems began with pictures. Early scripts work by using pictures of things that can be represented easily; the trick is to find a way to extend these to cover ideas that cannot be expressed pictorially. This breakthrough seems to have been made first in southern Mesopotamia, by the people known as the Sumerians, at some date after 3200 B.C. The method used is known as paronomasia (punning): pictures are substituted for other words that happen to sound alike, or nearly so. (Sumerian has many such homonyms, or word-pairs, and the language lends itself readily to such a process.) In Mesopotamia, the use of recognizable picture-signs soon gave way to simplified designs based on the marks made by a wooden stylus on clay tablets, but the essentials of the system remained unchanged (Robinson 1995:62-90). Another method used in the development of writing is the cartoon, in which signs are combined to carry derived meanings, without reference to the way they are pronounced. This idea is common in Chinese writing, but is not of much importance in the Near East.

In Mesopotamia, we can follow the development of writing over several centuries: it seems it was at home among the Sumerians and their Semitic-speaking compatriots. In Egypt, things happened more suddenly. Until recently it was thought that the hieroglyphic script was created at the beginning of the First Dynasty (c. 3000 B.C.), or just before this. However, recent excavations, mostly German, at the site of Abydos in Upper Egypt and Buto in the Delta have pushed this date back by at least a century; and it has been known for some time that there were kings of a sort in Egypt before the traditional beginning of history.
This period is increasingly referred to, illogically but understandably, as Dynasty 0. Dockets and jar-labels from a quasi-royal tomb at Abydos, dated no later than 3050 B.C., bear most of the hallmarks of later hieroglyphic texts, and may well be earlier than this. Yet, even with this new evidence, hieroglyphs do not show the same gradual, experimental development that we see in Mesopotamian writing. They seem from the outset to be connected with the royal administration rather than the needs of individual merchants, and they give the impression of having been devised to order, as if a prototype already existed that had overcome the conceptual problems involved. Where would such a prototype be found, if not in Mesopotamia?

Early Egypt soaked up ideas from Mesopotamia, in architecture and the arts, and imported Mesopotamian pottery was found at several Protodynastic sites in Egypt, especially Buto (Rice 1990:57-67). This influence is so strong that at one point the idea was seriously entertained that an early Mesopotamian state had even conquered Egypt and turned it into a province. This theory has long been discredited, and a more convincing analogy is to liken early Egypt to a child learning to walk, looking around for a prop to help it to do so. This prop was the advanced city culture in Mesopotamia. When Egypt had found its confidence, it was able to throw away the prop, and many Mesopotamian motifs came to be discarded in favor of Egyptian ones. Writing, however, was an exception. It was too useful to be abandoned.

How much of the Mesopotamian writing system did the Egyptians adopt? The best answer seems to be the simplest: they adopted the underlying idea, namely that pictures of the natural world could be used to express notions that were otherwise impossible to draw. Such an idea could travel fast, and this may well explain the short period of time between the appearance of writing in Mesopotamia and its adoption on the banks of the Nile. The method on its own was sufficient for the fertile minds of the Egyptians, and there was no necessity for them to learn cuneiform in order to try it out. The Egyptians did not take over the Mesopotamian picture-forms, since they already had an extensive pictorial repertoire of their own. However, they were obliged to adapt the phonetic principle underlying Mesopotamian writing to the peculiarities of their own language, in particular the fact that it tends to express variations of meaning by altering the vowels within a word, like Hebrew and Arabic. The Egyptian answer was brilliantly simple: to ignore vowels completely, and to use picture-signs for other words that happened to contain the same consonants (for general principles, see Davies 1987). Ambiguity was lessened by the use of determinatives, signs with no sound-value that indicate what category of objects a word falls into. Mesopotamian writing also uses determinatives, though less systematically. Determinatives also have the useful function of indicating where words come to an end, since ancient scripts do not mark gaps between words, and they also mark out particularly important classes, such as gods, sums of trade goods, or place-names. Perhaps because of the vowellessness of the script, which encouraged thinking in terms of individual consonants, the Egyptians soon developed a form of alphabet, which was used to eke out the value of pictorial signs, and to mark things such as grammatical endings, which were otherwise difficult to express. A smaller difference was that the Egyptians' numbering system was decimal, whereas Mesopotamia's was sexagesimal. But on balance, the adoption of writing in Egypt falls into a general pattern. Mesopotamian culture, and its writing, was the prop that helped ancient Egypt find its feet (Ray 1986).

REFERENCES CITED

Davies, W. Vivian
1987 *Egyptian Hieroglyphs*. London: British Museum Publications.

Ray, John D.
1986 The emergence of writing in Egypt. *World Archaeology* 17(3): 307-16.

Rice, Michael
1990 *Egypt's Making: The Making of Ancient Egypt 5000-2000 B.C.* New York: Routledge.

Robinson, Andrew
1995 *The Story of Writing*. New York: Thames & Hudson.

MOTHER AND CHILD FIGURES

Mother and Child Figures in Africa

Martha J. Ehrlich
Associate Professor of Art History
Southern Illinois University at Edwardsville

In both ancient Egyptian and other traditional African cultures, mother and child images embodied the continuity of the life cycle. For these cultures, children were guarantors of parental security in old age, proper burial, and spiritual continuity as ancestors. A woman's most important biological, social, and religious function was to produce children who in maturity would secure lineage continuity (Sieber and Walker 1987:28-31). Failure to obey this reproductive imperative was ultimately disastrous for both the woman and her lineage.

In keeping with this concern for the perpetuation of lineage, maternity figures from sub-Saharan Africa rarely depict birth, but instead show a young, beautiful mother at the height of her reproductive powers. Her child is either a generalized image (ills. 16, 19) or a small adult in a childlike pose (ill. 18). Rarely is the child given an entirely infantile, childlike or adult appearance; it usually has a large head and may sometimes display adult sexual characteristics, but lacks any expression of character, personality, or self-awareness. It is displayed, almost as an accessory, by the mother, who almost never looks at her child. Power and awareness lie with the mother; the child's figure is proof of her ability and the image of continuity (ills. 16, 18-19). This is also true of some ancient Egyptian works (ill. 15), where the child is a miniature but passive adult in his clothing and body proportions.

ill. 16
carver: Nana Osei Bonsu
Asante people
Ghana (Western Africa)

royal mother and child figure
wood, pigment, gold leaf;
h. 17 11/16 in.
1930s

Lent by The Seattle Art Museum
Gift of Katherine White and The Boeing Company
81.17.323

ill. 15
ancient Egyptian people
Saqqara
Egypt (Northeastern Africa)

Pharaoh Pepy II
and mother figure
alabaster; h. 15 7/16 in.
Old Kingdom, 6th Dynasty
about 2350-2250 B.C.

Lent by The Brooklyn Museum
Charles Edwin Wilbour Fund
39.119

Mother and child images from sub-Saharan Africa are almost always spiritually connected to the living, with their concerns about continuity, whereas much surviving Egyptian art is in service of the dead. However, these differences may be more apparent than real, since West and Central Africans included ancestors, the living, and those yet to be in their sense of continuity, while the ancient Egyptian dead, immanent and never entirely separated in their afterlife from the living, still were involved in the lives of their descendants (Robins 1993). There are few direct parallels between representations of Egyptian deities such as Isis and Horus (ill. 20) and maternity images from sub-Saharan Africa, which focus on ancestor and other spirit forces rather than on gods.

Two royal images, one from ancient Egypt and one from twentieth-century West Africa, demonstrate similar forms and functions (ills. 15-16). The Egyptian sculpture of Pepy II and his mother was probably made early in the long reign of this 6th Dynasty king who came to power as a small child, because he is smaller and clearly subordinate to her. The figure was perhaps intended for the queen mother's tomb or a shrine dedicated to her memory (Romano 1995:73-74). Frontality relieved by the right-angle placement of the child across its mother's lap is also demonstrated by the Asante queen mother figure (ill. 16), probably used as display sculpture by popular secular drum ensembles in the late 1930s (Cole and Ross 1977:176). Focus is clearly on the mother; the child is a tiny accessory lying on her lap in a V-shape rather than sitting up, while most detail is lavished on the mother's elaborate hairstyle, large face with high, back-sloping forehead, sharp and elegant features, and fat-ringed neck. All these characteristics denote ideal female beauty for the Asante. An imported European chair, her upright, graceful, and dignified "royal" pose, with knees apart and feet flat on the ground, combine with the gold leaf to produce an image of composure proper for a queen mother, a close relative, or mother of a king. Her function in a matrilineal society was to give and maintain the continuity of the state (Thompson 1974:68).

Nonroyal maternity figures, while still frontal, are sometimes less ideal and less formal (ills. 17-18). The Egyptian sculpture (ill. 17) is from the last Old Kingdom dynasty, a period of regionalism caused by changes in central authority. Sculptures of parents with children are relatively common from this period, but examples showing only a mother and child or children are scarce. This woman's unclothed upper body displaying sagging breasts and an unideal figure perhaps indicate her status as a servant, represented with her children in her master's tomb to serve him in the afterlife. The nineteenth-century bronze casting from the Fante people (ill. 18) shows the mother seated on a stool while holding two children on her lap in a more symmetrical pose. Each child holds a breast. Although the mother is dignified, not looking at her children, their active, linear quality destroys the feeling of stability and calm. Twins were given special, favorable notice by the Asante, and presumably in related matrilineal societies like that of the Fante as well (Rattray 1923:99). This small casting was used as a counterweight on balance pan scales in the African-European gold trade.

Although mothers with two or three children occur in African art, maternity figures normally show one child,

ill. 18
probably Fante people
Ghana (Western Africa)

mother figure with two children counterweight for measuring gold
bronze; h. 2 1/4 in.
late 19th century

Lent anonymously
TR 8538/1

ill. 17
ancient Egyptian people
Saqqara
Egypt (Northeastern Africa)

mother figure with two children
limestone; h. 4 1/16 in.
Old Kingdom, 6th Dynasty
2410-2250 B.C.

Lent by The Metropolitan Museum of Art
Edward S. Harkness Gift, 1926
26.7.1405

as does the Soso figure (ill. 19). Mothers stand, sit, or kneel, carrying children in their arms or on their backs, but in every case attention is focused on the mother, not the child. Again, this reflects continuity, which is in the hands of the mother, the child being tangible proof of her capability. Only in servant figures (ill. 17) does ancient Egyptian art approach this idea because most extant maternity sculptures represent gods and individuals of high status. Children in group portraits, though stylized, represent real people, who share the viewer's attention with their parents. Yet, whether figures were made of stone, metal or wood, for the living or for the dead, the messages of biological and social continuity carried by both ancient Egyptian and more recent sub-Saharan African maternity figures are identical.

ill. 19
Soso people
Zaire (Central Africa)

mother and child figure
wood; h. 13 ⅜ in.
20th century

Lent by Marc Felix
TR 8545/1

REFERENCES CITED

Cole, Herbert M., and Doran H. Ross
1977 *The Arts of Ghana.* Los Angeles: Museum for Cultural History, UCLA.

Rattray, Robert Sutherland
1923 *Ashanti.* London: Oxford University Press.

Robins, Gay
1993 *Women in Ancient Egypt.* Cambridge: Harvard University Press.

Romano, J. F.
1995 Statue of Queen Ankhnesmerye II and King Pepy II. In *Africa, the Art of a Continent.* T. Phillips, ed. pp. 73-74. London: Royal Academy of Arts.

Sieber, Roy, and Roslyn Adele Walker
1987 *African Art in the Cycle of Life.* Washington, D.C.: National Museum of African Art, Smithsonian Institution Press.

Thompson, Robert F.
1974 *African Art in Motion:Icon and Act.* Los Angeles: UCLA Press.

Mother and Child Imagery in Egypt and Its Influence on Christianity

Frank J. Yurco
Research Associate
Field Museum of Natural History

Mother and child imagery in ancient Egypt is inextricably associated with Isis, the mother of Horus. Isis is one of the oldest and most powerful deities of Egypt, attested in texts from the 1st Dynasty, about 3100 B.C., onwards (Frankfort 1978:44). Considered as an offspring of Geb and Nut (earth and sky deities), she thus derived from Atum, the creator deity and his offspring, Shu and Tefnut, in the Heliopolitan creation myth. Nephthys was her sister, and Osiris and Seth were her brothers. Her name, in Egyptian, means "seat, throne" (Frankfort 1978:43); as wife of Osiris, prototype of Egypt's kings, Isis became linked to the royal tradition, a role already affirmed for her in the Pyramid Texts, of Old Kingdom date (Frankfort 1978:40-44, 120-122). As wife of Osiris, Isis played key roles in the myth, as the one who raised Osiris from the dead after Seth had murdered him, and as mother of Horus, her child by Osiris. Sorrowfully mourning him, Isis created the first mummy out of Osiris, and so she came to be a central figure in the resurrection of the dead through Osiris, a deeply held belief in ancient Egypt. Isis reared the young, helpless Horus as a widowed mother (ill. 20), with the aid of her sister Nephthys, other deities, and humans. After maturing, Horus went on to rule after avenging Osiris by defeating Seth (Lichtheim 1976:214-223). Since Horus also was manifested through the pharaoh, Isis came thereby to be associated with the queen-mother and was the prototype of every mother, royal (ill. 15) and commoner (ill. 17). She became a very powerful deity in other ways; in one myth, she works her will on Atum-Re, the creator deity, to learn his secret name after a serpent had stung him and he sought a cure from her (Pinch 1994:29-31). In the Late Period, Isis's tears for the murdered Osiris came to be viewed as the source of the Nile flood, even as Osiris himself was seen as the flooding Nile, which annually gave new life to Egypt (Frankfort 1978:190-195).

These multifaceted roles in Egyptian religion made Isis an inspiration to women especially, as she was known as wife and widow to Osiris and as the single mother who had reared Horus with divine and human help. She was a very sympathetic figure and became much beloved and popular, especially as the murder and mourning for Osiris and his resurrection were performed annually in a mystery play enacted at Abydos. Isis thereby played a key role in underpinning the high status women held in pharaonic Egypt (Lesko 1987).

Worship of Isis and Osiris as saviour deities who provided resurrection and life after death grew in the Late Period (663 B.C. and later). Foreign cultures in contact with Egypt took some notice of these beliefs, and Greeks and Jews who had settled in Egypt were noticeably attracted. Vibrant Egyptian belief in resurrection and afterlife through Isis and Osiris must have been appealing to these settlers, whose ill-defined concepts of an afterlife were shadowy at best. The Greeks, especially, adopted these Egyptian beliefs (Bell 1957:9-63).

In the syncretistic religious atmosphere of Late Antiquity, Isis and Osiris gained an ever-stronger following. The Ptolemaic Kingdom of Egypt (323-30 B.C.) for a time politically controlled Lower Syria-Palestine and Greek Ionia and some Greek Islands. They introduced in those regions the cult of Serapis, a synthesis of Osiris and Apis (ill. 53, Animal Deities and Symbols section), and Isis, both of whom are savior deities. In the Greek context, this echoes in the creed texts of Isis (Mueller 1972). Among the Greeks, women were an underclass, and none of the Greek female deities had the powers and magic of Isis. Following the Egyptian pattern, she became patroness of marriage and of women's equality. How powerful she was is demonstrated by the Ptolemaic queen Cleopatra VII (51-30 B.C.), who portrayed herself as Isis manifest (Bell 1957:63).

ill. 20
ancient Egyptian people
possibly Saqqara
Egypt (Northeastern Africa)

Isis and Horus figure
bronze; h. 10 11/16 in.
Late Period, 25th-26th Dynasties
712-525 B.C.

Lent by The University of Pennsylvania Museum of Archaeology and Anthropology
E14293

ill. 21
Nubian people
Faras
Sudan (Northeastern Africa)

Virgin, Christ Child, and bishop
wall painting from cathedral at Faras
plaster, pigment
10th century

Photograph from K. Michalowski, *Faras: Wall Paintings in the Collection of the National Museum in Warsaw*, 1974, pl. 45

In the Roman world of which Egypt became a province after 30 B.C., this role of Isis as champion of women, protectress of marriage, and pathway to resurrection after death through Osiris had a powerful appeal. In Rome itself, despite the early emperors' efforts to ban her cult, by the late first century A.D., they relented, and Isis appeared with yet more powers, as protectress of navigation, and as a deity having power even over fate (Apuleius, *The Golden Ass*). Shrines of Isis spread throughout the Roman Empire as a result. Isis gained a very large following among the Roman Empire's varied peoples, especially in her role as a pathway to resurrection after death through Osiris.

Little wonder that as Christianity spread, Isis came to be identified with the Virgin Mary, especially in her aspect as mother of Horus (ill. 20). Egyptian depictions show this transition directly into Christianity (Lewis 1983:95-106; Bowman 1986:184, fig. 113; 194-202). Isis's cult remained strong in Egypt, especially at Philae, until 577 A.D., and among Nubians prior to their conversion to Christianity, under the emperor Justinian (MacQuitty 1976:49-90). In many ways Isis remains as a model for women today, and her name echoes in female names such as Isadora and Isabella. The iconography of the Virgin and Christ Child in Nubian and Ethiopian medieval Christianity echoes the image of Isis and Horus (ill. 21). Isis also is reflected strongly in the Black Madonna imagery in Europe (Morenz 1976:243-250, 255-257; David 1982:174-177; Riad 1981:188-189). These dark-complexioned images might derive from earlier Isis images done in the Nubian-Meroitic style, especially since Meroitic Africans helped spread the cult of Isis throughout Europe (Riad 1981:189; Leclant 1976:282; Snowden 1976:112-116). In her aspect as "seat, throne," Isis, when associated with royalty, represents the importance culturally of the royal throne or stool in African tradition (Frankfort 1978:43-44); and in her aspect as a cow-headed deity (Lurker 1980:42, lower left illustration), she recalls the pastoral tradition of Egypt, which is part of the great Saharan and East African cattle pastoral substratum (Frankfort 1978:6, 162-180).

REFERENCES CITED

Apuleius
1951 *The Golden Ass*. Translated by Robert Graves. New York: Noonday Press.

Bell, Idris H.
1957 *Cults and Creeds in Graeco-Roman Egypt*. Liverpool: School of Archaeology and Oriental Studies.

Bowman, Alan K.
1986 *Egypt After the Pharaohs*. Berkeley, Los Angeles: University of California Press.

David, A. Rosalie
1982 *The Ancient Egyptians: Religious Beliefs and Practices*. London, New York: Routledge & Kegan-Paul.

Frankfort, Henri
1948 *Kingship and the Gods*. Chicago: University of Chicago Press.

Leclant, Jean
1976 Egypt, Land of Africa, in the Greco-Roman World. In *The Image of The Black in Western Art*, vol. 1. *From the Pharaohs to the Fall of the Roman Empire*. Jean Vercoutter, Jean Leclant, Frank M. Snowden, Jr., Jehan Desanges, eds. p. 282. New York: William Morrow and Company Inc.

Lesko, Barbara
1987 *The Remarkable Women of Ancient Egypt*. 2nd ed. Providence: B.C. Scribe.

Lewis, Naphtali
1983 *Life in Egypt Under Roman Rule*. Oxford: Clarendon Press.

Lichtheim, Miriam
1976 *Ancient Egyptian Literature*, vol. 2. Berkeley, Los Angeles: University of California Press.

Lurker, Manfred
1980 *The Gods and Symbols of Ancient Egypt*. Translated by Barbara Cumming. London: Thames and Hudson.

MacQuitty, William
1976 *Island of Isis: Philae Temple of the Nile*. New York: Scribner's.

Morenz, Siegfried
1976 *Egyptian Religion*. Translated by Ann E. Keep. Ithaca: Cornell University Press.

Mueller, Dieter
1972 I am Isis. In *Orientalische Literaturzeitung LXVII*, no. 3-4, March-April. pp. 117-130.

Pinch, Geraldine
1994 *Magic in Ancient Egypt*. Austin: University of Texas.

Riad, H.
1981 Egypt in the Hellenistic Era. In *General History of Africa*, vol. 2. G. Mokhtar, ed. pp. 184-207. Berkeley: UNESCO-University of California Press.

Snowden, Frank M., Jr.
1976 Iconographical Evidence on the Black Populations in Greco-Roman Antiquity. In *The Image of The Black in Western Art*, vol. 1. *From the Pharaohs to the Fall of the Roman Empire*. Jean Vercoutter, Jean Leclant, Frank M. Snowden, Jr., Jehan Desanges, eds. pp. 135-245. New York: William Morrow and Company Inc.

African Headrests

Rebecca L. Green
Assistant Professor of Art History
Bowling Green State University (Ohio)

Frank J. Yurco
Research Associate
Field Museum of Natural History

ill. 22
ancient Egyptian people
Saqqara, Tomb of Mehu
Egypt (Northeastern Africa)

wall painting with headrest
stone, pigment
Old Kingdom, 5th Dynasty
2535-2410 B.C.

Photograph from Ahmed Moussa and Fritz Junge, *Two Tombs of Craftsmen*, 1975, pl. 2

Headrests have been used in Africa for thousands of years. The earliest African headrests we know of come from ancient Egypt, but these may not be the oldest examples. While ancient Egyptian headrests survived because they were put in sealed, dry tombs, ancient headrests might also have existed in other parts of Africa, but may not have survived the wetter climates or termites (Dewey 1993:17).

Although apparently once widespread, headrests are now disappearing in Africa (Dewey 1993:20, 26, 28). Headrests were used in ancient Egypt from the Early Dynastic Period to the end of Egyptian pharaonic history (30 B.C.). Many scholars believe headrests were invented when Egyptians developed beds, with accompanying headrests that elevated the sleeper's head to keep it cool in the subtropical climate. Although most known Egyptian examples were placed in tombs for use in the afterlife, evidence exists that headrests were also used in daily life (ill. 22) and as commodities traded in the market.

The earliest datable examples of sub-Saharan headrests have been found in burial caves of the Tellem people, who lived in Mali during the eleventh to fourteenth centuries (Dewey 1993:18) (ill. 23). The ancestral association "continues today, as demonstrated by the inclusion of headrests in ancestor altars of the Baule people in Côte d'Ivoire (Ravenhill 1991:14). Today, most examples of headrests used as head supports are found in Central and Eastern Africa, as among the Kuba people of Zaire (ill. 24) and the Shona people of Zimbabwe (ill. 25).

ill. 23
Tellem people
Mali (Western Africa)

headrest
wood; h. 6 ½ in.
11th-17th centuries

Lent by Roy and Sophia Sieber
TR 8283

ill. 24
Kuba people
Zaire (Central Africa)

headrest
wood; h. 4 ⅞ in.
20th century

Indianapolis Museum of Art
Gift of Carole and Richard Darst
1991.68

ill. 25
Shona people
Zimbabwe (Southern Africa)

headrest
wood; h. 4 15/16 in.
20th century

Indianapolis Museum of Art
Gift of Mr. and Mrs. Harrison Eiteljorg
1989.1278

ill.26
ancient Egyptian people
Giza
Egypt (Northeastern Africa)

headrest
alabaster; h. 8 $\frac{1}{4}$ in.
Old Kingdom,
3rd-8th Dynasties
2735-2230 B.C.

Lent by the Museum of Fine Arts, Boston
Harvard University-Museum of Fine Arts Expedition
21.2790

ill. 27
Turkana people
Kenya (Eastern Africa)

man resting on headrest
20th century

Photograph from David Keith Jones, *Shepherds of the Desert,* 1984, p. 53

The importance of the head is significant throughout Africa. It is often considered the seat of a person's wisdom and life. In many areas of Africa, knowledge is equated with power. The possession and control of knowledge is, therefore, a form of empowerment. Headrests are important because they cradle, comfort, and protect one's head during life and sometimes into the afterlife. Some Africans equipped the deceased with a headrest during burial. In ancient Egypt (ill. 26), the *Book of the Dead* describes headrests as elevating, preserving, and protecting the deceased's head (Petrie 1914:15, no. 34; Faulkner 1985:16; Andrews 1994:95-96, fig. 95). Egyptian headrests also evolved into miniature symbolic funerary amulets that were placed inside a mummy's wrappings (Petrie 1914:15, no. 34). Ancient Nubian headrests were more than mere tomb furnishings and actually supported the deceased's head. In other areas of Africa the headrest of a deceased important person is buried in that person's stead if the deceased's body is unavailable, as occurs among the Luba people of Zaire (Nooter 1990:64).

ill. 31
Boja people
Sudan (Northeastern Africa)

headrest
wood, hide; h. 7 $\frac{1}{2}$ in.
20th century

Indianapolis Museum of Art
Emma Harter Sweetser Fund
1994.37

ill. 28
unidentified people
Chad (Western Africa)

headrest
ceramic; h. 5 $\frac{1}{8}$ in.
probably 12th century

Lent by Wilford H. Morris
TR 8546

A headrest supports a person's head during rest or sleep. It cradles the head and supports the neck or jaw of a person lying on his or her side (ill. 27). But most headrests are hard, not soft like a pillow. The hard, smooth surface helps protect an elaborate hairstyle. Depending on region and ethnicity, headrests may differentiate individuals of varying social standings. For example, specific hairstyles correspond to particular social ranks, and the accompanying headrests used to protect these hairstyles may also come to symbolize one's rank (Dewey 1993:21; 1995:136). For Somali people living in Somalia and Kenya, style differentiation denotes differences in age, status, and gender. Thus, younger men use simpler styles than elder men, and women use broader-based headrests than do men (Dewey1995: 128). In this way, headrests can visually declare one's identity.

ill. 29
ancient Egyptian people
Thebes-Luxor
Egypt (Northeastern Africa)

headrest
wood; h. 5 1/16 in.
Middle-New Kingdom,
12th-18th Dynasties
1991-1550 B.C.

Lent by The Metropolitan Museum of Art
Rogers Fund, 1927
27.3.160

A headrest's size is also significant of its overall importance; it is portable and therefore publicly visible and manipulable. Headrests are often objects of prestige. For example, they have been used as political gifts and as symbols that legitimate leadership. In some regions, they serve as links with the ancestors, inducing dreams that relay the ancestors' wishes (Dewey 1993:22). Headrests can also have secondary utilitarian uses. For example, a hollowed-out headrest may be used as a storage container, as among the Zande people of Zaire (Sieber and Walker 1988:112).

ill. 30
probably Sidamo people
Ethiopia (Eastern Africa)

headrest
wood; h. 7 1/16 in.
20th century

Indianapolis Museum of Art
Emma Harter Sweetser Fund
1994.122

African headrests are most frequently made of wood, some with decorative additions of other materials. A few examples in ceramic (ill. 28) and in ivory are known. Most known ancient Egyptian headrests are stone (ill. 26), perhaps because stone was used in tombs. Both ivory and glazed ceramic (faience) headrests were also used in ancient Egypt, although wooden headrests may have been used more frequently in daily life.

Headrests provide a smooth horizontal or slightly curved surface upon which to lay one's head. This elevated surface may be achieved with a relatively simple block shape (ills. 29-30). Known from both ancient Egypt and Nubia, block-shaped headrests suggest a strong continuity of style and form. The most prevalent and oldest-known type, however, consists of a base, vertical support, and horizontal resting surface. Generally, the support displays the greatest amount of creativity and has, therefore, been used as the basis of typological categories by scholars such as Jaques and Nettleton (Becker 1995:206).

Headrest decoration varies depending on regional, ethnic, and personal style. Among some peoples, such as the Somali, and the Shilluk of Sudan, headrests are created by specialists as well as by individuals for their own personal use (Dewey 1995:128, 136). Decoration may be incised, carved, molded, or added. A carver may incise designs over all or part of a headrest's surface (ill. 24). Embellishment of ancient Egyptian headrests included writing (generally the names and titles of the owner) and, more rarely, images or symbols of deities as references to their protective associations (Davies 1995:90). Similarly, images referring to dangerous animals or situations may be rendered on headrests to ward off the potential danger they represent, as on headrests of the Somali people (Dewey 1995:129).

Geometric patterns can be abstract or representative, depicting objects or corresponding to local ethnic scarification patterns. Embellishment is complex and may have multiple meanings. Thus, concentric circles on a Shona headrest (ill. 25) may represent female breasts, scarification, a cross-view of a white conus seashell, or the ripple of water in a pool. Or they may make suggestive reference to all four images, which refer to fertility or divination, which in turn are associated with the ancestors (Nettleton 1995:204-205).

Carved embellishment may have a strong three-dimensionality. Ancient Egyptian headrests often had fluted, column-like supports (ill. 26), while headrests of the Songye and Zande peoples, for example, include figurative forms. Some headrests incorporate human figures, although the Mbala people of Zaire reserved them for their chiefs (Mack 1995:255), thereby visually indicating status. African headrests are often carved to represent or suggest animals.

Embellishment is also achieved by attaching materials to headrests. Beads, tacks, metal wire, plaiting, inlays, and leather strapping, as in the Beja example (ill. 31), visually enhance a headrest and sometimes serve an additional utilitarian function. For example, straps can create a handle by which to carry the headrest. Eastern African pastoralists, whose portable headrests symbolize a warrior's status, often carry additional objects such as tweezers, knives, or tobacco by attaching them to their headrests (Mack 1995:141). Additions—some decorative—may also result from repair work, as when headrests are mended with strapping or stitching.

Headrests provide us with a distinct example of a cross-cultural, cross-geographical, and cross-temporal African continuity. They are and were made throughout African society, in all parts of the continent, for thousands of years. Thus, headrests are one of the strongest forms of evidence for the commonality of African traditions, from antiquity to the present, and from one end of the continent to the other.

REFERENCES CITED

Andrews, Carol
1994 *Amulets of Ancient Egypt*. Austin: University of Texas.

Becker, Rayda
1995 Untitled article on South African headrests. In *Africa: The Art of a Continent*. p. 206. New York, Munich: Prestel.

Davies, Vivian
1995 Untitled article on an ancient Egyptian headrest in the form of a hare. In *Africa: The Art of a Continent*. p. 90. New York, Munich: Prestel.

Dewey, William J.
1993 *Sleeping Beauties: The Jerome L. Joss Collection of African Headrests at UCLA*. Los Angeles: University of California Press.

1995 Untitled article on Ethiopian and Somali headrests. In *Africa: The Art of a Continent*. pp. 128-129. New York, Munich: Prestel.

1995 Untitled article on Sudanese headrests. In *Africa: The Art of a Continent*. p. 136. New York, Munich: Prestel.

Faulkner, Raymond O.
1985 *The Ancient Egyptian Book of the Dead*. Carol Andrews, ed. New York: Macmillan.

Mack, John
1995 Untitled article on two Karamajong headrests. In *Africa: The Art of a Continent*. p. 141. New York, Munich: Prestel.

1995 Untitled article on Mbala headrests. In *Africa: The Art of a Continent*. p. 255. New York, Munich: Prestel.

Nettleton, Anitra
1995 Two untitled articles on three Shona headrests. In *Africa: The Art of a Continent*. pp. 204, 205. New York, Munich: Prestel.

Nooter, Polly
1990 Contributor, *Art of Central Africa: Masterpieces from the Berlin Museum für Völkerkunde*. Hans-Joachim Koloss, ed. New York: The Metropolitan Museum of Art.

Petrie, William Matthew Flinders
1914 *Amulets*. London: Constable and Co.

Phillips, Tom, ed.
1995 *Africa: The Art of a Continent*. New York, Munich: Prestel.

Ravenhill, Philip L.
1991 *Exploring African Art: The Art of the Personal Object*. Washington D.C.: National Museum of African Art, in association with University of Washington Press, Seattle and London.

Sieber, Roy, and Roslyn Adele Walker
1988 *African Art in the Cycle of Life*. Washington D.C. and London: National Museum of African Art.

DEPICTION OF HUMANS IN AFRICAN ART

Depiction of Humans in African Art
Theodore Celenko
Curator of African, South Pacific, and Precolumbian Art
Indianapolis Museum of Art

Frank J. Yurco
Research Associate
Field Museum of Natural History

Is there an African way of depicting people in sculpture and painting, a cultural feature shared throughout the continent? The answer is both "yes" and "no." In Africa, the use of symbolic size and color in the depiction of humans in works of art may have first occurred in Saharan rock art over 9,000 years ago. There is evidence of its use in ancient Nile Valley works as early as 5,000 years ago and in sub-Saharan works as early as 500 years ago. The Saharan rock scene (ill. 7, Early African Cultures section) depicts people of different sizes and colors, which may symbolize differences in gender, age, social status or ethnicity. However, it is important to acknowledge that these figures may have been painted at different times by different people.

ill. 33
Yoruba people
Meko
Nigeria (Western Africa)

Sango staff with multi-figured group
wood, glass, fiber; h. 18 ¾ in.
20th century

Indianapolis Museum of Art
Gift of Mr. and Mrs. Harrison Eiteljorg
1989.736

ill. 32
ancient Egyptian people
Egypt (Northeastern Africa)

seated male noble figure flanked by two small females
stone (quartzite); h. 14 in.
Middle Kingdom,
late 12th Dynasty
1848-1786 B.C.

Lent by The Field Museum, Chicago
105188

An ancient Egyptian seated noble, flanked by two smaller females (ill. 32), demonstrates hierarchical sizing of human images. The male noble is large and centrally placed, while the socially inferior flanking figures, probably a wife and daughter or mother, are rendered in miniature size.
A twentieth-century ritual staff (ill. 33) from the Yoruba people of West Africa also employs symbolic size. The staff's large, central figure is a Sango priest. His left hand rests on the head of a worshiper, and on his other side is a small male drummer, both depicted in diminutive scale because of their subordinate social positions.

Two commemorative sculptures, one from ancient Egypt (ill. 34) and another from the Benin Kingdom (ill. 35) of West Africa, clearly illustrate the use of relative size to depict a figure's social standing. The small Egyptian carving has a prominent woman as its central, largest, and most

By the late Old Kingdom, the growing presence of Nubians from the south may have contributed to the occasional appearance of a new color convention. In this convention both males and females had brown complexions. However, the older color scheme continued through the Late Period. One should be cautious in basing interpretations of the physical appearance of ancient Egyptians on color in works of art because of the artificial and changing nature of artistic conventions.

The colors of deities also varied greatly. Some were depicted red-brown or yellow-gold, like humans, but others were green-blue or black. Green, and sometimes black, usually denoted fertility and fecundity. Blue represented air, invisibility, or water. Black also symbolized night and death. Hence, coffin faces were often painted green or black, symbolizing Osiris, god of the

ill. 34
ancient Egyptian people
Egypt (Northeastern Africa)

female figure flanked by husband and son
stone (steatite); h. 4 ¾ in.
Middle Kingdom, 11th-12th Dynasties
2020-1786 B.C.

Lent by the Petrie Museum of Egyptian Archaeology, University College, London
UC 16650

important person, flanked by smaller figures, her less socially significant son (left) and husband (right). Similarly, the central figure in the plaque from West Africa is a large man in high relief, a high-ranking military leader. He is flanked by somewhat smaller, lower-ranking soldiers. The other figures, musicians and attendants, in miniature form appropriate for their low status, serve as attributes of leadership.

An ancient Egyptian relief (ill. 36) incorporates both symbolic sizing and coloring. The seated couples to whom this funerary relief is dedicated appear in both rows of figures. The socially less important adult sons and brother stand before them. All figures adhere to the gender-based color convention of red-brown males and yellow-white females, which appeared throughout Egyptian history, but was strongest in the Old Kingdom.

ill. 35
Edo people
Benin Kingdom
Nigeria (Western Africa)

commemorative plaque
brass; h. 18 ¾ in.
16th-17th centuries

Lent by The University of Pennsylvania Museum of Archaeology and Anthropology
AF2066

ill. 36
ancient Egyptian people
Egypt (Northeastern Africa)

funerary relief
limestone; h. 16 5/16 in.
New Kingdom,
Early 18th Dynasty
1550-1389 B.C.

Lent by The Metropolitan Museum of Art
Gift of Mrs. S. W. Straus, 1925
25.184.3

ill. 38
ancient Egyptian people
Saqqara
Egypt (Northeastern Africa)

male figure
limestone; h. 21 1/4 in.
Old Kingdom, 5th Dynasty
2535-2410 B.C.

Indianapolis Museum of Art
Gift of Dr. George A. Reisner, through Alex R. Holliday
28.222

afterlife, and fertility of the soil. Likewise, representations of deceased kings were often painted black for this reason. The solar god Amun, whose name means "the hidden," was generally depicted as golden and sometimes as blue (Wilkinson 1994:104-125).

Symbolic color in masks, figures, textiles, beadwork, body painting, and other art forms is found in other parts of the continent. The Pende masquerader mbangu depicts a spiritually and physically afflicted character. Half of the mbangu mask's (ill. 37) twisted face is white, symbolizing death and the spiritual realm; the other half is black, symbolizing the precarious nature of life and the crises of illness. The white and black are a metaphor for the human condition (Mudiji 1989).

ill. 37
Pende people
Zaire (Central Africa)

mask with symbolic coloring
wood, pigment, cloth, fiber;
h. 8 1/2 in.
20th century

Lent by Dr. and Mrs. Wally Zollman
TR 8536/1

ill. 39
ancient Egyptian people
Egypt (Northeastern Africa)

male figure
stone; h. 23 3/16 in.
Late Period, 30th Dynasty
about 360 B.C.

Lent by The Metropolitan Museum of Art
Rogers Fund, 1908
08.202.1

ill. 40
Yoruba people
Nigeria (Western Africa)

male twin figure (ibeji)
wood, pigment; h. 12 ½ in.
20th century

Indianapolis Museum of Art
Gift of Mr. and Mrs. Harrison Eiteljorg
1989.714

Similarities in the postures of human figures from the ancient Nile Valley and from cultures south of the Sahara Desert have been previously cited (Willett 1971:110, 112). Freestanding depictions of people in Africa usually have consistent features: a frontal orientation, a rigidity of posture without contrapposto (the shift of body weight at the hips), formality of posture without casual gestures, and an idealization of the human form, particularly the face. Blemishes and wrinkles are rarely depicted on an ancient Egyptian pharaoh or a West African ancestor figure. For example, compare standing figures from ancient Egypt (ill. 38) and the Yoruba people of West Africa (ill. 40). With the exception of the striding pose with left foot forward, typical of many Egyptian male figures, the two carvings share many characteristics, although they are rendered in very different styles. Egyptian art was very conservative over a three-thousand-year period, and comparison of an Old Kingdom figure (ill. 38) and a Late Period figure (ill. 39), separated by more than two thousand years, makes this obvious (Iversen 1975). Indeed, figures from sub-Saharan Africa also come out of conservative traditions. Unfortunately, it is rare in sub-Saharan Africa—due in large part to environmental conditions and a lack of early collecting—to have a significant group of figures with a chronological range from one people or state. The thousands of objects dating from the fourteenth to twentieth centuries from the Benin Kingdom of West Africa, which include many human figures, are the primary exception.

Many figures from sub-Saharan Africa have a dynamism and animation in large part created by a bent-leg posture, animated arm gestures, and a subtle twist of body alignment, as illustrated in the carving from the Chokwe people of Central Africa (ill. 41). These qualities are absent from freestanding figures from ancient Egypt. Another feature common in sub-Saharan Africa, but uncommon in ancient Egypt, is a disproportionately large head, apparent in the above-cited Yoruba (ill. 40) and Chokwe figures (ill. 41).

It must be acknowledged that the formal characteristics outlined above are not solely African phenomena. For example, ancient Sumer in Western Asia, contemporary with early Egyptian culture, produced rigid, frontally posed figures and reliefs with hierarchical sizing. Much European art of the Middle Ages shares many conventions with African art. One only has to compare many Byzantine icons or mosaics and Gothic cathedral portals to a Benin plaque to find similar centralized, symmetrical compositions with hierarchical sizing and frontal, sometimes rigid postures.

Certainly, it would be incorrect to speak of one African sculptural or painting style. However, there are broad similarities in the way African artists from many cultures over millennia have portrayed human beings. The contrast

ill. 41
Chokwe people
Angola (Central Africa)

royal male figure
wood; h. 19 in.
19th century

Indianapolis Museum of Art
Gift of Mr. and Mrs. Harrison Eiteljorg
1989.1213

with European art, particularly from Classical Greece and Rome, and since the Renaissance, is clear. European art often has been naturalistic and illusionistic; African art generally has been abstract and symbolic.

REFERENCES CITED

Iversen, Erik
1975 *Canon and Proportions in Ancient Egyptian Art.* 2nd ed. Warminster: Aris and Philips.

Mudiji, Malamba Gilombe
1989 *Le langage des masques africains: étude des formes et fonctions symboliques des "Mbuya" des Phende.* Kinshasa, Zaire: Facultés catholiques de Kinshasa.

Wilkinson, Richard H.
1994 *Symbol and Magic in Egyptian Art.* London: Thames and Hudson.

Willett, Frank
1971 *African Art: An Introduction.* New York: Praeger Publishers.

ANCESTOR WORSHIP AND DIVINE KINGSHIP

Ancestor Worship and Divine Kingship in the Ancient Nile Valley

Lanny Bell
Associate Professor of Egyptology, Emeritus
Oriental Institute Museum, University of Chicago

Ancestor worship and divine kingship in Egypt conformed to similar institutions documented in many cultures. Together these institutions governed religious, social, political, and economic life. Through the kinship system, the cult of the ancestors provided foundations for divine kingship. Kinship in any homogeneous culture establishes parameters of behavior—authorizing and limiting the exercise of power; prescribing rights and privileges, duties and obligations; controlling marriage, inheritance, and succession. New Kingdom Egypt was a patrilineal society, lineage descent being traced through the father's bloodline (Bell 1991; Franke 1986). Kingship was based on paternal authority in the family: the Egyptian word for "sovereign" was an extension of the word "father." Female pharaohs were portrayed and referred to as males. Marriage was a contractual alliance between families, and many pharaohs chose nonroyal women from prominent families as their chief queens. Queens acquired prestige as consorts and/or mothers of the living god. The pharaoh's legitimacy did not depend on marrying a princess, nor did brothers usually marry their sisters. However, as god-kings,pharaohs could, and sometimes deliberately did, violate incest taboos, particularly in conjunction with their thirty-year jubilees, when they were rejuvenated and ritually incorporated into their sons' generation (Troy 1986:102-114; Robins 1993:15, 29-30; Meyer 1984).

Most direct evidence for ancestor worship comes from the royal sphere, but evidence confirms that it was also fundamental in the private domain. Relative status of the king, nobility, and commoners was determined by ancestry. Hierarchical ranking was symbolized in the ka-concept, the Egyptian expression for creative fertility or generational power of the ancestors (Bell 1985; 1996a; 1996b). Indeed, the Creator himself was the ancestor of the divine king. According to myth, Amun-Re of Karnak selected a human woman to bear his son. Assuming the guise of her husband (paradigmatically, the reigning king), the god impregnated her with his divine seed. The royal ka (thus implanted in the egg that the woman had produced) resided in this holy babe from its conception. But the king's divine status was not confirmed publicly until his coronation, when his origins were revealed and depicted in retrospect, to demonstrate that he had been predestined to rule (Berlev 1981:362-365). Every family had its ka-ancestor. Acting through the agency of male descendants, these

ill. 42
ancient Egyptian people
Hierakonpolis (Nekhen)
Egypt (Northeastern Africa)

Palette of Narmer
stone; h. 25 $^{9}/_{16}$ in.
Early Dynastic Period
about 3100 B.C.

Egyptian Museum,
Cairo, Egypt
CG14716
Photograph courtesy of The Metropolitan Museum of Art

ill. 43
ancient Egyptian people
Egypt (Northeastern Africa)

head fragment from figure of Pharaoh Senwosret II
diorite; h. 8 ½ in.
Middle Kingdom, 12th Dynasty
1897-1878 B.C.

Lent by The Walters Art Gallery,
Baltimore, Maryland
22.351

spiritual beings were credited with responsibility for every pregnancy in their families. Because a single ancestor was progenitor of a whole family, similar inherited genetic traits could be explained; individual differences were the mother's contribution.

Family ties were not broken by death, and the ritual reunions of the living and dead members of a family were celebrated. The king's divine ancestry was confirmed during the Opet Festival, statues of deceased kings were paraded during the festival of the fertility god Amun-Min-Kamutef, and the Festival of the Valley celebrated royal and nonroyal forebears alike (Bell 1996b). Life expectancy was short, and few grandparents got to know their grandchildren. The grandfather's generation was as far back as anyone could remember. Deceased grandfathers quickly merged with more remote nameless ancestors, who collectively constituted the ka. The referent for the paternal grandfather was father's father, a term also used of ancestors in general. Personal names were recycled, the first-born son being named after his father's father. Since one's name signified identity, the grandfather was essentially reborn in his grandson. The basic kinship configuration was grandfather-father-son. In view of inevitable death, families were conceived of as immortal corporations, outliving their mortal constituents. Family continuity was achieved in the smooth succession of generations. In this way the wealth and positions of fathers could be preserved for their sons. Ancient kings were archetypes to be emulated by their successors (ill. 42). Stereotyped royal statues portrayed the timeless nature of kingship (ill.43). All pharaohs, as incarnations of the royal ka, were theoretically descended from a common ancestor in an unbroken line, conceptualized in the fictive royal clan, of which each ruler became a member regardless of who his earthly father had been. A dutiful eldest son was expected to conduct his father's funeral rites, ensure a proper burial, and maintain his daily mortuary service, thereby guaranteeing him safe passage to the afterworld. In this way, the son asserted his claim to succeed his father as head of the family. Likewise, to legitimate his own kingship, each claimant to the throne had to control the body of his predecessor and bury him.

Two other means occasionally employed to secure succession for a particular heir were coregency and adoption. There was royal adoption in the 25th Dynasty, when the sister or daughter of the pharaoh was adopted by the daughter of a previous monarch, so she could inherit the important priestly position of God's Wife of Amun. The appointment enhanced the new ruler's claims in Thebes, where divine kingship had its theological base. This practice reflected a major difference between the New Kingdom Egyptian system and the Kushite kinship system, where succession was secured matrilineally, through the females of the royal line. According to the Sudanese version of divine kingship, the ruler was conceived by Amun of Gebel Barkal and born to the queen in her role as god's wife; princesses could similarly be espoused to the god. Kingship normally passed to the king's brother or his sister's son, although many queens ruled in their own right (Haynes 1992:25-26, 31-32; Priese 1981).

As early as the late Old Kingdom, the authors of letters to the dead pled with the ghosts (akh-spirits) of close relatives to stop afflicting them or to intervene to stop their suffering at the hands of others (Wente 1990:210-220). Uninscribed sculpted "ancestor busts," generic disembodied heads, have been found at the New Kingdom Egyptian craftsmen's village of Deir el-Medina. Along with related stelae and offering tables, these artifacts were placed in household shrines dedicated to recently deceased family members (akhs) who, supported in this way by their survivors, we successfully in transition to becoming ancestors (Friedman 1994:111-

ill. 44
ancient Egyptian people
Egypt (Northeastern Africa)

male ancestor bust of the scribe Ahmose
granite; h. 4 ⅞ in.
3rd Intermediate Period, 22nd Dynasty
945-712 B.C.

Lent by The Field Museum, Chicago 105172

117). This custom continued into the first millennium B.C., when the portraits were particularized with inscriptions (ill. 44). Just as official king lists—highly edited compilations—purported to give the family history of the pharaohs (with the reigning scion depicted as the pinnacle of family glory), so some first millennium B.C. private monuments contained detailed genealogies, tracing remote ancestry over many generations (Wildung 1975).

REFERENCES CITED

Bell, Lanny
1985 Luxor Temple and the Cult of the Royal Ka. *Journal of Near Eastern Studies* 44:251-94.

1991 *Family Priorities and Social Status: Preliminary Remarks on the Ancient Egyptian Kinship System.* Abstracts of Papers. Sixth International Congress of Egyptology. pp. 96-97. Turin.

1996a The Meaning of the Term Ka in the Instructions of Ptahhotep. In *Program & Abstracts. Annual Meeting of the American Research Center in Egypt.* pp. 30-31. New York: American Research Center in Egypt.

1996b The New Kingdom 'Divine' Temple: The Example of Luxor. In *Ancient Egyptian Temples: Rituals, Functions, and Meanings.* Byron E. Shafer, ed. In press. Ithaca, New York: Cornell University.

Berlev, Oleg D.
1981 The Eleventh Dynasty in the Dynastic History of Egypt. In *Studies Presented to Hans Jakob Polotsky.* Dwight W. Young, ed. pp. 361-377. East Gloucester, Massachusetts: Pirtle & Polson.

Franke, Detlef
1986 Verwandtschaftsbezeichnungen. In *Lexicon der Ägyptologie.* 7 vols. 1975-1992. Wolfgang Helck, Eberhard Otto, and Wolfhart Westendorf, eds. VI: cols. 1032-1036. Wiesbaden: Otto Harrassowitz.

Friedman, Florence D.
1994 Aspects of Domestic Life and Religion. In *Pharaoh's Workers: The Villagers of Deir el Medina.* Leonard H. Lesko, ed. pp. 95-117. Ithaca, New York: Cornell University.

Haynes, Joyce L.
1992 *Nubia: Ancient Kingdoms of Africa.* Boston: Museum of Fine Arts.

Meyer, Christine
1984 Zum Titel *"hmt njswt"* bei den Töchtern Amenophis' III. und Ramses' II. *Studien zur Altägyptischen Kultur* 11: 253-263.

Priese, Karl-Heinz
1981 Matrilineare Erbfolge im Reich von Napata. *Zeitschrift für Ägyptische Sprache und Altertumskunde* 108:49-53.

Robins, Gay
1993 *Women in Ancient Egypt.* London: British Museum.

Troy, Lana
1986 *Patterns of Queenship in Ancient Egyptian Myth and History.* Uppsala: Uppsala University. Boreas. Uppsala Studies in Ancient Mediterranean and Near Eastern Civilizations, 14, Acta Universitatis Uppsaliensis.

Wente, Edward F.
1990 *Letters from Ancient Egypt.* Edmund S. Meltzer, ed. Society of Biblical Literature Writings from the Ancient World, 1. Atlanta: Scholar's Press.

Wildung, Dieter
1975 Ahnenkult. In *Lexicon der Ägyptologie.* 7 vols. 1975-1992. Wolfgang Helck, Eberhard Otto and Wolfhart Westendorf, eds. I: cols. 111-112. Wiesbaden: Otto Harrassowitz.

Ancestor Worship and Divine Kingship in Sub-Saharan Africa

Chapurukha M. Kusimba
Curator, Department of Anthropology
Field Museum of Natural History

ill. 46
Edo people
Benin Kingdom
Nigeria (Western Africa)

commemorative head of king
brass, iron inlays; h. 18 in.
19th century

Lent by The University of Pennsylvania Museum of Archaeology and Anthropology AF5081 BT

Ancestor worship is one of the central features in most African religious institutions. It serves to spiritually bind living and dead kin members. Both humans and ancestors are responsible for maintaining the social, cultural, and moral order of the relationship, each playing an important part (Ray 1976:147). Ancestors protect the living from evil and reward goodness (Fiawoo 1976:263). They occupy the ontological position between the spirits and the living. They are, therefore, an intermediary between the living and the High God, known by various names throughout Africa. Thus, ancestors "speak a bilingual language of humans whom they 'left' through physical death, and of spirits to whom they are now nearer than they were when they were in their physical life" (Mbiti 1970:69; Uchendu 1976:291).

The concept of divine kingship in Africa is often associated with ancient Egypt. Divine kingship was less well-developed in sub-Saharan Africa, where a king sometimes had divine aspects but may not have been an actual god, as in ancient Egypt. Divine kingship gave spiritual power or godship to the king, making him, the royal palace, and the ancestral altar the focal point of political and ritual life of the kingdom. Among the Edo of the Benin Kingdom of West Africa, for example, the Oba was divine, his person mysterious, and his power limitless (ill. 45). The Oba presided at the ancestral altar (ill. 46), a ritual of national importance (Ben-Amos 1980:64). The health and well-being of the kingdom depended upon the health of the king (Bradbury 1957:40). To protect the kingdom, healthy and powerful kings were needed. A good king was one who instilled in his people awe, fear, admiration, and pride. These attributes were also universally applied to ancestors in many African societies.

ill. 45
Edo people
Benin Kingdom
Nigeria (Western Africa)

royal procession leaving the city of Benin
17th century

From Armand Duchâteau, *Benin Tresor Royal*, 1990, p.15

The relationship between the living and the dead is commonly maintained in Africa through ritual sacrifices undertaken in personal, lineage, or royal shrines and in public arenas or private homes to honor the dead or renew or strengthen the bond between the two entities. The reverence of dead predecessors is often referred to as ancestor worship. Parenthood, death, and good moral character are conditions for attaining ancestorhood (Fortes 1961:174; Levine 1982; Sangree 1976; Uchendu 1976:293). The medium of relationship with ancestors often takes the form of prayer, libation, and sacrifice (Fortes 1976).

Humans are responsible for the immortality of the lineage. Indeed the stigma associated with childlessness in African societies is the fear of death—the total death of a lineage. Without humans to maintain the bond through sacrifice to reaffirm the relationship, ancestors cannot exist. The sanctity of life for most African societies was best articulated by R. E. Bradbury, who showed that among the Edo of Benin, Nigeria:

> *To die childless, or sonless, is the most dreaded fate, and when one asks "why do you want many children?" the reply is often "so that they can bury me well." The Edo believe that one who is not properly "buried" cannot enter the society of his dead kin and associates. For his survival as a social being he is dependent on the performance of the mortuary ritual by his children. Again and again, at the climaxes of these rites one hears the song: "This is what we bear children for." In a sense, the funerary ritual is the most potent symbol of the parent-children relationship as it is ideally conceived in Edo culture* (1965:97-98).

ill.47
Kota people
Gabon (Central Africa)

reliquary figure
wood, copper, brass; h. 16 ¼ in.
19th-20th centuries

Indianapolis Museum of Art
Gift from the Joseph Cantor Collection
1991.292

To become an ancestor one must die and leave a legitimate filial successor. One only remains an ancestor as long as one's legitimate lineal successors survive (Fortes 1961:174). Living a transparent and moral life provides legitimacy and credibility to the memory of the dead, thus conferring ancestral honor (Levine 1982:27-28; Sangree 1976:299; Uchendu 1976:295).

Africans traditionally believe that the ultimate destiny of each individual is to reach the ancestral spirit land. They know, however, that in order to achieve ancestorhood, they must satisfy certain conditions. First, they should live honorably and maintain active membership in their lineage through participation in the lineage activities (McCall 1995:264). Membership in a lineage and maintaining ties by building a home, being generous, and having offspring insure entry into ancestorhood. Those who meet these conditions have higher chances of receiving honorable burials, without which they cannot reach the world of the ancestors (Ray 1976). Honorable burials take place in the homeland in the lineage or family cemetery, and receive full funeral rites (Bloch 1971; Mack 1986; McCall 1995:265). Many African societies believe that dead people who fail to receive honorable funeral and post-burial rituals to prepare their spirits for the long and arduous journey to the ancestral world become wandering, homeless, discontented, and evil spirits (Griaule 1965:189; Mbiti 1970). These spirits may return to punish their relatives through illnesses, fatal or near fatal accidents, miscarriages, childlessness, infant mortality, and poor harvests (Fortes 1959; Ray 1976:147). Not all misfortune is the work of disgraced ancestors, however (Parrinder 1949). Some misfortunes result from sorcery, witchcraft, or accidents. Oracles and diviners are usually consulted to determine the true source and cause of problems before the remedy is sought (Uchendu 1976).

Belief in the afterlife symbolically unites the living and the dead and serves to maintain order. This union is maintained through animal sacrifices, prayer, libation, or erection of ancestral memorials, often at the homes, grave sites, tombs, or shrines of the dead (McCall 1995). In kingdoms, the kings presided over these ceremonies at the royal ancestral altars as national ceremonies to reaffirm their spiritual and political power.

Ancestors are memorialized in various forms. Fetishes, twin figures, masks, reliquary figures (ill. 47), stools, shrines, and commemorative heads (ill.46) illustrate the interdependent relationship between the human and ancestral world (Ben-Amos 1980; McCall 1995; Udvardy 1995). Thus, to the makers and users of African art, these objects constitute a life source and a constant reminder that life is an ongoing and continuous process that does not stop with physical death (Bascom 1973; Idowu 1973; Willett 1971).

Masks and masquerades used at ceremonies honoring ancestors show them returning from heaven to restore order and bring stability and prosperity (Sangree 1976:301). These rituals often involve the most elaborate of Africa's art (Bascom 1973; Willett 1971). For example, Egungun masks (ills. 57-58, Masking section) worn during the festival of ancestor worship served to bind the living Yoruba to their dead ancestors and strengthen the relationship between them (Idowu 1973; Ray 1976:144).

Ancestors form an integral part of the social structure of Africans. Superior and powerful, beyond human challenge, the rights and duties sanctioned by the ancestors both define and regulate basic social and political relations (Ray 1976:147). In both stateless societies and large-scale kingdoms, ancestors constitute the basic categories of moral and legal thought. This responsibility raises ancestors and divine kings above transitory human level and invests them with sacred significance. Sages, diviners, griots, and the oracle serve as spokespeople of their respective societies (Griaule 1965; McCall 1995; Ray 1976). Ritual sacrifices at the shrines and memorials of ancestors bind humans and ancestors together, ensuring the stability and prosperity of the community and society.

REFERENCES CITED

Bascom, William
1973 *African Art in Cultural Perspective: An Introduction.* New York: W.W. Norton and Company.

Ben-Amos, Paula
1980 *The Art of Benin.* London: Thames and Hudson.

Bloch, Marc
1971 *Placing the Dead: Tombs, Ancestral Villages, and Kinship Organization in Madagascar.* London: Seminar Press.

Bradbury, R. E.
1957 *The Benin Kingdom and the Edo-speaking Peoples of South-Western Nigeria.* London: International African Institute.

1965 Father and Senior Son in Edo Mortuary Ritual. In *African Systems of Thought.* M. Fortes and G. Dieterlen, eds. London: Oxford University Press.

Fiawoo, D. K.
1976 Characteristic Features of Ewe Ancestor Worship. In *Ancestors.* William H. Newell, ed. pp. 263-282. The Hague: Mouton Publishers.

Fortes, Meyer
1959 *Oedipus and Job in West African Religion.* Cambridge: Cambridge University Press.

1961 Pietas in Ancestor Worship. *Journal of the Royal Anthropological Institute, Man* 91:201-255.

1976 An Introductory Commentary. In *Ancestors.* William H. Newell, ed. pp. 1-16. The Hague: Mouton Publishers.

Griaule, Marcel
1965 *Conversations with Ogotemeli.* London: Oxford University Press for the International African Institute.

Idowu, Bolaji, E.
1973 *African Traditional Religion: A Definition.* London: SCM Press Limited.

Levine, Robert A.
1982 Gusii Funerals: Meaning of Life and Death in an African Community. *Ethos* 10(1):26-65.

Mack, John
1986 *Madagascar: Island of the Ancestors.* London: British Museum Publications.

Mbiti, John S.
1970 *African Religions and Philosophy.* New York: Doubleday and Company, Inc.

McCall, John C.
1995 Rethinking Ancestors in Africa. *Africa* 65(2): 256-270.

Parrinder, G.
1949 *West African Religion.* London: Epworth Press.

Ray, Benjamin C.
1976 *African Religions: Symbol, Ritual, and Community.* Englewood Cliffs, New Jersey: Prentice-Hall, Inc.

Sangree, Walter H.
1976 Youth as Elders and Infants as Ancestors. The Complementarity of Alternate Generations, Both Living and Dead in Tiriki, Kenya, and Irigwe, Nigeria. In *Ancestors.* William H. Newell, ed. pp. 297-306. The Hague: Mouton Publishers.

Uchendu, Victor C.
1976 Ancestorcide! Are African Ancestors Dead? In *Ancestors.* William H. Newell, ed. pp. 283-296. The Hague: Mouton Publishers.

Urdvardy, M.
1995 Notes From the Field: The Culture of Fertility Compared-Preliminary Research on Ancestral Cults Among the Digo of Tanzania. *Anthropology Newsletter* 36(9):18-19.

Willett, Frank
1971 *African Art: An Introduction.* New York: Praeger Publishers.

ANIMAL DEITIES AND SYMBOLS

Animal Deities and Symbols in Africa

Chapurukha M. Kusimba
Curator, Department of Anthropology
Field Museum of Natural History

Frank J. Yurco
Research Associate
Field Museum of Natural History

ill. 49
Karagwe people
Tanzania (Eastern Africa)

cattle figure
iron; h. 16 ⅛ in.
19th-20th centuries

Lent anonymously
TR 8545/3

Interaction between humankind and animals in Africa has profoundly affected Africa's cultural and ecological landscape. This interaction has been captured in the archaeological record, in ancient rock art, in more recent wood carving, and in oral traditions. Chroniclers, storytellers, and artists have passed on knowledge and ethnic experiences in the form of proverbs, legends, epics, and myths.

ill. 48
Edo people
Benin Kingdom
Nigeria (Western Africa)

leopard head vessel lid
brass; h. 7 ¾ in.
15th-16th centuries

Indianapolis Museum of Art
Alliance Income Fund
1992.61

Many mythological and popular stories in Africa prominently feature animals (e.g., Beier 1966; Bleek and Lloyd 1911; Hambly 1949). Some were hunted for food, clothing, and shelter. Some were respected for their might, wit, and cunning. The belief that spirituality is deeply rooted in most aspects of African life may explain why many animals or composite animal forms were adopted as totems and as deities of particular groups and societies (Mbiti 1970; Hornung 1983). For example, the ancient Egyptians revered Sobek, the crocodile deity, and Sekhmet, the lioness, and some of the snake deities such as Edjo, the cobra, for their dangerous qualities. Seth, whom the Egyptians considered a trickster (Evans-Pritchard 1967; Hambly 1949; Te Velde 1977), was manifested as a hippopotamus, pig, or donkey. As a trickster, Seth was very much in an African mold. Characteristics of frogs, lizards, and insects were used to express aspects of deities. Composite animal forms in Egypt included Taweret, part female hippopotamus, part crocodile, and part lioness, and Bes, the bandy-legged household deity, benign, but with a leonine face. Composite animal forms sometimes constitute the imagery of sub-Saharan masks. Other ancient Egyptian deities, like Hathor and Isis, both having cow aspects, were beneficent (Goedicke 1970). That both Egyptians and Kushites worshipped rams as deities, especially Amon of Karnak, underscores the cultural interaction between Egypt and the Nubian cultures of Kush (Kendall 1982). Rams have also had ritual significance among the Yoruba, Edo, and other West African peoples. Moreover, most of the animals of special importance in ancient Egypt have ritual and social significance in sub-Saharan Africa (ills. 48-49).

Thus, Egyptian religious culture depicted in engravings and in art and sculpture points to the common African substratum of Egypt's culture (Frankfort 1948). What have

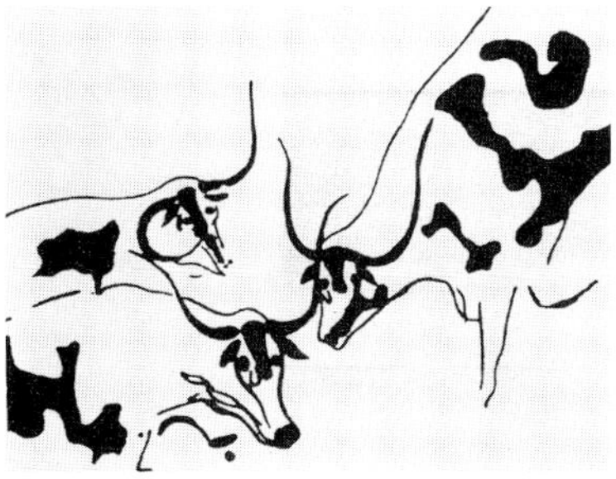

ill. 50
unidentified people
Tassili Plateau
Algeria (Northern Africa)

pastoral scene of cattle with deformed horns
rock art
Neolithic Period
7000-2000 B.C.

Drawing from Jean-Dominique Lajoux, *The Rock Paintings of Tassili,* 1963, p. 108

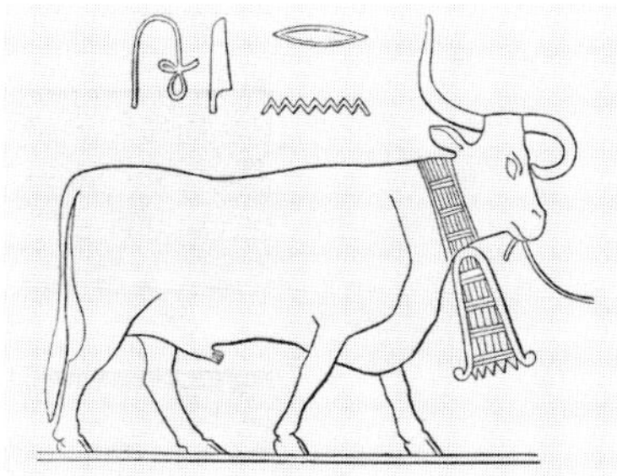

ill. 51
ancient Egyptian people
Saqqara
Egypt (Northeastern Africa)

cattle with deformed horns
tomb relief
Old Kingdom, 5th Dynasty
2535-2410 B.C.

Drawing from C. G. Seligman, *Pagan Tribes of the Nilotic Sudan,* 1935, fig. 8

ill. 52
Dinka or Nuer people
Sudan (Northeastern Africa)

cattle with deformed horns
20th century

Drawing from Henri Frankfort, *Kingship and The Gods,* 1948, fig. 38b

been interpreted as masked priests portraying animal deities in Egyptian ceremonies depicted in murals are reminiscent of common African rituals. The proliferation of animal representation in rock art in Africa probably illustrates the practical, emotional, and spiritual ties between Africans and animals. For example, depictions of people wearing animal masks and animals with discs, aureoles, and rods on their heads, often found together in southern Oran and Oued Djerat in Algeria, suggest people praying in front of animals (Ki-Zerbo 1981:670).

A myth of the San of Southern Africa, which tells of the sun growing tired of being carried on a zebra's back and taking refuge between the horns of a bull (Bleek and Lloyd 1911), is very similar to depictions showing oxen bedecked with the solar disc in Egypt, southern Oran, and the Sahara. The origins of the cow-goddess Hathor may be rooted in a pan-Africanist myth (Ki-Zerbo 1981:669). Ki-Zerbo makes a very strong case for the cultural unity of Africa based on his analysis of African prehistoric art:

> *Art of the Egyptian Nile flourished much later than that of Saharan and Sudan Africa. The Saharan representations of oxen with discs between their horns is much earlier than those of the cow-goddess Hathor. The hawk delicately carved on the sandstone plaque at Hammada el Guir is much earlier than the ram of Amon [known from the 12th Dynasty onwards]. When André Malraux looked at the animal heads at Oued Djerat, he considered them to be "forerunners of the Egyptian animal deities." The same no doubt holds for the bird-headed goddess at Jabbaren. Semi-naturalism only appears in Egypt in the Gerzean period and is derived from Saharan ox period carvings. . . . Egypt had a tremendous influence on the interior of Africa. . . . but what is even more certain is that the prehistoric civilization of the Sahara is earlier in time. . . . It was only from the so-called "historic" period onwards that Egyptian civilization achieved that splendor as a result of which everything is now attributed. But where art and technology is concerned, the focal points were originally in the modern republic of the Sudan, in East Africa, and the Near East. Moreover, the prehistoric Sudan owed much more to southeastern influences than to those from the Near East (1981:676).*

Thus, the ancient Egyptian belief that divinity can be manifested in any form has strong pan-Africanist roots. Among cattle-owning societies in Africa, cattle are symbols of wealth and serve to define as well as distinguish status. Old Kingdom tombs depict cattle as large parts of a noble's holdings. Cattle provided the means for forging new relations of cooperation and interdependence. Cattle were valued for milk and cheese, but were occasionally slaughtered for religious offerings (Beidelman 1960; Bloch 1971; Rigby 1969). In common with other African pastoralists, the Egyptians practiced horn deformation on special cattle (ills. 50-52). Egyptians worshipped cattle as beneficent

ANIMAL DEITIES AND SYMBOLS

ill. 53
ancient Egyptian people
Saqqara
Egypt (Northeastern Africa)

Apis bull figure
bronze; h. 4 ⅞ in.
Late Period, 26th Dynasty,
Ptolemaic (Greek) Period
663-30 B.C.

Lent by
The Walters Art Gallery,
Baltimore, Maryland
54.538

deities. Deities with bovine aspects echoed the importance of cattle in Egyptian society. Apis (ill. 53), the bull deity of Memphis, was a national deity. A bull with special markings and color was sought and, once located, was enshrined at Memphis with great honor. When the Apis died, he was embalmed with solemn ceremony and buried in the vast catacomb at Saqqara, called the Serapaeum. It should be noted that some ox masks (ill. 54) of the Bidjogo people of West Africa and Apis bulls have a triangular forehead design. Beside Hathor and Isis, Neith and a lesser-known deity, Bat, occasionally were depicted in bovine form. Cow deities provided milk and nourishment to the pharaoh.

Egyptian myths and stories feature cattle. In the *Story of the Two Brothers* (Lichtheim 1976:203-210), a pair of brothers are grazing animals, and one brother takes on the appearance of a bull. Cattle formed an important part of the booty in Egyptian and other African military raids on neighboring peoples. The Maasai, for example, believe that God gave them all the cattle in the world. They thus feel that they have strong kinship ties with cattle (Rigby 1992). This culture is well illustrated in the earlier prehistoric art, in the legends and myths of many African societies, in the archaeological record, and in modern African religious and cultural practices. Animal deities and animals, then and now, continue to play a central role in the everyday spiritual, cultural, and economic life of African people.

ill. 54
Bidjogo people
Guinea-Bissau (Western Africa)

ox mask
wood, horn, pigment, glass, iron; h. 18 in.
19th-20th centuries

Indianapolis Museum of Art
Gift of
Mr. and Mrs. Harrison Eiteljorg
1989.375

REFERENCES CITED

Beidelman, T. O.
1960 The Baraguyu. *Tanganyika Notes and Records* 55:244-278.

Beier, Ulli
1966 *The Origin of Life and Death: African Creation Myths.* London: Heinemann Educational Books Limited.

Bleek, W. W. I., and L. C. Lloyd
1911 *Specimens of Bushman Folklore.* London: George Allen and Company, Limited.

Bloch, Marc
1971 *Placing the Dead: Tombs, Ancestral Villages, and Kinship Organization in Madagascar.* London: Seminar Press.

Evans-Pritchard, E. E.
1967 *The Zande Trickster.* Oxford: Clarendon Press.

Frankfort, Henri
1948 *Kingship and the Gods.* Chicago: University of Chicago Press.

Goedicke, Hans
1970 The Story of the Herdsman. *Chronique d'Egypte* 45(90):244-256.

Hambly, Wilfrid D.
1949 *Talking Animals.* Washington, D.C.: The Associated Publishers, Inc.

Hornung, Erik
1983 *Conceptions of God in Ancient Egypt: The One and the Many.* Translated by John Baines. Ithaca, New York: Cornell University Press.

Kendall, Timothy
1982 *Kush: Lost Kingdom of the Nile.* Brockton: Brockton Art Museum.

Ki-Zerbo, J.
1981 African Prehistoric Art. In *General Prehistory of Africa I: Methodology and African Prehistory.* J. Ki-Zerbo, ed. pp. 656-686. Paris: UNESCO.

Lichtheim, Miriam
1976 *Ancient Egyptian Literature,* vol. II. Berkeley: University of California Press.

Mbiti, John S.
1970 *African Religions and Philosophy.* New York: Doubleday and Company, Inc.

Rigby, Peter
1969 *Cattle and Kinship Among the Gogo.* Ithaca, New York: Cornell University Press.

1992 *Cattle, Capitalism, and Class: Ilparakuyo Maasai Transformations.* Philadelphia: Temple University Press.

Te Velde, Hermann
1977 *Seth, God of Confusion.* Leiden: E.J. Brill.

The Beast of Kings: Male Lion Imagery and Kingship in the Ancient Nile Valley

James F. Romano
Curator of Egyptian, Classical, and Ancient Middle Eastern Art
The Brooklyn Museum

In the fifth year of his reign, King Ramesses II (c. 1290-1224 B.C.) led his soldiers into battle against the Hittite army lying in wait at Qadesh, on the Orontes River in Syria. On the eve of battle, Ramesses slept confidently in his tent, knowing that his pet lion lay just outside, ready to maul anyone foolish enough to venture too close to pharaoh. When the battle began, the Egyptians withstood the initial Hittite onslaught. Then Ramesses struck. He charged the enemy in a light chariot with an image of a springing lion decorating the cab. According to the Egyptian version of the events, the Hittite forces broke ranks and ran from Ramesses's assault. The texts accompanying the depiction of the battle relate that Ramesses "was behind them [the fleeing Hittites] like a ferocious(?) lion" (Wit 1951:24).

ill. 55
ancient Egyptian people
Saqqara
Egypt (Northeastern Africa)

male lion head
alabaster; h. 7 in.
Old Kingdom, 3rd Dynasty
2735-2640 B.C.

Lent by The Brooklyn Museum
Charles Edwin Wilbour Fund
68.152

These three examples of leonine imagery in the Qadesh account—one a living lion, one a representation, and one a simile—underscore the importance of the lion as a symbol of Egyptian kingship. From the first moment humans entered the Nile Valley, they were, no doubt, awed by the lion's ferocity, strength, and majestic appearance. Precisely when the Egyptians began associating the animal with their own rulers, however, is impossible to know. Certainly this connection had been made sometime before the founding of the pharaonic state. A ceremonial palette of the late Predynastic era (c. 3100-2920 B.C.), of which only a fragment remains, originally showed seven animals—a scorpion, a falcon, a pair of falcons on standards, and a lion are all that remain—each holding a hoe and standing on the crenelated walls of a town (Lange and Hirmer 1968: pl. 3 [below]). Since the first three images all served as royal symbols in late Predynastic Egypt, the lion must have also embodied some aspect of royalty at this time.

In the Early Dynastic Period (c. 2920-2649 B.C.) and Old Kingdom (c. 2649-2134 B.C.), the lion was one of the most conspicuous of all royal symbols. Early kings kept lions as palace pets (Wit 1951:10-11; Houlihan 1996:91-95), and one First Dynasty king was buried with seven juvenile lions (Dreyer 1990:86-87). Old Kingdom artisans often added leonine details to royal furniture. A chair and bed of 4th Dynasty Queen Hetepheres, for example, featured legs modeled like a lion's legs and paws (Smith 1981:87-93), and the famous statue of King Chephren shows him on a throne with leonine legs and armrests terminating in lions' heads (Lange and Hirmer 1968:pls. 30 and IV; Smith 1981:110-111). Even offering tables from several Old Kingdom pyramid complexes were carved in the form of lions supporting a tray (ill. 55) (Saleh and Sourouzian 1987:no. 18). Also at this time royal sculptors created the sculptural type known as the sphinx: a composite form with the head of the reigning king and a lion's body (Schweitzer 1948:32-38).

To understand this intimate connection between kings and lions, it is necessary to examine both Egyptian religious beliefs and the behavior of male lions in the wild (Grapow 1924:69-70; Bonnet 1971:428-429; Rössler-Köhler 1980:cols. 1081-1082). Several Old Kingdom reliefs represent leonine goddesses, such as Bastet and Sakhmet, nursing the king. These lionesses played the role of divine mothers who imparted to their son, through their milk, the indomitable power and vigilance of their species. Such traits were obligatory for pharaoh. On the mundane level, he was responsible for guarding Egypt's borders from attack; on a more celestial plane, he maintained Ma'at, the divinely ordained equilibrium between established order and the forces of Chaos that always threatened to engulf Egypt. Not surprisingly, the Egyptians placed sphinx statues—part man and part lion—on their frontiers to define emphatically the boundaries between the stability of Egypt and the confusion characteristic of all foreign lands.

The male lion's behavior made it an ideal paradigm for the king as defender of Universal Order. While guarding their prides, lions spend most of their time in a state of torpidity punctuated by occasional paroxysms of carnage. Egypt's vast military power meant that she was rarely subjected to foreign aggression. When Egypt was threatened, however, pharaoh responded with ruthless leonine fury. Both Thutmose III and Sety I became "a ferocious(?) lion who transforms his enemies into corpses" (Wit 1951:20, 24); Ramesses II was "like a lion when he tasted combat" (Wit 1951:25); and when Merenptah confronted a host of Libyan invaders, he "became enraged against them like a lion (Wit 1951:26)."

Given the infrequency with which these powers were released, it is not surprising that the pantheon of Egyptian deities contained few gods who took the form of male lions. The most important were a series of composite deities, with lion heads and human bodies, that first appeared in the Old Kingdom (Romano 1980:39-50). They seem to have guarded women and children, particularly during the perilous nighttime hours. By the middle of the 18th Dynasty these demi-gods had adopted a new physical appearance: a lion-headed being with the body of an achondroplastic dwarf. In this form, the gods, including Aha ("the Fighter"), Bes, and Hayet, served primarily as guardians of the household. Just as pharaoh defended Egypt's borders, these deities were capable of unleashing their relentless fury on snakes, scorpions, or evil spirits that threatened the Egyptian home.

In contrast to their Egyptian neighbors to the north, the ancient Nubians did worship a powerful leonine deity. Apedemak, who most frequently appears with a lion's head and human body (ill. 56), or as a serpent with the head of a lion and human arms, was venerated in Nubia during the Meroitic Period (c. 270 B.C.-A.D. 350). Certain features of his iconography, particularly his characteristic bow and arrow, signal his role as Meroitic god of war (Žabkar 1975:13-17).

ill. 56
ancient Nubian-Meroitic people
Sudan (Northeastern Africa)

double-sided plaque with king and the lion deity Apedemak
slate; h. 7 in.
Meroitic Period
593 B.C.-330 A.D.

Lent by the Walters Art Gallery, Baltimore, Maryland 22.258

REFERENCES CITED

Bonnet, Hans
1971 Löwe. In *Reallexikon der Ägyptischen religions geschichte*. 2nd ed. Berlin: Walter de Gruyter.

Dreyer, Günter
1990 Umm el-Qaab; Nachuntersuchungen im frühzeitlichen Königsfriedhof 3./4. Vorbericht. *Mitteilungen des Deutschen Archäologischen Instituts Abteilung Kairo* 46:53-81.

Grapow, Hermann
1924 *Die bildlichen Ausdrücke des Aegyptischen vom Denken und Dichten einer altorientalischen Sprache*. Leipzig: J.C. Hinrichs'sche.

Houlihan, Patrick F.
1996 *The Animal World of the Pharaohs*. Cairo: American University in Cairo Press.

Lange, Kurt, and Max Hirmer
1968 *Egypt; Architecture, Sculpture, Painting in Three Thousand Years*, with Contributions by Eberhard Otto and Christiane Desroches-Noblecourt. 4th ed. London: Phaidon.

Romano, James F.
1980 The Origin of the Bes-image. In *Bulletin of the Egyptological Seminar* 2:39-56.

Rössler-Kohler, Ursula
1980 Löwe, L.-Köpfe, L.-Statuen. In *Lexikon der Ägyptologie 3*. Wiesbaden: Otto Harrassowitz:cols. 1080-1090.

Saleh, Mohamed, and Hourig Sourouzian
1987 *Official Catalogue, The Cairo Museum*. Mainz: Philipp von Zabern.

Schweitzer, Ursula
1948 Löwe und Sphinx im Alten Ägypten. *Ägyptologische Forschungen 15*. Glükstadt: J.J. Augustin.

Smith, William Stevenson
1981 *The Art and Architecture of Ancient Egypt*, revised with additions by William Kelly Simpson. New York: Penguin Books.

Wit, Constant de
1951 *Le rôle et le sens du lion dans l'Égypte ancienne*. Leiden: E.J. Brill.

Žabkar, L.V.
1975 *Apedemak, Lion God of Meroe; A Study in Egyptian-Meroitic Syncretism*. Warminster: Aris & Phillips Ltd.

Masking in Sub-Saharan Africa

Arthur P. Bourgeois
University Professor of Art History
Governors State University

Masked performances in sub-Saharan Africa involve the transformation of a human actor into a being of another order who intervenes in village life. Ancestors are frequently commemorated and honored, as illustrated by Egungun masks of the Yoruba of Nigeria (ills. 57-58). The cultural domain of the masquerade might include initiations, funerals, agricultural cycle festivals, healing, and entertainment. Masks generally entail some symbolic transformation, but this transformation concerns not just the power-object, consisting of head or facial covering and body costume, but, equally, the transformation of participants, audience, and social situation. Sets of relationships are involved whereby power is exchanged, transformed, or otherwise manipulated. As extensions of chiefly authority or that of the elders, this power includes the capacity to nominate others as equals or unequal and to open potentiality and possibility. The metaphor of an extra-human agency (e.g., god, gods, or spirits) is commonly used as effecting this change, but the derivation of this power is not a single dominant source. Rather, power derives from diverse centers of influence within the community, similar in a way to that which confers authority on leaders.

ill. 58
Yoruba people
Nigeria (Western Africa)

Egungun helmet mask
wood, pigment; h. 12 in.
20th century

Indianapolis Museum of Art
Gift of Mr. and Mrs. Harrison Eiteljorg
1989.750

ill. 57
Yoruba people
Nigeria (Western Africa)

Egungun masking scene
20th century

Photograph courtesy of
John Pemberton III

Masking can be viewed as a protection from danger for the masked wearer within a ritually ambiguous situation. The mask serves as an outer projection of deeper symbolic structures evoking primal narratives and events and past situations. It is a repeat performance, and its repetition is the means by which the beings represented are made manifest in the present. The present and the past are united in intentional ambiguity. Within the masking context, with its concentration of ritual and symbol, a new dimension is created. Performers are transformed and transported into the setting out of which the ancestors, their tutelary spirits, and protective charms originally transformed society. In this way they become their founding ancestors and the past shapes the present.

The masked performance is "framed" by special preparations, rules, clothing, visitors, names, dances, and songs, which create a heightened significance, and the total context becomes isolated from everyday existence. Performers and audience are caught up in a mutual exchange, participation, and willing suspension of disbelief. The mask depends on this whole; detached from its ritual and ceremonial frame, it makes no sense.African masks of wood either cover the face, completely envelope the head, or ride above the head as a cap, although they are usually embellished with natural materials, textiles, or unwoven raffia, which assist in concealing the wearer. Paint, clay, metal appliqué, hide, or composites of horns, bones, seeds, beads, or shells might further adorn the surface. Widespread conventions in rendering human or animal imagery on masks include such features as the heart-shaped face, multiple heads, skin coverings, and elaborate superstructures. Elaborate coiffures, either carved or built up of other materials, further enhance the mask and reflect special identities and prestige status. Representation ranges from high naturalism, as demonstrated by the Bidjogo ox helmet mask (ill. 54, Animal Deities and Symbols section) from Guinea Bissau, to the highly conventualized Mama bush cow cap masks from Nigeria.

The symbolism of mask elements makes reference to opposing categories that are mediated through ritual intervention, namely, village and bush, humankind, and the supernatural, male and female, initiated and uninitiated, life and death. Ritual display of the colors black, white, and red on masks in initiatory settings refers to death, life

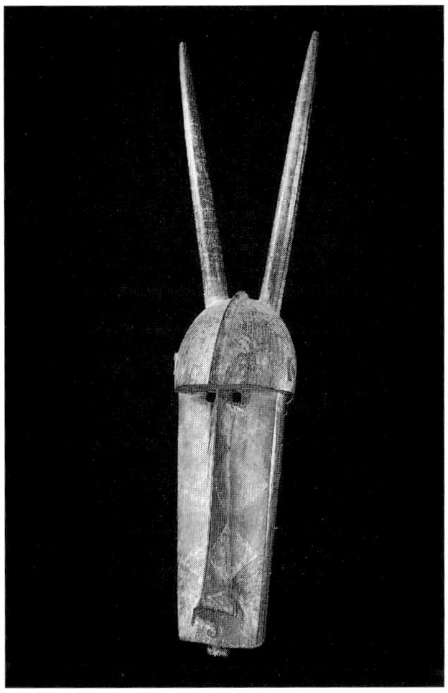

ill. 60
Bobo people
Burkina Faso (Western Africa)

mask
wood, pigment, fiber; h. 58 ½ in.
20th century

Gift of Mr. and Mrs. Harrison Eiteljorg
1989.249

ill. 59
unidentified people
Tassili Plateau
Algeria (Northern Africa)

rock art masker outline
Neolithic Period
8000-4000 B.C.

Drawing from Henri Lhote,
The Search for the Tassili Frescoes,
1959, pl. 37

fluids, blessing of ancestors, and uncertainty. As a mode of abstraction, the masked personage occupies a betwixt-and-between position, taking on attributes of two or more categories.

Although the age of masking as a life-sustaining activity and dominant artistic expression remains unknown, several rock paintings (ill. 59) dating from 4000 B.C. or earlier in Tassili-n'Ajjer in the Algerian Sahara suggest an early appearance of masks and masquerades (Lhote 1973). Animal forms and imaginative composite masks worn by costumed performers are carefully depicted in red ochre and white pigment and bear a resemblance to mask types still in use today (ill. 60). Moreover, ceramic helmet masks surmounted by animal figures, dating from A.D. 500, have been found in South Africa at Lydenburg (ill. 61) (Maggs 1981), and a ceramic face mask of the Jenne culture, dating from the eleventh through seventeenth centuries, has been found in Mali (Roy 1985:14). Due to the perishable nature of wood and difficulties in preserving wood in tropical Africa, no known complete examples of wooden masks are older than 150 years.

ill. 61
unidentified people
Eastern Transvaal
South Africa (Southern Africa)

mask
ceramic, pigment; h. 15 in.
500-700 A.D.

Photograph courtesy of the South African Museum, Cape Town
UCT 701/1

Masking forms and functions in sub-Saharan Africa manifest power and presence whether in rites of transition, policing, entertainment, or satirical plays. The critical place of masking in unifying basic human values and furthering community cooperation is beyond question. The secrecy implied and anonymity of mask wearers and the severity of the regulations that surround the performance and material accoutrements demonstrate the seriousness with which the mask intervenes in human affairs.

In sum, masking in Africa incorporates pictorial, oral, and functional traditions that involve the roles of masker and audience, mythology, ritual symbolism, and the broader ceremonial and social organization. Yet, the masked event is not conducted primarily to impart specific information; rather it actualizes an upheaval and recentering of daily life from that of a self-centered existence of individuals to one of collective experience.

REFERENCES CITED

Lhote, Henri
1973 *The Search For the Tassili Frescoes.* London: Hutchinson.

Maggs, Tim, and Patricia Davidson
1981 The Lydenburg Heads. *African Arts* 14(3):28-33.

Roy, Christopher D.
1985 *Art and Life in Africa: Selections from the Stanley Collection.* Iowa City: The University of Iowa Museum of Art.

The Case for Ceremonial Masking in Ancient Egypt

Arlene Wolinski
Professor of History
San Diego Mesa College

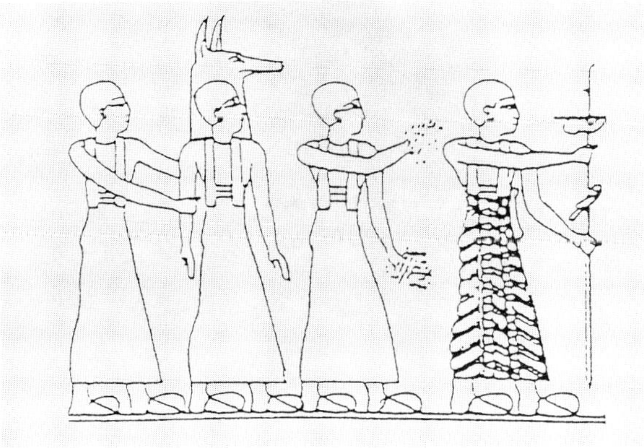

ill. 63
ancient Egyptian people
Dendera
Egypt (Northeastern Africa)

line drawing of wall relief in Temple of Hathor showing Anubis helmet-masked priest
Ptolemaic(Greek)-Roman Periods
332 B.C.-330 A.D.

Drawing from Auguste Mariette, *Denderah IV*, 1873, pl. 31

In July 1899, Gaston Maspero, director general of Egyptian Museums, commented that the figures depicted with animal heads and human bodies in temple reliefs at Deir el Bahri were actually priests and priestesses wearing animal masks and costumes appropriate to their respective gods and goddesses while witnessing the birth of a future pharaoh (1899:406).

By 1934 Margaret Murray, an eminent British Egyptologist, expressed surprise in a short article that no scholars had pursued Maspero's idea (1934:251-255). Ironically, her article was generally ignored. In 1984, I discovered her article and published my research (Wolinski 1986:47-53; 1987:22-29; 1995:30-37; 1996). Initially, the bibliography from "die Maske" in *Lexikon der Ägyptologie* (1980:1196-1199) had directed me to Murray, Mariette, and the Pelizaeus Museum in Hildesheim, Germany.

A photograph in the Hildesheim museum's catalog of a terracotta Anubis priest's mask (Kayser 1966:plate 74) (ill. 62) made me ponder its wearability, and so a hands-on, or heads-on, experiment seemed worthwhile. What could actually wearing the mask tell me? At the museum, I asked Dr. Bettina Schmitz, the curator, if I could try on the mask. Carefully, it was lowered over my head, and its eighteen pounds settled into place over my back, shoulders, chest and head. Inside, the jackal's snout balanced against my forehead. The weight of the mask would not have been a problem for a priest who regularly wore it since many modern African masks weighing between twenty-five and fifty pounds still are worn and danced with today.

Two rectangular slits in the neck area of the mask were in the proper place for my eyes, but the lack of peripheral vision meant that another person's assistance was necessary when walking. This very fact is illustrated in a carving on a doorpost in the temple of Dendera (ill. 63; see also ill. 64) (Wolinski 1995:33; Mariette 1873, plate 31). This carving shows the jackal mask "around" the head of the priest who is being led, and his eyes in the neck area, exactly as the Hildesheim mask had fit me (Wolinski 1995:30,33). The art is confirmed by the artifact.

Other holes in the sides of the mask enabled me to hear conversation, so the priest, dressed as the god Anubis, might act as an oracle in public processions (Hornung 1982:135-136) and hear questions addressed to him. Masks still act as oracles in African societies (McNaughton 1979:30). The long neck meant the mask rose above shoulder level, ensuring that the wearer would stand out in a crowd.

The painted designs on the Hildesheim mask end at four protrusions (two on each side) perhaps allowed for attachment of cloth, fiber, or leather. Masker garments are still worn this way in Africa today (Sieber and Walker 1987:55).

Ceramic seems an unusual material for the construction of a mask, but in Africa mud or clay can be a sacred substance, particularly in riverine areas where the mixture of water and earth has a deep religious significance (Ben-Amos 1973:28-31). That the Hildesheim mask was crafted of clay was similarly symbolic of the annual Nile flooding, which carried and deposited the fertile regenerating silt along its banks. How appropriate that the mortuary priests of Anubis, liminally placed between the living and the dead, wore molded mud masks.

Lower levels of priests probably wore molded or starched linen animal masks, precursors of ancient Greek theater masks, similar to the cartonnage (linen and gesso) Bes mask found by Petrie at Kahun (Petrie 1890:30). We can consult

ill. 62
ancient Egyptian people
Egypt (Northeastern Africa)

Anubis (jackal) helmet mask
ceramic, pigment;
h. 19 5/16 in.
Late Period
probably 600-300 B.C.
(or later)

Lent by Pelizaeus Museum Hildesheim, Germany 1585

New Kingdom painted tombs or carvings on the walls of the 19th Dynasty mortuary temple of Sety I at Abydos or the Ptolemaic temple of Horus at Edfu. At both Abydos and Edfu, a "train of priests" (Brooklyn Museum 1988:37), masked, are carrying a litter on poles (David 1981:190-191). Molded linen masks would not only have been ritually correct, but also more practical for priests carrying the shrine in a procession. Since linen clothing was supposed to be worn by the priests in the temple (David 1982:136), the ceramic mask was the perfect symbolic companion for the priests of Anubis, who wrapped the mummy in linen.

The Louvre's collection has a miniature wooden Anubis jackal mask (no. 4096) with holes in place of the eyes, an articulated jaw, which can be controlled with a cord, and holes all around the edge. The mask could have been sewn onto a quilted, lined hood with lappets down the front and back as seen on New Kingdom wall paintings.

On most wall carvings or paintings that show a man wearing a stitched cloth animal hooded mask, the two lappets with gold weights on the bottom, evident over both shoulders and the back, hold the cloth mask in place. This artistic convention of the double lappet is found in most periods (Wolinski 1995:31). In a tomb wall painting of a person wearing a headdress, crown, wig, or even long hair (but not an animal helmet mask), the headdress, crown, wig, or hair hangs down only over the shoulder closest to the viewer.

Ancient Egyptian women, like other African women today, rarely wore animal masks, but instead wore animal emblems on their headdresses. The few exceptions, such as Bast and Sekhmet, were usually face masks, and not helmet masks as worn by men. In wall carvings, a ridge along the jaw line indicates a face mask tied under a woman's hair or wig. Even today African women rarely wear ceremonial face masks (Mack 1994:42).

Why did ancient Egyptians wear ceremonial masks? Worldwide, past or present, the most convincing reason given is that masks are worn to attract the spirit and power of the deity into the mask or the wearer. A properly garbed ancient Egyptian priest could impersonate the animal deity, aware that the divinity might take up his abode in an animal (Hornung 1982:137) and, by extension, in the mask. Clearly, the ancient Egyptians believed in visual attraction of a spirit into a mask, because the death mask placed over the wrapped mummy served to attract the spirit of the person back into the correct body. This attraction concept still is found in Africa today (Cole 1985:10).

Another pervasive reason for masking is the need for anonymity. Theoretically, "the king alone was the high priest of every god" (David 1980:73), performing the daily temple ritual everywhere in Egypt. Obviously high priests of each temple impersonated pharaoh, and wearing the Horus falcon mask facilitated the fiction. A crucial time for the priests to be concealed in masks would be during the coronation of pharaoh, because only gods could perform these rituals. Anonymity often is desired by people who handle the dead, and the priests of Anubis performing the mummification procedures are depicted wearing jackal masks.

ill. 64
ancient Egyptian people
Egypt (Northeastern Africa)

papyrus painting with masked priest of Anubis
1300 B.C. New Kingdom, 19th Dynasty

Photograph from Stephon Quirke and Jeffrey Spencer,
The British Museum Book of Ancient Egypt, 1992, ill. 113

Egyptologists disagree on a hieroglyph for the word "mask," but neither do some groups in modern Africa have a specific word for masks (Cole 1985:20,28). Surprisingly, our English word "mask" does not derive from a Latin or Greek root, as expected (the Latin is "persona," and the Greek, "prosopon"), but from the Arabic "mskr," from which we derive both "mask" and "mascara." Two important meanings are found in Faulkner's *Concise Dictionary of Middle Egyptian* (1962:118) and *Wörterbuch der Ägyptischen Sprache* (v2:150), with regard to the root "msk": 1. skin and 2.

leather (depending on the determinative). These are significant because they lead us back to the earliest Predynastic cosmetic palettes, which show warriors or hunters wearing animal masks, skins, or hides of animals (see examples in Ashmolean Museum, Oxford; Manchester Museum, ill. 65). These palettes were used to mix face paints, and face painting is a form of masking. Was it for war paint, as suggested by the Narmer Palette? Were the earliest masks made of leather? Now masking can be traced from the earliest Predynastic period pictorially, and through the texts in the Middle Egyptian and New Kingdom examples. Perhaps we have missed reading the determinative for a masked priest because the actual painting or illustration of a masked priest is the determinative (Fischer 1976:73).

The reasons for masking are consistent with anthropological, ritualistic, artistic, linguistic, and religious theory and practices. Examples from more recent African societies indicate possible continental continuities (ill. 57).

ill. 65
ancient Egyptian people
Egypt (Northeastern Africa)

detail of stone palette with masked hunter stalking ostriches
Protodynastic Period
Naqada III
3300-3100 B.C.

Photograph courtesy of The Manchester Museum, University of Manchester, England
5476

REFERENCES CITED

Ben-Amos, Paula
1973 Symbolism in Olokun Mud Art. *African Arts* 6 (4), 28-31,95.

The Brooklyn Museum
1988 *Cleopatra's Egypt*. Brooklyn, New York: Brooklyn Museum.

Cole, Herbert
1985 *I Am Not Myself: The Art of African Masquerade*. Los Angeles: Museum of Cultural History, University of California.

David, Rosalie
1980 *Cult of the Sun: Myth and Magic in Ancient Egypt*. London: J. M. Dent.

1981 *A Guide to Religious Ritual at Abydos*. Warminster, Wilts, England: Aris & Phillips.

1982 *The Ancient Egyptians, Religious Beliefs and Practices*. London, New York: Routledge & Kegan Paul.

Erman, A., and H. Grapow
1926 *Wörterbuch der Ägyptischen Sprache*. Leipzig: J. C. Hinrichs.

Faulkner, Raymond
1962 *A Concise Dictionary of Middle Egyptian*. Oxford: Griffith Institute at the University Press.

Fischer, Henry
1976 Redundant Determinatives in the Old Kingdom. *Ancient Egypt in the Metropolitan Museum Journal*. (1968-76). New York: Metropolitan Museum of Art.

Hornung, Erik
1982 *Conceptions of God in Ancient Egypt: the one and the many*. Translated by John Baines. Ithaca, New York: Cornell University Press.

Kayser, Hans
1966 *Die Sammlung Ägyptischer Altertumer in Roemer-Pelizaeus Museum in Hildesheim*. Plate 74. Hildesheim: A. Lax.

Lexicon der Ägyptologie
1980 Die Maske. 1196-1199. Wiesbaden: O. Harrassowitz.

Mack, John, ed.
1994 *Masks and the Art of Expression*. London: The Trustees of the British Museum.

Mariette, Auguste
1873 *Denderah IV*. Plate 31. Paris: A Franck.

Maspero, Gaston
1899 Book Review of Deir el Bahri. *Journal des Savants*. July. 401-414. Le Caire: Imprimerie de l'Institut Francais d'Archeologie.

Mc Naughton, Patrick
1979 Secret Sculptures of Komo: Art and Power in Bamana Initiation Associations. Philadelphia: Institute for the Study of Human Issues.

Murray, Margaret
1934 Ritual Masking. *Melanges Maspero*. Paris.

Petrie, W. M. Flinders
1890 *Kahun, Gurob, and Hawra*. London: K. Paul, Trench, Trubner.

Sieber, Roy, and Roslyn Walker
1987 *African Art in the Cycle of Life*. Washington, D.C.: Smithsonian Press.

Wolinski, Arlene E.
1986 Ancient Egyptian Ceremonial Masks. *Discussions in Egyptology* 6:47-53.

1987 Egyptian Masks: The Priest and His Role. *Archaeology* 40(1):22-29.

1995 *Ancient Egypt, Personal Perspectives*. El Cajon. InterAct Publishers.

1996 *Ceremonial Masks of Ancient Egypt*. El Cajon. InterAct Publishers.

The Case Against Extensive Masking in Ancient Egypt

Robert Steven Bianchi
Independent Egyptologist
New York

One of the hallmarks of ancient Egyptian representation is the composite figure, a harmonious design in which common objects are often composed in uncommon compositions. Of these, the most familiar are depictions of deities in both two- and three-dimensional representations with the heads of animals and the bodies of human beings. The zone of transition between the human body and the animal head is invariably masked by a broad collar, effectively rendering the image somewhat innocuous to Western sensibilities. The resulting creatures are never sublime in the same way that Western composite beasts associated with Halloween are because they are designed in accordance with the principles governing the design of the hieroglyphs, a system of pictograms in which a certain percentage of signs are composite representations as well (Fischer 1986). Relying exclusively on a formal analysis rooted in Western art historical exegesis, some modern commentators have identified such ancient Egyptian composite figures as mask-wearing human beings (Wolinski 1986). The application of the empathetic theorem by which one's own subjective feeling is imposed upon the interpretation of an animate object has been cogently rejected by F. Junge (1990) in his assessment of ancient Egyptian art. It is, therefore, proper to remember J. G. Herder's (1892) observation, adduced over a century ago, that one ought not to judge ancient Egyptian art by Greek and, by extension, Western standards, because ancient Egyptian art was produced neither for the Greeks nor for us. Ancient Egyptian art is symbolic, not representational (Bianchi 1995). It is, therefore, inappropriate to identify such composite ancient Egyptian figures as masked human beings simply because *they would be so identified if they appeared in that way in Western art.* Such identifications ignore both the hieroglyphic and symbolic nature of ancient Egyptian art, the principles of which not only dictate the form of the image, but also its content. Accordingly, such images qualify simultaneously as a word for the deity depicted and an image of the deity itself, because in ancient Egyptian representations, word and image are one (Fischer 1986; Te Velde 1986). In accepting this position, one must repudiate E. Panofsky's (1924) acceptance of I. Kant's epistemology that idea and image are incapable of resolution because idea and image are essentially the same in ancient Egyptian art (Fischer 1986:140). Furthermore, ancient Egyptian visual conventions stress visual clarity to the exclusion of replications of reality. As a result, a complex and consistent visual vocabulary was developed for the representation of an object within an object in accordance with the canonical nature of ancient Egyptian art (Bianchi 1995; Davis 1992). So, for example, it was customary to omit the front panels of containers in an effort to reveal the contents of their interiors. One of the best known examples of this visual conceit is to be found in that vignette from the Tomb of Tutankhamun that has been described as a train of nobles of the realm drawing the royal catafalque (Desroches-Noblecourt 1963, fig. 144). The front panel of the catafalque is not represented in order that the spectator can clearly see the anthropoid sarcophagus within. As a result of this consistent use of that convention, it should be patently clear that ancient Egyptian visual design tenets were developed whereby all ambiguity regarding the contexts within an object was removed. Those two-dimensional representations that are often offered as clear examples of a masked human being include a fragmentary relief from the funeral temple of Sahure (Sourdive 1984:113, fig. 2), which has no context whatsoever and preserves only the upper torso and head of a composite figure; a relief from the Old Kingdom, without an archaeological context (Sourdive 1984:48-52), in which the interpretation of the scene where the figure in question appears has received no scholarly consensus (Pinch 1994:121), and an enigmatic register from the Tomb of Khereuf (Sourdive 1984:57), in which the figures in question are damaged, but on which the accompanying inscription sheds no light whatsoever (The Epigraphic Survey 1980:46-48). In all of these examples, and others as well, there is not one accompanying text to support the identification of such images as masked human beings. The same can be said for the representations on the Manchester (ill. 65) and Ashmolean palettes (Davis 1992:73, fig. 25;76, fig 26, respectively), the identification of which as masked human beings fails to heed Davis's caveat that the material culture of the Predynastic horizons cannot be interpreted in accordance with what is known from the later historical epochs.

If any of the composite representations of animal-headed human beings actually represented masked individuals, the animal mask would be rendered in accordance with established ancient Egyptian artistic conventions, such as those observed for the crafting of the masked priest shown in one of the reliefs from the Temple of Hathor at Dendera. As a result, one should avoid interpreting all animal-headed depictions in ancient Egyptian art as masked human beings unless those depictions are rendered in strict accordance with these established and documented design tenets.

Observations gained from a study of the *textual evidence* can be added to these formal objections to identifying such animal-headed humans as masked individuals. These texts all reveal that in the pharaonic periods, pharaoh and pharaoh alone was accorded the right of masking (Meeks 1986). According to these *texts*, priests did not enjoy that privilege.

The only exception to this generalization, to my knowledge, is the depiction of an Anubis-masked priest in one of the scenes from the Temple of Hathor at Dendera (ill. 63). The depiction of this masked priest finds its parallel in an actual mask in the collections of the Pelizaeus Museum in Hildesheim (ill. 62). Since the Hildesheim mask has no archaeological context and since the scene from Dendera comes from a temple, and not a tomb context, one ought not claim that the Hildesheim mask was used by a human priest during rites of mummification of mortals, as has often been claimed in the past. The use of masks in temple contexts, then, requires further investigation. The enigmatic "Bes-like *face*" that Petrie (1890) found at Kahun is fragmentary but does relate to typologically similar funerary masks, contemporary in date, from Mirgissa (Vercoutter 1976). To associate this object with a wooden statuette (Sourdive 1984:113, fig. 5; Bourriau 1988:111, fig. 1) and claim that the latter is a depiction of a masked human being is a circular argument damaged by the uncritical application of the empathetic theorem.

Western formal approaches to the significance of the funerary arts of ancient Egypt have likewise resulted in misconceptions regarding what one commonly terms a "face mask/death mask," created in a variety of media, and in which the deceased was often enclosed. Calling such objects "masks" obfuscates their true significance. Their functions are clearly defined within the corpus of ancient Egyptian funerary texts. On the one hand, these texts specify that such masks magically guaranteed the deceased the ability to see in the hereafter (Meeks 1986). On the other hand, such masks were intended to disguise the deceased so that he/she would not fall prey to the inimical forces intent on aborting his/her aspired resurrection (George 1981; Meeks 1991). The deceased becomes unknown (Meeks 1991).

As these brief discussions suggest, masking was practiced in ancient Egypt, but within certain, limited contexts. It is necessary, therefore, to avoid interpreting the pictorial record of ancient Egypt in a vacuum, relying solely on the application of Western, formal analyses and the application of the empathetic theorem. Masking was a royal prerogative, associated with pharaoh. This is confirmed by the textual evidence and documented by one representation of a mask, attested in a temple, rather than in a purely funerary context. As a rule, then, ancient Egyptian priests did not go about the performance of their rituals adorned in masks of animals.

REFERENCES CITED

Bianchi, R. S.
1995 Ancient Egyptian Reliefs, Statuary, and Monumental Paintings. In *Civilizations of the Ancient Near East* IV. Jack M. Sasson, ed. pp. 2533-2554. New York.

Bourriau, J.
1988 *Pharaohs and Mortals, Egyptian Art in the Middle Kingdom*. New York: Cambridge.

Davis, Whitney
1992 *Masking the Blow*. Berkeley: University of California Press.

Desroches-Noblecourt, C.
1963 *Tutankhamen. Life and Death of a Pharaoh*. New York and London: Penguin Books.

The Epigraphic Survey
1980 *The Tomb of Kheruef, Theban Tomb 192*. Oriental Institute Publication, vol. 102. Chicago: The University of Chicago.

Fischer, Henry George
1986 *L'écriture et l'art de l'Égypte Ancienne. Quatre leçons sur la paléographie et l'épigraphie pharaoniques*. Paris: Presses Universitaires de France.

George, Beate
1981 Geheimer Kopf—Kopf aus Lapislazuli. *Medelhavsmuseet Bulletin* 16:15-38.

Herder, J. G.
1892 *Sämtliche Werke*. edition Suphan, VIII:476-477. Berlin: Weidman.

Junge, F.
1990 Versuch zu einer Ästhetik der ägyptischen Kunst. In *Studien zur ägyptischen Kunstgeschichte*. M. Eaton-Krauss and E. Graefe, eds. pp. 1-38. Hildesheim: Gerstenberg.

Meeks, D.
1986 Zoomorphie et image des dieux dans l'Égypte ancienne. *Le temps de la réflexion 7, Corps des dieux*. 171-191. Paris: Gallimard.

1991 Dieu masqué, dieu sans tête. *Archeo-Nil Bulletin* 1:5-16.

Panofsky, I.
1924 *Idea*. pp. 71-72. Berlin: B. G. Teubner.

Petrie, W. M. Flinders
1890 *Kahun, Gurob, and Hawara*. London: K. Paul. Trench, Trubner.

Pinch, Geraldine
1994 *Magic in Ancient Egypt*. London: British Museum Press.

Sourdive, C.
1984 *La main dans l'Égypte pharaonique, Recherches de morphologie structurale sur les objects égyptiens comportant une main*. Berne: Lang.

Te Velde, Herman
1986 Egyptian Hieroglyphs as Signs, Symbols, and Gods. *Visible Religion* 4-5:63-72.

Vercoutter, J., et al
1976 *Mirgissa* III. Paris: Direction général des relations culturelles scientifiques et techniques avec la collaboration du centre national de la recherche scientifique.

Wolinski, Arelene
1986 Ancient Egyptian Ceremonial Masks. *Discussions in Egyptology* 6:47-53.

Body Art in Africa: Painting, Tattooing, and Scarification

Chike C. Aniakor
Professor of African Art
Howard University

"When a wound is healed, men see the scar."
— Fon proverb

"Yet body for body, they are weaker than we."
—Ibibio comment on women's secret powers

"Our love affair with paint goes back a long, long way... four hundred thousand years, and probably more...when retreating body hair first uncovered enough skin for canvas."
—Olivia Vlahos in Body: The Ultimate Symbol

"When a woman wishes to gossip, she paints uli on the upper lip."
—Igbo body painter

ill. 67
Makonde people
Mozambique or Kenya (Eastern Africa)

woman with tattoos
20th century

Photograph from Michel Leiris and Jacqueline Delange, *African Art,* 1968, ill. 121

In Africa, body art seems to have emerged early in the dimness of the past. It would appear as if the other arts had waited for this to happen so as to be graced by it and be given external plumage. Body art had indirect echoes in the Paleolithic landscape over 7,000 years ago in the form of rock outcrops that were painted, engraved, or incised and sheltered from the elements at various sites in the Sahara and other regions of Africa. Colors used included pulverized oxides, and possibly chalk, charcoal, and plant juices—from monochrome to polychrome. Among the scenes depicted are men, women, and hunting; possibly rituals and dance; performance in crisis-laden conditions, and predators and prey (Willett 1971). The human body was exaggerated, distorted and transformed, or even masked. Examples of body art are found in Saharan rock paintings (ill. 66).

ill. 66
unidentified people
Algeria (Northern Africa)

body art depicted on rock art
Neolithic
7000-2000 B.C.

Photograph from Henri Lhote, *The Search for the Tassili Frescoes,* 1959, fig. 39

With the emergence of Neolithic cultures with stable institutions of kingdoms and lesser polities, body art acquired greater momentum in its thrust, range of designs, and deeper filiations to and interconnections with the human environment. Body parts—nostril, bridge of the nose, ear, forehead, thigh, arms, belly, chest, breasts, chin and others—were manipulated with diverse techniques. These were contracted, exaggerated, expanded, punched, hollowed, painted, scarred, tattooed with designs schematized for clear communication. They were laden with meanings and associations: political, economic, familial, ritual, fecund, moral, ontological, sexual, and aesthetic. As armature, the body was sculpted. As canvas, it was painted. Whether the designs were inscribed or painted, body art acted as a protective envelope (Prussin 1976), as medicine (Brain 1979), and was implanted in rites of passage, birth, growth and death, status, rank, and wealth (Paulme 1973). It soon filtered into the various arts. It was incised on surfaces, carved, hammered, drawn,

ill. 68
Berber people
Morocco (Northern Africa)

woman with skin painting and tattoos
20th century

Photograph from Angela Fisher, *Africa Adorned,* 1984, p. 226

painted on masks (Aniakor 1995), costumes, wood, rock, hide, architecture, and sacred grounds. Body art is tranquil and mobile, simultaneously processual and permanent.

Three techniques of adorning the skin are body painting, tattooing, and scarification. These techniques in turn define two kinds of body art, namely: the transient (painting) and the permanent (scarification and tattooing), underpinned by two distinct social states. Victor Turner found that among the Ndembu people of Central Africa red, black, and white are considered "body colors, colors of the body products and fluids associated with the process of living. These were colors not merely perceived but *felt*" (Vlahos 1979: 1921). Among the Igbo people of Nigeria, yellow was rubbed round the eyes of diviners and elders for safety of passage (Basden 1921). As indigo juice extracted from plant pods (Ardener 1954), cursive lines were painted on the skin of Igbo nubiles for initiation and marriage to enhance beauty or disguise ugliness because "the maiden who entered marriage with uli body painting, uli has faded and beauty has gone." The successful Sherbro dancer in Sierra Leone was painted with grease; a young Akan bride in Ghana was painted with red and white marks on the face (Alldridge 1901:139; Hair and Jones 1987). Black and red check patterns were painted round the eyes in boys' dance in the Congo(Gide 1927).

If body painting is transient, repetitive, and differentiative, tattooing and scarification leave permanent impressions on the skin (Buckland 1888) from the very flat to the very highly raised, thus altering the body in the more ultimate sense within the cycle of life (Sieber and Walker 1987). Whether with a razor, pin, needle, sharp bone, thorn, or any other instrument, the skin was cut slightly or deeply, punched or simply pulled up and sliced. Colorant was added for pigmentation or medicated with charcoal or dye insertion for delayed healing with the resultant keloid welts or body sculpture. Nuba boys and girls of the Sudan were scarred after puberty; the Bangwa child of the Cameroon was marked with solar or linear discs; the Kete royal marks from Zaire were along the line and structure of the face (Faris 1972; MacRow 1958). The zigzagging geometric marks of the tattooed Makonde female of East Africa (ill. 67) contrast with the lyrical marks of the tattooed Berber female from Morocco (ill. 68). Others included the keloid welts of Ramesses III's Nubian enemies (ill. 74) and Hausa markings that memorialized travels and pilgrimage (Paulme 1973). Among the Nuer of Sudan, a man's forehead markings were transformed into body sculpture like those of Igbo titled elders. Still others included the markings on female ceramic figures (ills. 70-72) and tattooed mummy markings of ancient Egyptian people (ill. 71), Tiv girls of Nigeria (Bohannan 1956), and the alluring tattooed facial marks of the Fulani of West Africa. Complex body markings among the Yoruba distinguished status, sex, persons, family, lineage, and royalty (Adepegba 1976). So also are the dramatic markings of the Tetela women of Zaire and body markings of the Mbembe and Bamileke peoples of Cameroon (Cole 1970). Others enveloped the body like an all-over surface embroidery or the painted markings on Kuba sculpture from Zaire (ill. 69) and of Igbo nubiles collaged with other body accessories (Cole and Aniakor 1984).

All said, African body art has celebrated and transformed the human body into mobile sculpture. Its continuity as an Africanism can be seen from its early appearance in rock paintings and its greater proliferation in the other arts with the emergence of the more stable Neolithic cultures. While its range of designs is a product of human inventiveness and institutional demands, it is on the human body that it focuses in its formal address.

ill. 69
Kuba people
Zaire (Central Africa)

female figure with scarification or other form of body art
wood, pigment; h: 25 ¾ in.
19th-20th centuries

Lent by Dr. and Mrs. Wally Zollman
TR 8536/2

REFERENCES CITED

Adepegha, Cornelius O.
1976 A Survey of Nigerian Body Markings and Their Relationship to Other Nigerian Arts. Unpublished Ph.D. dissertation. Bloomington, Indiana.

Alldridge, J. J.
1901 *The Sherbro and Its Hinterland.* London: Macmillian and Co. Ltd.

Aniakor, Chike C.
1995 Female Imagery and Presence in Igbo Arts: The Example of Maiden Spirit Masking. *Baessler-Archiv* XLIII:67-88.

Ardener, E. W.
1954 Some Ibo Attitudes to Skin Pigmentation. *Man* 54:71-73.

Basden, G. T.
1921 *Among the Ibos of Nigeria.* London: Seeley Service & Co. Ltd.

Bohannan, Paul
1956 Beauty and Scarification among the Tiv. *Man* 56: 117-121.

Brain, Robert
1979 *The Decorated Body.* New York, Hagerstown, San Francisco, London: Harper and Row.

Buckland, A. W.
1988 On Tattooing. *Journal of Royal Anthropological Institute.* pp. 318-326.

Cole, Herbert M.
1970 *African Arts of Transformation.* Santa Barbara: Art Galleries, University of California.

Cole, Herbert M., and Chike C. Aniakor
1984 *Igbo Arts: Community and Cosmos.* Los Angeles: Museum of Cultural History.

Faris, James C.
1972 *Nuba Personal Art.* Toronto and Buffalo: University of Toronto Press.

Gide, André
1927 *Travels in Congo.* Translated by Dorothy Bussy. New York: Alfred A. Knopf.

Hair, P.E.H., Adam Jones and Robin Law, eds.
1987 *Barbot on Guinea, The Writings of Jean Barbot on West Africa 1678-1712.* London: The Hakluyt Society.

MacRow, D.W.
1958 Bamenda Art. *Nigeria Magazine.* 57:132-153.

Paulme, Denise
1973 Adornment and Nudity in Tropical Africa. In *Primitive Art and Society.* Anthony Forge, ed. New York: Oxford University Press.

Prussin, Labelle
1976 Fulani-Hausa Architecture. *African Arts* 10(1): 8-19, 97.

Sieber, Roy, and Roslyn Adele Walker
1987 *African Art in the Cycle of Life.* Washington D.C.: Smithsonian Institution.

Vlahos, Olivia
1979 *Body The Ultimate Symbol.* New York: J. B. Lippincott Company.

Willett, Frank
1971 *African Art, An Introduction.* New York and Washington: Praeger Publishers.

Tattooing and Skin Painting in the Ancient Nile Valley

Robert Steven Bianchi
Independent Egyptologist
New York

Although the ancient Egyptians themselves were reticent about tattoo and made almost no mention of it in their preserved written records, tattoo did exist in ancient Egypt (Bianchi 1988; 1985), as is demonstrated by a small but exceedingly important group of mummies on which tattoos are actually preserved. These mummies are, however, far too few in number and too separated from each other in time to provide an adequate framework for generalization. To the data provided by these physical remains can be added inferences about body adornment derived from examples of ancient Egyptian art. Here, however, one must exercise caution, because that art is often symbolic, rather than representational, and was crafted in accordance with the same specific conventions that governed the designs of the hieroglyphs.

The earliest evidence for tattoo and other forms of body art in Egypt during the Predynastic Period (4500-3650 B.C.) is equivocal, although certain female figurines in clay from this period, such as an example in the Metropolitan Museum of Art (ill. 70), are decorated with intricate linear patterns. Whether these designs are to be regarded as actual tattoo or as another form of body art, such as painting, remains moot because there is no independent method of corroborating either suggestion. Physical remains are of little value because the processes of mummification, which would have preserved the epidermis, were not sufficiently developed until the 4th Dynasty. Nevertheless, the exclusive appearance of such designs on female, rather than male, figurines is not surprising and is in keeping with the practice in the later historical periods of confining tattoo exclusively to women. On the other hand, one must admit that many of the motifs depicted on these female figurines are identical to those that decorate some types of pottery. For the moment, these pottery motifs do not appear to be derived from the tattoos. Nevertheless, the possibility does exist that both belong to a common repertoire of decorative elements and have nothing whatsoever to do with tattoo.

ill. 70
ancient Egyptian people
Thebes-Luxor
Egypt (Northeastern Africa)

female ceramic figure with body art
Predynastic Period
Naqada I or II
4500-3300 B.C.

Lent by the Metropolitan Museum of Art
07.228.71

With the exception, therefore, of this small group of female figurines, there are neither physical remains nor other works of art that suggest the presence of tattoo in ancient Egypt until the Middle Kingdom. Actual tattoo appears for the very first time preserved on the mummy of a woman named Amunet, who served as a priestess of the goddess Hathor at Thebes during the 11th Dynasty. This mummy was in an excellent state of preservation and the tattoos were arranged in a series of abstract patterns of individual dots or dashes randomly placed upon the body with apparent disregard for formal zoning. A second mummy (ill. 71) of approximately the same date, identified as that of a female dancer who lived about the same time, was also discovered. Her tattoos were composed of dots arranged into diamond-shaped patterns on the upper arms and chest. In addition, this second mummy exhibits a remarkable cicatrix across her lower abdomen in the zone of the pubic region. This incision, whether made by knife or cautery, does not invade the muscles of the abdominal wall and thus cannot be explained as either a scar from surgery or from a wound. A third female mummy of contemporary date exhibits tattoos similar to those adorning the second mummy.

Reflections of these tattoos from the Middle Kingdom are preserved on a series of faience figurines that are traditionally called "Brides of the Dead," an example of which is in the Metropolitan Museum of Art (ill. 72). All of these figures are highly abstract, and have been interpreted, in certain contexts, as guarantors of the deceased's procreative abilities on analogy with those of the

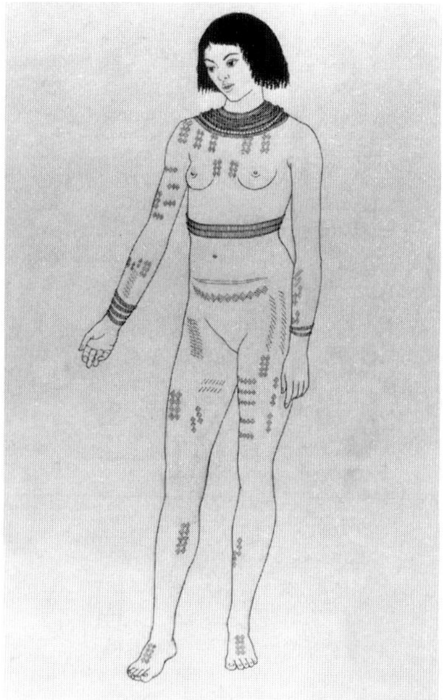

ill. 71
ancient Egyptian people
Thebes-Luxor
Egypt (Northeastern Africa)

drawing of tattooed woman based on a mummy from tomb complex of Nebhepetra Mentuhotep II
Middle Kingdom
11th Dynasty
2060-2010 B.C.

Drawing courtesy of The Metropolitan Museum of Art

goddess Hathor. These were interred with the deceased to insure resurrection. The priestess Amunet and the figurines just described have an undeniably carnal overtone. The eroticism that is undoubtedly associated with Egyptian tattoo of the Middle Kingdom correlates with the prevailing religious attitude that linked physical procreation with the loftier aspirations of resurrection in the Hereafter.

Some scholars maintain that the introduction of tattoo into Egypt during the Middle Kingdom is due to influences from Nubia. Indeed, Amunet and the two mummies contemporary with her have demonstrated connections with Nubia. This suggestion is supported by results of excavations in a cemetery assigned to the Nubian C-Group at the village of Kuban, which is contemporary with the culture of Middle Kingdom Egypt. Here, fragments of the epidermis of a female mummy, roughly contemporary with that of Amunet, revealed tattoo of similar design in similar patterns. Such a tattoo tradition appears to have had a long life in Nubia. At least one figural ostrakon, from the Egyptian New Kingdom, depicts a female Nubian dancer whose thigh is adorned with a representation of a tattoo in the form of a dotted triangle. This tradition continued well into the fourth century B.C., as demonstrated by mummies of both adolescent and adult women of the Meroitic Period uncovered at the Nubian site of Aksha. Their tattoos conform to precisely the same configurations as those found on the Middle Kingdom mummies of Amunet and her contemporaries. Whether or not tattoo had the same erotic overtones for the Nubian peoples as it apparently did for the Egyptians is open to discussion, but one observation seems certain. Namely, tattoo appears to have been introduced into Egypt from Nubia.

During the course of the Egyptian New Kingdom, tattoo became firmly established, but its use appears to have been reserved exclusively as body art for women. The use of dots and dashes gives way to representations, the most common of which is a figure of Bes, a curious deity thought to derive from a leonine god of the Predynastic Period. This image often decorates the thighs of female figures in

ill. 72
ancient Egyptian people
Egypt (Northeastern Africa)

female figure with tattoos or body painting
glazed ceramic (faience);
h. 5 in.
Middle Kingdom, 12th Dynasty
1991-1786 B.C.

Lent by The Metropolitan Museum of Art
Rogers Fund, 1908
08.200.18

ill. 73
ancient Egyptian people
Thebes-Luxor
Egypt (Northeastern Africa)

Libyan with body art from tomb of Sety I
New Kingdom
1291-1279 B.C.

from Ippolito Rosellini, *Monumenti dell' Egitto e della Nubia, Monumenti istorici,* 1834
plates CLV and CLVI

Egyptian art, as depicted in wall paintings, vessels, and cosmetic implements, such as on the bronze mirror from the Brooklyn Museum (60.27.1). In certain limited contexts from the Egyptian New Kingdom, particular male figures are often adorned with abstract patterns that have been traditionally interpreted as depictions of tattoo or body art (ill. 73). These figures are associated with Northeast Africa, and it has been suggested that they represent Libyans. More research is required in order to ascertain whether this body art is either tattoo or body painting. In either case, this cultural phenomenon does not appear to be related to either that of the ancient Egyptian tattoo or its Nubian antecedents.

REFERENCES CITED

Bianchi, Robert Steven

1985 Tätowierung. In *Lexicon der Aegyptologie* 6, 1. W. Helck and W. Westendorf, eds. pp. 145-146. Wiesbaden: Harrassowitz.

1988 Tattoo in Ancient Egypt. In *Marks of Civilization. Artistic Transformations of the Human Body.* Arnold Rubin, ed. pp. 21-28. Los Angeles: Museum of Cultural History, University of California, Los Angeles.

Scarification in the Nile Valley from Antiquity to the Present

Timothy Kendall
Associate Curator of
Egyptian, Nubian, and Near Eastern Art
Museum of Fine Arts, Boston

ill. 74
ancient Egyptian people
Egypt (Northeastern Africa)

relief of Nubian with forehead scarification
stone
New Kingdom, 20th Dynasty
Ramesses III
1181-1150 B.C.

Photograph courtesy of the Oriental Institute Museum, University of Chicago
14648

Traditional among peoples of the Upper Nile regions—and among many peoples of equatorial Africa—is the custom of cutting the face in established designs to create distinctive permanent scars. These scars vary from one group to another and serve as a mark of one's group affiliation or as an indicator of a youth's initiation or other important life event. Justification for them is that they enhance appearance and that they have efficacy in preventing eye diseases, headaches, and other maladies of the head (Brain 1979:70; Nur 1956:86; Seligman 1913:646-648). Several types of facial scars seen today in the Sudan are very ancient, for identical marks are depicted on faces of non-Egyptian Africans represented in Egyptian art from the fourteenth century B.C., and their continuity is documented in later Meroitic and Greco-Roman art.

In Egyptian art there are very naturalistic renderings of non-Egyptian Africans as captives, for example, those depicted in reliefs in the tomb of General Horemheb at Saqqara (Vercoutter et al. 1976:85-87, figs. 61-63; Martin 1989:pls.81-84, 87-93). In many respects these figures correspond to the so-called Nilotic physical type, today represented by the Shilluk, Nuer, and Dinka peoples of the upper White Nile and its tributaries. Like these peoples, the figures in Horemheb's reliefs are unusually tall and thin; the hair of some of them is short overlapping rows of tight curls, a style still typical among many modern peoples of the southern Sudan and northwest Kenya (Seligman and Seligman 1932:pl. 43; Bernatzik 1929:Abt. 123, 154, 189; Saitoti and Beckwith 1980:127). Others have thick untextured mats of hair, suggestive of the mud- or dung-pack coiffures still worn by modern Shilluk, Nuer, Dinka, and related peoples (Westermann 1912:pl. 24; Bernatzik 1929:Abt. 28, 111; Saitoti and Beckwith 1980:127). Most remarkable, however, is the care with which the Egyptian sculptor has indicated the facial scars. Most have four or five prominent horizontal lines incised across their foreheads. Such marks also appear on a dancer represented in the Opet Festival reliefs of Luxor Temple (Vercoutter et al. 1976:fig. 32; Epigraphic Survey 1994:pl. 74) and among the ethnically similar wrestlers represented in reliefs at Medinet Habu (Vercoutter et al. 1976:fig. 32; Epigraphic Survey 1932:pls. 111, 112; Hölscher 1941: pl. 33c, d). The sculpted Nilote's head in the Oriental Institute (ill. 74), which once projected from the base of pharaoh's "window of appearances" at Medinet Habu, displays six horizontal forehead scars (Ibid. pl. 33f; Epigraphic Survey 1932:pl. 111).

ill. 75
Nuer people
Sudan (Northeastern Africa)

man with forehead scarification
20th century

Photograph from C. G. Seligman, *Pagan Tribes of the Nilotic Sudan,* 1932, pl. XX

Six horizontal forehead scars are still the identifying mark of the modern Nuer people, who dwell in the southern part of the present-day nation of Sudan. The Nuer forehead scars, called gar, comprise six parallel incisions extending from the center of the forehead around each side of the head. They are given to groups of boys, usually between the age of 14 and 16, as an initiation into manhood (ill. 75). That such scars are identified with certain similar peoples in Egyptian art reveals that they have continued within the same groups to the present day (Jackson 1923:145-146; Seligman and Seligman 1932:223-224; Titherington 1927:205, pl. 22; MacDermot 1972:104-116).

In northern Sudan ("Upper Nubia"), various Nubian peoples customarily have three cuts on each cheek. These scars are given to very young children by females skilled in the art, who are contracted by the parents. Particular care is taken cutting the scars of girls' faces, as the beauty of a face is measured by the length and width of the scars (Halim 1939:46). Scars of the Dongolawi and Shaigiya are typically horizontal, with the middle mark being in line with the mouth (Crowfoot 1913:131). Among Rubatab and Ja'aliyyin peoples, scars are more or less vertical. The Abdullab wear three similar scars on each cheek but also cross them with single horizontal lines. Sometimes, as among sedentary Arabs south of Khartoum and among the Baggara in the Western Sudan, scars are long and wide and extend prominently across each cheek. In the case of Kababish people in midwestern Sudan, cuts are made so cleanly that in middle age they are hardly visible (Seligman and Seligman 1918:151). Many peoples of the eastern Sudan wear the same scars, although some scars are quite short. Among the Rashaida at Kassala, and among some of the other nomadic peoples of the Bayuda Desert, women wear the same marks in tattoo or wear a combination of scars and tattoos.

Cheek scars of this type also appear in ancient Egyptian art, but they are quite rare. Deep cheek furrows—apparently cheek scars—appear, for example, on some of the Nubian captives carved on the base of colossi of Ramses II at Luxor (Vercoutter et al. 1976:figs. 38, 40). Curiously, no such scars appear earlier than this in Egyptian art, which may suggest that cheek scars were quite unusual or nonexistent among the Nubian peoples from the Aswan-Kerma area, whom Old and Middle Kingdoms contacted, and only became prevalent when Egyptian armies of the New Kingdom penetrated farther south.

In many areas of the Sudan, some people have, besides their tribal scars, one or more short scar lines directly behind each eye or other places on the body. These are related to tribal identity, but are worn as a protective folk-cure or preventative for eye diseases and other maladies (Brain 1979:70). This custom is very old. Herodotus, writing in the fifth century B.C., noted that "wandering Libyan" cattle nomads west of the Nile on the southern edge of the Sahara burned the veins on their childrens' temples when they reached the age of four in order to protect them from disease, "and such they declare is the reason why they are so much more healthy than other men" (Rawlinson 1942:366).

The forehead scars and cheek scars of modern Sudanese type found in New Kingdom art do not appear in later Egyptian art. Not a single surviving image of a Nubian ruler or bureaucrat from the 25th Dynasty (c. 750-660 B.C.), when kings from Upper Nubia ruled Egypt, exhibits such facial markings. Perhaps, Kerma-Napata ruling elite did not practice scarification. Such scars only recurred in the art of Meroitic Nubia, toward the end of the first century B.C., when they occasionally appeared in relief representations of royalty (Lepsius 1842-46, Abt. 5:Bl. 60; Wenig 1978:88, 101, n. 58; Chapman and Dunham 1952:pl. 17); on small clay heads from more southerly Meroe (Shinnie and Bradley 1980:180, figs. 70-72); on faces decorating painted pottery (Woolley and Randall-MacIver 1910: pls. 49, 62, 70), and on heads of some funerary statues and coffins from Meroitic cemeteries (ibid: pls. 2, 10). The scars appear either as three short incised marks on each cheek or as one or two horizontal lines (or two curving lines forming a crescent-like mark) on the forehead (Bates and Dunham 1927:pl. 36, 2-3; Wenig 1978:88-89, 227-234, 286, 288, 291; Vercoutter et al. 1976:128-131; Nur 1956:86-87). While many images of people display no marks, others wear combinations of both types. Occasionally, the same types of scars appear in small Roman caricatures of Nubians (Vercoutter et al. 1976:234), and Juneval (*Satyricon* 170) lists "forehead scars" as an essential feature of an "Ethiopian" (i.e., Meroitic) disguise.

Why some of these figures exhibit scars, while others do not, why some have combinations of scars, and why scars appear and disappear in art throughout the centuries we cannot know. Artists may have chosen not to render them or forgot to render them; in other cases they perhaps rendered them only in paint, which since has disappeared. Nevertheless, there can be little doubt that these scars have been a feature of ancient Nubian and Nilotic life for many thousands of years.

Note: The present article is an abridged version of Kendall 1989: 672-680.

REFERENCES CITED

Bates, Oric, and Dows Dunham
1927 Excavations at Gammai. *Harvard African Studies*, vol. VIII: *Varia Africana IV*. Cambridge, Massachusetts: Peabody Museum: 3-121, pls. 1-72.

Bernatzik, H.A.
1929 *Zwischen Weissem Nil und Belgisch-Kongo*. Vienna: Seidel.

Brain, R.
1979 *The Decorated Body*. New York: Harper & Row.

Chapman, Suzanne, and Dows Dunham
1952 *Royal Cemeteries of Kush*, vol. III: *Decorated Chapels of the Meroitic Pyramids at Meroe and Barkal*. Boston: Museum of Fine Arts.

Crowfoot, J. W.
1918 Customs of the Rubatab. *Sudan Notes and Records* 1:119-134.

Epigraphic Survey
1932 *Medinet Habu*, vol II: *Later Historical Records of Rameses III*. Chicago: University of Chicago Press.

1994 *Reliefs and Inscriptions at Luxor Temple*, vol. 1: *The Festival Procession of Opet in the Colonnade Hall*. Chicago: The Oriental Institute of the University of Chicago.

Halim, A. A.
1939 Native Medicine and Ways of Treatment in the Northern Sudan. *Sudan Notes and Records* 22:27-48.

Hölscher, Uvo
1941 *The Excavations of Medinet Habu*, vol. III: *The Mortuary Temple of Rameses III, Part I*. Chicago: University of Chicago.

Jackson, H. C.
1923 The Nuer of the Upper Nile Province. *Sudan Notes and Records* 6:59-189.

Kendall, Timothy
1989 Ethnoarchaeology in Meroitic Studies. Meroitica, vol. 10: *Studia Meroitica 1984*. Berlin: Akademie Verlag.

Lepsius, Karl Richard
1842-46 *Denkmaeler aus Aegypten und Aethiopien*. 12 vols. Berlin: Nicholai.

MacDermot, B. H.
1972 *Cult of the Sacred Spear*. London: Hale.

Martin, Geoffrey T.
1989 *The Memphite Tomb of Horemheb, Commander-in-Chief of Tutankhamun*. London: Egypt Exploration Society.

Nur, Sadik el
1956 Two Meroitic Pottery Coffins from Argin in Halfa District. *Kush* 4:86-87.

Rawlinson, George, trans.
1942 *Herodotus: The Persian Wars*. New York: The Modern Library.

Saitoti, Tepilit O., and Carol Beckwith
1980 *Maasai*. New York: Harry N. Abrams.

Seligman, C. G.
1913 Some Aspects of the Hamitic Problem in the Anglo-Egyptian Sudan. *Journal of the Royal Anthropological Institute* 43:583-705, pls. 25-38.

Seligman, C. G. and Brenda Z. Seligman
1918 *The Kababaish, a Sudan Arab Tribe. Harvard African Studies*, vol. II: Varia Africana, Part II. Cambridge, Massachusetts: Peabody Museum.

1932 *Pagan Tribes of the Nilotic Sudan*. London: Routledge & Kegan Paul.

Shinnie, Peter, and Rebecca Bradley
1980 The Capital of Kush, vol. I. *Meroitica* 4. Berlin: Akademie Verlag.

Titherington, G.N.
1927 The Raik Dinka of Bahr el-Ghazal Province. *Sudan Notes and Records* 10:159-209.

Wenig, Steffen
1978 *Africa in Antiquity: The Arts of Ancient Nubia and the Sudan*, vol. II. Brooklyn: The Brooklyn Museum.

Westermann, Dietrich
1912 *The Shilluk People: Their Language and Folklore*. Philadelphia: Board of Foreign Missions of the United Presbyterian Church of North America.

Woolley, C. Leonard, and D. Randall-MacIver
1910 *Karanog: The Roman-Nubian Cemetery*. Philadelphia: The University Museum.

Vercoutter, Jean, Jean Leclant, Frank M. Snowden and Jehan Desanges
1976 *The Images of the Black in Western Art*, vol. I: *From the Pharaohs to the Fall of the Roman Empire*. Cambridge, Massachusetts: Harvard University Press.

CIRCUMCISION AND MALE INITIATION

Circumcision and Male Initiation in Africa

Susan Bailey
Department of Anthropology
Indiana University

ill. 76
ancient Egyptian people
Saqqara
Egypt (Northeastern Africa)

circumcision scene from tomb of Ankh-ma-hor
limestone
Old Kingdom, 6th Dynasty
2410-2250 B.C.

Photograph courtesy of Frank J. Yurco

People in the West are most familiar with the practice of circumcision as an ancient Hebrew custom that has spread throughout the world, particularly to those areas where Judaism, Christianity, and Islam are prevalent. In reality, circumcision is far older and had its origins somewhere in Africa. Herodotus, a Greek from the fifth century B.C., wrote that the Jewish people borrowed the practice from the Phoenicians, who in turn borrowed it from ancient Egypt (Wilkinson 1883:25), although it is also possible that the Jews adopted the practice during their stay in Egypt. The Jewish people altered it from its original practice into the infant circumcision Western peoples are familiar with. In ancient Egypt, circumcision was an adolescent matter that involved a complex of traditions very different from those practiced in the rest of the world. This type of ancient circumcision is still practiced throughout the African continent by many adherents of traditional religious custom (de Rachewiltz 1964:282).

The earliest archaeological evidence for circumcision was found in the southern Nile Valley and dates from the Neolithic Period, some 6,000 years ago. The dry, hot climate has naturally preserved the remains of some circumcised individuals (Strouhal 1992:29). In later periods numerous stele, statues, tomb murals, and mummified remains show that as the peoples of the area flourished and grew into the great civilizations of Egypt and Nubia, the practice of circumcision remained with them (Helck and Otto 1985:728-729).

How and why the removal of the foreskin developed into tradition is not clear. The Egyptian *Book of the Dead* describes an act of creation by the sun-god Ra that involves genital mutilation (de Rachewiltz 1964:31). But not only is it unclear if this act is indeed circumcision, there is no evidence to suggest that the myth dates back to Neolithic times, when the practice began (Jonckheere 1951:215).

Some have suggested that circumcision might have served a medical rather than religious purpose. Although many modern physicians see the removal of the foreskin as a hygienic advantage in the hot climates of Africa, the ancient Egyptians probably did not. Their theories of disease and healing were not based on a knowledge of bacteria and other microorganisms, and in ancient medical texts circumcision was not recommended to prevent infection (Strouhal 1992:29).

On the contrary, ancient writings discuss circumcision in religious terms, as an act of ritual purification carried out by priests using the same hooked flint knife intended for the initial incisions made during the process of mummification (Strouhal 1992:29). The murals found on the 6th Dynasty tomb of Ankh-ma-hor offer one of the few clear illustrations of the actual practice of circumcision (ill. 76). Here the person performing the procedure is identified as the "circumcising priest" rather than as a physician (Ghalioungui 1963:95).

This practice of circumcising by religious, rather than medical, authorities is still common throughout Africa today. In areas where people practice traditional religions, the person doing the cutting is often a blacksmith or some other individual possessed of supernatural knowledge (de Rachewiltz 1964:192). For these societies, circumcision plays a vital social role. In many African societies, young children are seen as androgynous; thus, when they reach the age of puberty, a transitional ritual is performed to

ill. 77
Yaka people
Pasanganga
Zaire (Central Africa)

male initiation scene immediately after circumcision

Photograph courtesy of
Arthur P. Bourgeois, 1976

render them adults. For boys, this often includes the removal of the foreskin, which is perceived as a female element (de Rachewiltz 1964:181).

When a young man reaches puberty, between the age of 13 and 15, he and other boys of similar age are grouped together for initiation. They are stripped of their belongings, given uniform costume to wear, and secluded in some private area where they are taught the knowledge necessary for an adult life. It is during this seclusion that they undergo a number of mental and physical trials, one of which is circumcision. Then, after a short convalescence, they are returned to society and allowed to begin taking on more adult responsibilities, such as marriage and land ownership (ill. 77) (For a wide-ranging discussion of such traditions within contemporary African societies, see Murdock 1959).

Evidence indicates that the current practice of isolating young men in groups for circumcising is not very different from what was practiced in pharaonic times. Young men who underwent circumcision were probably the same age as contemporary African boys. Mummies of royal children as old as ten still bear their childhood side locks of hair and remain uncircumcised (Smith and Dawson 1924:93). Surviving depictions of circumcision like that found at Ank-ma-hor show that the initiates are adolescent and that the side lock of hair has been removed.

A rare text on a stele at Naga ed-Deir (ill. 78) states: "When I was circumcised with 120 men, there were none whom I struck and none who struck me among them...." (Dunham 1937:103). This text is fascinating not only because it indicates a mature age for the practice of circumcision, but because it alludes to the circumcising of young men in large groups. Just as in contemporary societies, this act of group circumcision was one of a series of practices included in the ritual in ancient Egypt. Secluded huts were built where circumcision and physical trials took place, and ancient candidates were often given a specific ceremonial garment to wear (Stracmans 1959:7-15).

In those contemporary African societies where circumcision initiation occurs, the operation is a mandatory one. Uncircumcised individuals are denied the rights of adult status (Murdock 1959). In ancient Egypt, there is no clear evidence of such a strict requirement. Some have suggested that circumcision was an obligatory, general practice that only later became linked to priests and purification rites, while others have declared it a privilege of the upper classes (de Wit 1972:43). Occasional Old Kingdom portrayals of unclothed laborers and craftsmen in mastaba murals show that they had been circumcised, and mummified remains show that it was common among lower classes at this time. It could be that it was mandatory for royals and priests, but that the lower classes were allowed greater leeway in compliance (Ghalioungui 1963:96).

ill. 78
ancient Egyptian people
Naga ed-Deir
Egypt (Northeastern Africa)

funerary relief with circumcision text
limestone, pigment
1st Intermediate Period, 9th-11th Dynasties
2230-2020 B.C.

Photograph courtesy of The Oriental Institute Museum, University of Chicago
16956

Despite this debate, circumcision played an important part in the ancient Egyptian sense of identity. Uncircumcised peoples were considered barbaric, and uncircumcised Egyptians were no exception (Wilkinson 1883:386). Prisoners of war were separated into the circumcised and the uncircumcised. Circumcised captives had their hands removed, while those uncircumcised had both their hands and their genitalia cut off (Strouhal 1992:29).

This sense of circumcision as a civilizing force is a heritage passed down from ancient Egypt and still survives among many peoples today. From Egypt it traveled to the Middle East and, through the religions of that region, spread to large portions of the world. But perhaps its strongest and purest representation remains in the Africa of today, where young men still undergo adolescent initiation rituals as part of their passage into manhood.

REFERENCES CITED

de Rachewiltz, Boris
1964 *Black Eros*. New York: Lyle Stuart Inc.

de Wit, Constant
1972 La Circoncision chez les anciens Egyptiens. *Zeitschrift fur Agyptische Sprache*. 99:41-48.

Dunham, Dows
1937 Naga ed Dêr Stelae of the First Intermediate Period. Boston Museum of Fine Arts.

Ghalioungui, Paul
1963 *Magic & Medical Science in Ancient Egypt*. New York: Barnes & Noble.

Jonckheere, Frans
1951 La circoncision des Anciens Egyptiens. *Centaurus*. 1:212-234.

Murdock, George P.
1959 *Africa, Its Peoples and Their Culture History*. New York: McGraw-Hill.

Otto, Ebarhard, and Wolfgang Helck, eds.
1985 *Lexicon der Agyptologie*, vol. I. Wiesbaden: O. Harrasowitz.

Smith, G. E., and W. R. Dawson
1924 *Egyptian Mummies*. p. 93. London: G. Allen and Unwin Ltd.

Strouhal, Eugen
1992 *Life of the Ancient Egyptians*. Norman: University of Oklahoma Press.

Stracmans, M.
1959 Encore un texte peau connu relatif à la circoncision des anciens Egyptiens. *Archivio Internazionale di Ethnografia e Preistoria*. 2:7-15.

Wilkinson, J. G.
1883 *The Manners & Customs of the Ancient Egyptians* vol. 3. Boston: Caccino & Co.

NUBIA

An Outline of Nubian History

Peter Lacovara
Assistant Curator of Egyptian, Nubian, and Near Eastern Art
Museum of Fine Arts, Boston

Prehistoric Nubia
7000 B.C.-3100 B.C.

Near modern-day Khartoum is the oldest known record of settled African civilization. This civilization, called Khartoum Mesolithic culture (c. 7000 B.C.), is noted for its settled way of life and pottery production that seemingly preceded agriculture, unlike development in early Near Eastern cultures. These early Nubians subsisted on hunting and fishing, but their remarkably sophisticated ceramics are among the oldest known. Fashioned from low-fired Nile mud and decorated with impressed dots and wavy lines, this pottery dispersed throughout the African continent and remained unchanged for thousands of years. The earliest evidence from Egyptian civilization shows a strong affinity with Khartoum Neolithic (c. 6000 B.C.). Later (c. 4000-3500 B.C.) Predynastic Upper Egyptian and Lower Nubian materials are strikingly similar. Human figurines, cosmetic palettes, and black-topped red pottery were common to both cultures.

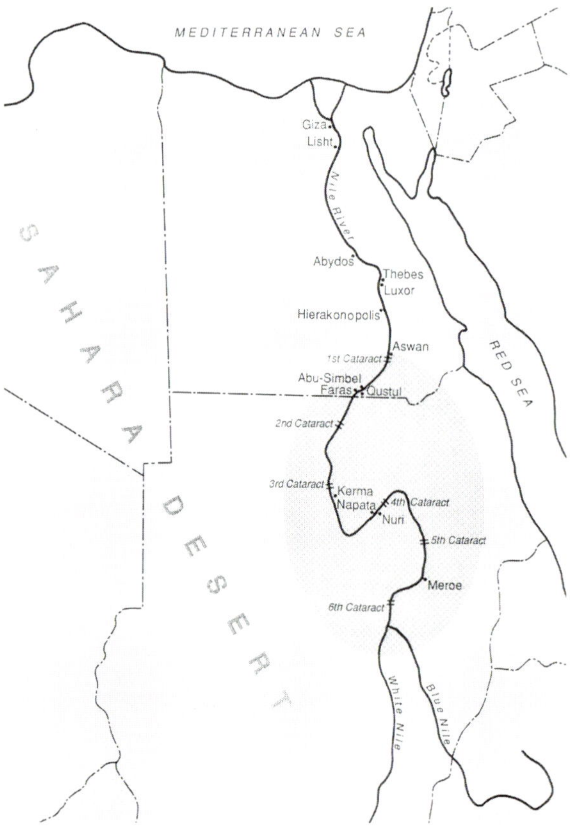

ill. 79
map of ancient Nubia and Egypt
4000 B.C.-1000 A.D.

Indianapolis Musem of Art

The A-Group
3100 B.C.-2800 B.C.

A-Group, Lower Nubia's earliest civilization, appeared around 3100 B.C., immediately preceding Egypt's unification. Although finely painted ceramics imitating basketry and a spectacular mace head with a gold handle were excavated from A-Group graves, this civilization formerly was dismissed as a chiefdom of nomadic cattle herders.

Qustul's royal burial ground was excavated by the University of Chicago's expedition in the 1960s, and the large, rich graves of local kings were revealed (ill. 84-85). These contained Egyptian imports as well as local artifacts. Despite theories that Qustul's kingdom preceded the early Egyptian proto-states found at Nubt-Naqada and Nekhen-Hierakonpolis, all these states probably developed simultaneously, some with contacts with Syrian Amuq Valley Mesopotamian civilization.

Raids by pharaohs of the Egyptian 1st and 2nd Dynasties (c. 2800 B.C.) ended the A-Group kingdom. The next centuries of Nubian history are sparsely documented; archaeological information about Nubia is more available from Egypt's late Old Kingdom (c. 2300 B.C.).

The C-Group
c. 2300 B.C.-1300 B.C.

Perhaps the lapse of Egyptian control during the late Old Kingdom to the First Intermediate Period (c. 2350-2250 B.C.) enabled the indigenous civilization to arise anew in Lower Nubia. Known as C-Group, it may be related to the A-Group. C-Group people inhabited Lower Nubia, from Aswan south to the Second Cataract. They were sheep and cattle herders, best known for excellent black-topped red bowls decorated with white geometric designs. They also produced figurines of men and animals, fine jewelry, and intricate beadwork.

C-Group settlements were small, rudimentary, dry-stone fortified encampments. Their dry-stone tombs were in squat cylinder shapes, with stelae marking their offering places. The C-Group shared Lower Nubia with a nomadic group, the "Pan-Grave" culture, who roamed the eastern desert areas and into Egypt, where they were employed as mercenary soldiers, called "Medjay" in Egyptian texts.

Kerma: The First Kingdom of Kush
c. 2000 B.C.-1550 B.C.

South of the Second Cataract, centered in the Dongola

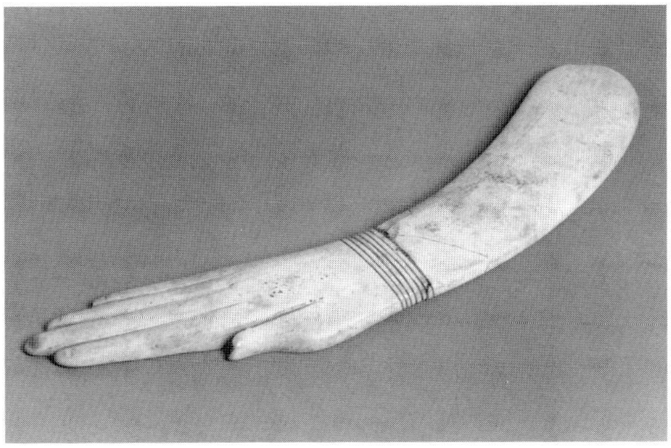

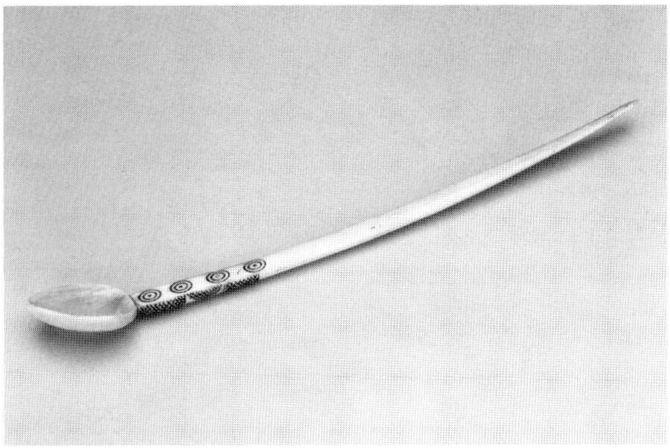

ill. 81
Zulu people
South Africa (Southern Africa)

snuff spoon
ivory; l. 6 1/8 in.
20th century

Lent by Roy and Sophia Sieber
TR 8457

ill. 80
ancient Egyptian people
Lisht
Egypt (Northeastern Africa)

musical clapper
ivory; l. 7 7/8 in.
Middle Kingdom, 12th Dynasty
1991-1786 B.C.

Lent by the Indiana University Art Museum
William Lowe Bryan Memorial
58.20

Reach at Kerma, another Nubian civilization developed, starting perhaps as early as 2500 B.C. Kerma people were the "fierce Nubian bow-men" of Egyptian texts. Bows and arrows, axes, and short daggers were found at Kerma, attesting its military prowess.

Recognizing Kerma's threat to its southern frontier, Egypt's Senwosret I (c. 1900 B.C.) constructed a series of forts in Lower Nubia, which were extended by Senwosret III, and utilized as garrisons and trading posts. Throughout Nubia's prehistory and history there was trade with, and sometimes tribute to, Egypt. Gold, ivory, animal pelts, and other materials entered Egypt through Nubia (ills. 80, 82). These massive mud brick forts, with their moats, parapets, crenelated battlements, and drawbridges, resembled medieval castles and housed the Egyptian garrison and their families. Mud seals from documents indicate the forts communicated with Egypt, and pharaonic records document expeditions sent to battle "Kush," now called the Kerma Kingdom.

Weakening Egyptian central authority in the Second Intermediate Period (c. 1750-1550 B.C.) led to Kush's asserting control over Lower Nubia and the lucrative trade passing through it. Some occupants of the forts switched allegiance to the "King of Kush." Kerma's kingdom grew powerful, allying itself with Egypt's foreign Hyksos kings. The Kerma kings were buried in huge circular earth-mound graves nearly 300 feet across. Royal bodies were placed on carved and inlaid beds along with pottery, weapons, food, and clothing for the afterlife, and sacrificial offerings of animals and humans. Nearly 400 people were buried alive in larger royal mounds. Large mud-brick funerary chapels, decorated with wall paintings and inlaid with faience tiles, were built near these graves.

Another large mud-brick temple, at Kerma's center settlement, was surrounded by workshops and storehouses containing raw and manufactured materials and imported Egyptian goods. The Kerma kings imported much plundered Egyptian material to decorate their chapels and tombs, including jewelry, stone vessels, and sculpture.

The New Kingdom Occupation of Nubia 1550 B.C.-1100 B.C.

After Thebes's rulers expelled both sets of invaders and established the 18th Dynasty (c. 1550-1293 B.C.), Tuthmosis I destroyed the kingdom of Kerma and extended Egyptian control to the Fourth Cataract. The Second Cataract forts were restored and reoccupied by Egyptian forces. Later, temples were built in the forts and throughout Nubia. A viceroy administered Kush, the "King's son of Kush," and reported directly to pharaoh. Both C-Group and remaining Kerma people were thoroughly indoctrinated, practicing Egyptian burial rites and religion and wearing Egyptian dress.

Temples now were centers of Egyptian control. Ramesses II, of the 19th Dynasty, built the great temples at Abu Simbel and others. The most important Egyptian temple, though, was at Gebel Barkal. Founded by Tuthmosis III, nearly every New Kingdom pharaoh added to this temple featuring Amun, the ram-headed god. It functioned long after Nubia again asserted its independence after the New Kingdom ended.

ill. 82
ancient Egyptian people
Lisht
Egypt (Northeastern Africa)

ornament in cowrie shell form
gold; l. 5/8 in.
Middle Kingdom, 12th-13th Dynasties
about 1991-1650 B.C.

Lent by The Metropolitan Museum of Art
Rogers Fund, 1909
09.180.1200

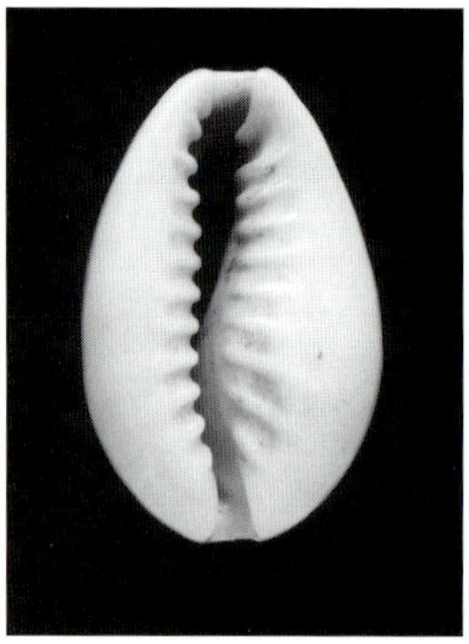

ill. 83
unidentified people
Western Africa

cowrie shell
l. 3/8 in.
19th-20th centuries

Indianapolis Museum of Art
unaccessioned object

The 25th Dynasty and the Second Kingdom of Kush
767 B.C.-656 B.C.

Egypt eventually lost authority over Nubia, and by the ninth century B.C. a powerful local kingdom had emerged around the Fourth Nile Cataract at Napata. By about 750 B.C. it controlled Nubia entirely, and later it conquered Egypt. These Kushites so devoutly worshipped Egypt's deities, especially Amun, that they were remembered for their extreme piety. They revered Egyptian culture and restored many Egyptian temples, and they sparked Egypt's last great cultural renaissance.

This vast kingdom ruled the entire Nile Valley until 663 B.C., as Egypt's 25th Dynasty. When Assyrian kings attempted to conquer the Levant, the Kushite kings mobilized against them. Constant warfare, from 670 to 663 B.C., resulted in Assyrian conquest of Egypt and the retreat of the Kushites into Nubia's heartland. Eventually the Saite rulers of the 26th Dynasty of the Delta removed the Assyrians and assumed control over Egypt.

The Napatan Period
c. 656-270 B.C.

This Second Kingdom of Kush was an African empire that lasted a thousand years. Most of this time, Kushite pharaohs maintained links with Egypt, and Egyptian remained the official written language. Since Napata remained the kingdom's chief cult center and nearby El-Kurru and Nuri were burial places of its kings, the early period of the Second Kingdom of Kush is called the "Napatan Period."

The Meroitic Period
c. 270 B.C.-350 A.D.

By the third century B.C., the Kushite political and religious capital shifted to the southern city of Meroe and became the center of "Meroitic" culture. The Kushites were influenced by both Greco-Roman and central African ideas. Many Meroitic gods were local, and art and architecture became highly original. The Kushites now wrote their language in their own alphabetic script, called Meroitic.

Meroe, an important city since the sixth century B.C., became capital of an empire controlling much of Lower and Upper Nubia and areas south of modern Khartoum. A vast settlement with a central great stone wall enclosed numerous stone palaces, temples, gardens of fruit trees, even royal baths. Some fifty royal pyramids were built atop two desert ridges east of the city. Meroe had a strong iron industry, and Kushite traders plied caravan roads south and east, to the Red Sea and up the Blue Nile. Rich trade flourished with Hellenistic Egypt and the Mediterranean world. In 24 B.C. a brief war with Rome for control of Lower Nubia concluded with a peace accord that endured until the collapse of Meroe in the fourth century A.D.

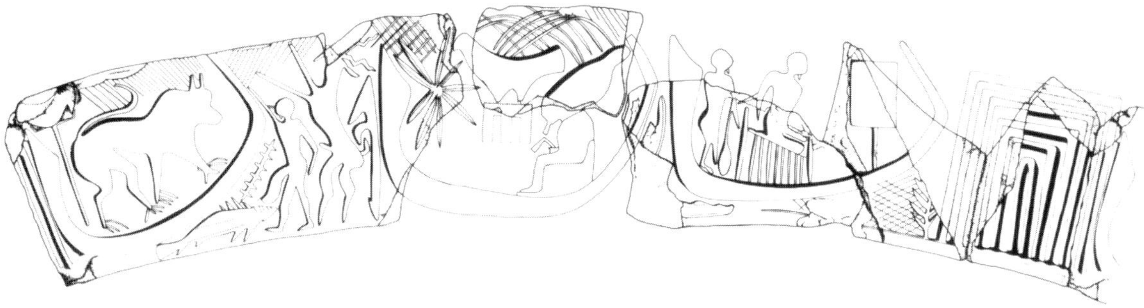

ill. 85
roll out drawing of Qustul incense burner

Drawing courtesy of The Oriental Institute, University of Chicago

The Qustul Incense Burner and the Case for a Nubian Origin of Ancient Egyptian Kingship

Bruce B. Williams
Independent Egyptologist
Chicago

The predominant view of Egypt's early institutional development has held that Egyptian kingship, administrative offices, writing, and religion developed in the last few generations before Hor-Aha, founding ruler of the First Dynasty. These institutions are documented by a series of carved objects with strictly pharaonic representations, and they are supported by a rapidly increasing wealth and complexity in the archaeological remains. These developments appeared in Egypt, strongly stimulated by influences from Asia, largely without reference to the rest of Africa (Baumgartel 1970:481; Trigger 1982:513-17, 521-28).

The successful restoration of the Qustul Incense Burner (ills. 84-85) in 1977 challenged the prevailing view on two grounds, although neither was readily apparent at the time. Carved from a block of hardened clay-like mineral in the recessed-silhouette style of many Egypto-Nubian rock drawings, the Qustul Incense Burner was found by the Oriental Institute Nubian Expedition in one of a dozen exceptionally large and rich A-Group Nubian (Predynastic) tombs in Cemetery L at Qustul (Williams 1980:12-18, 1986:138-45). The earliest of these tombs dates from the transition between the Naqada II (Gerzean) Period and the Naqada III (Semainean) Period or well before the start of the First Dynasty, and the Qustul Incense Burner was found in one of the earliest. Other objects in the cemetery indicated that it was the earliest of the carved monumental pharaonic documents (Williams 1986:172-83).

When restored, the Qustul Incense Burner was the earliest representation of an individual pharaoh (Williams 1980:18). However, its procession of sacred barks, or boats, and other elements bridged the gap between the sophisticated carved pharaonic objects of Naqada III, such as the famous Narmer palette, and earlier representations that had been considered pre-pharaonic, such as a painted tomb at Hierakonpolis in Upper Egypt and a painted textile from Gebelein, now in Turin. These paintings could be interpreted in light of the Qustul Incense Burner as completely pharaonic; and, by extension, all other art in the Naqada I and II periods was also pharaonic. For example, the painting at Hierakonpolis is centered on the ceremonial dance performed by pharaoh at the Heb Sed, the periodic festival of renewal. Other paintings have typical Egyptian symbols that are simply incipient writing (Williams and Logan 1987:245-82, Williams 1988:43-45). Egypt and Nubia shared a core of pharaonic institutions, rulers, deities, officials, and representations that began long before Egypt became a unified state.

To scholars of all types, the Naqada III representations seemed to be a major cultural innovation, a break. That proved illusory, for there are major monuments that date

ill. 84
ancient Nubian people
Qustul
Egypt (Northeastern Africa)

Qustul incense burner
clay
Protodynastic, A-Group
3300-3100 B.C.

Photograph courtesy of The Oriental Institute, University of Chicago
24069

from early Naqada III (Dreyer 1995), and there is no comparable break in culture stretching back as far as the beginning of Neolithic settlement in Upper Egypt, the Tasian Period. There is an increasing cultural development, and one might assume that this applied as much to society as material culture, but there is no break to indicate an institutional separation. The Tasian Period is significantly related to the Neolithic of Sudanese-Saharan tradition as found just north of Khartoum and near Dongola in Sudan. The relation continued, as many pottery vessels, for example, have counterparts in Nubia and Sudan and Egypt. The forebears of Egyptian culture arrived carrying the core of pharaonic culture (Williams 1991). Distilled, that core of a particular human being, inhabited or "possessed" by a deity, is responsible for ensuring a certain harmonious condition or ceremonial conduct on earth in order to ensure the deity's willingness, and possibly even ability, to make nature follow its proper course. Beliefs of this kind remain widespread in Southern Sudan to this day, notably in its most famous manifestation, the god-inhabited Reth, or King of the Shilluk, and it also appears among peoples with a much less complex formal social organization. Primarily a religious office, it requires no state apparatus for its existence, but the duty of assuring harmony is readily transformed into political power when the opportunity arises (Simonse 1992).

Since the Qustul Incense Burner is a Nubian object carved in a local rock-drawing style with precisely pharaonic representations, it indicates that monumental pharaonic culture was entirely at home in Nubia, much earlier than once thought. It thereby shows a much closer relation existed between Egypt and its neighbors in Africa than previously commonly admitted. The relationship was clearly reciprocal, for the incense burner and rock drawings show a creative use of pharaonic imagery. Most notable of these rock drawings is a raised relief from Gebel Sheikh Suleiman, located a short distance south of Qustul, which depicts the aftermath of a pharaoh's victory. Once attributed to a 1st Dynasty Egyptian ruler, the monument actually dates from an earlier time, when the Qustul dynasty controlled the region. Nubia played an active role in this as well as later periods when Nubians made use of explicitly Egyptian-style pharaonic formal culture. The repeated transitions to and from Egyptian-type formal culture indicate that competing ethics were at work to produce a harmonious universe in a complex of fundamentally pharaonic beliefs (Williams 1991:77-84). Changes of this sort often happened in Egypt, as shown by the Horus-Seth conflict in the 2nd Dynasty, the rise of Amun-Re at the start of the New Kingdom, and the religious revolution of the Amarna Period.

The two points of challenge to the isolation of early Egypt in Africa led to a third question: Could the A-Group kingdom itself have united Egypt? Seal impressions from northern Nubia indicate that A-Group rulers had united Nubia from the Second to the First Cataract along the Nile River. On these seals, the A-Group kingdom is explicitly named, Ta-Seti (Land of the Bow), surely the first such document in human history (Williams 1986:169-171, as is the name of King Pe-Hor from Qustul). Upper Egypt was not united, and the Nubian Kingdom would easily have been the most powerful of all the pharaonic kingdoms of the time. An early royal tomb found by a German expedition at Abydos has been taken as evidence against a Nubian conquest (O'Connor 1993:21), but pharaohs originating in one place were sometimes buried in another location. Nubian influence, in fact, appears in the A-Group royal design of a large tomb at Hierakonpolis, and, after a lapse of centuries, as a basis for the design of the tomb of the last ruler of the 2nd Dynasty at Abydos (Williams 1991:75). Because the details remain unknown, it is not possible to determine which dynasty actually united Egypt; but it is clear that A-Group Nubia and Egypt shared a common pharaonic heritage, and that heritage was completely African.

REFERENCES CITED

Baumgartel, Elise
1970 Predynastic Egypt. In *The Cambridge Ancient History, Third Edition.* vol. I, *Prolegomena and Prehistory.* I. E. S. Edwards, C. J. Gadd and N. G. L. Hammond, eds. pp. 463-497. Cambridge: Cambridge University Press.

Dreyer, Günter
1995 Die Datierung der Min-Statuen aus Koptos. In Kunst des Alten Reiches. Symposium im Deutschen Archäologischen Institut Kairo am 29. und 30. Oktober 1991. Rainer Stadelmann and Hourig Sourouzian, eds. pp. 49-56. Mainz am Rhein: Philip von Zabern.

O'Connor, David
1993 *Ancient Nubia, Egypt's Rival in Africa.* Philadelphia: University Museum, University of Pennsylvania.

Simonse, Simon
1992 *Kings of Disaster: Dualism, Centralism and the Scapegoat King in Southeastern Sudan.* Studies in Human Society, Vol. 5. Leiden: E. J. Brill.

Trigger, Bruce G.
1982 The rise of civilization in Egypt. In *The Cambridge History of Africa.* vol. I. *From the Earliest Times to c. 500 B.C.* J. Desmond Clark, ed. pp. 478-547. Cambridge: Cambridge University Press.

Williams, Bruce
1980 The Lost Pharaohs of Nubia. *Archaeology* 33(5): 14-21.

1986 *Excavations between Abu Simbel and the Sudan Frontier, Keith C. Seele, Director.* Part 1: *The A-Group Royal Cemetery at Qustul: Cemetery L.*The University of Chicago Oriental Institute Nubian Expedition, vol. III. Chicago: The Oriental Institute.

1988 *Decorated Pottery and the Art of Naqada III.* Münchner Ägyptologische Studien 45. Munich: Deutscher Kunstverlag.

1991 A Prospectus for Exploring the Historical Essence of Ancient Nubia. In *Egypt and Africa, Nubia from Prehistory to Islam.* W. V. Davies, ed. London: British Museum Press in association with the Egypt Exploration Society.

Williams, Bruce, and Thomas J. Logan
1987 The Metropolitan Museum Knife Handle and Aspects of Pharaonic Imagery before Narmer. *Journal of Near Eastern Studies* 46:245-85.

SUGGESTED READING

Adams, William Y.
1985 Doubts about the Lost Pharaohs. *Journal of Near Eastern Studies.* 44:185-92.

Williams, Bruce
1987 Forebears of Menes in Nubia, Myth or Reality. *Journal of Near Eastern Studies.* 46:15-26.

Interaction between the Nubian A-Group and Predynastic Egypt: The Significance of the Qustul Incense Burner

Joseph W. Wegner
Egyptologist
University of Pennsylvania

Over a period of nearly a thousand years (c. 3800-3000 B.C.), a distinctive Nubian culture, the A-Group, developed in the Nile Valley between the First and Second Cataracts. The last two centuries of this period (c. 3200-3000 B.C.), a phase known as the Classic/Terminal A-Group, witnessed the flowering of the A-Group culture. Developing wealth and complexity in the Classic A-Group occurred at the same time as the full emergence of complex society in Egypt. During the late Predynastic Period (Nagada II and III), the elaboration of the foundations of Egyptian civilization were occurring. These elements included the development of hieroglyphic writing and a complex governmental system at the head of which was the divine kingship.

The existence of close trade and exchange between Predynastic Egypt and the A-Group has long been known through the high frequency of Egyptian trade goods in A-Group burials. Indeed, economic interaction with Egypt appears to have been an important catalyst in the emergence of the A-Group itself as well as in the increasing wealth and complexity that characterize the Classic A-Group period (Nördstrom 1972; H. Smith 1991).

The extent of interaction between late Predynastic Egypt and the Lower Nubian A-Group has been highlighted recently by B. Williams in his publication of the finds from the important A-Group royal Cemetery L at Qustul (Williams 1986). The Qustul royal tombs have provided evidence for powerful A-Group kings who must have controlled a sizable part of Lower Nubia. Their tombs, although Classic/Terminal A-Group in material culture, included large quantities of imported Egyptian and Near Eastern goods. One of the most significant objects from Qustul is an incense burner (ills. 84-85) decorated with scenes that incorporate Egyptian-style pharaonic imagery. The scenes show a boat procession moving towards a niched palace facade and include the depiction of a king wearing the Upper Egyptian white crown, as well as the archaic Egyptian royal Horus title and serekh. Williams dates this object to the Nagada IIIA Period.

Objects of Egyptian design and manufacture had been found previously in Classic A-Group tombs: most significantly, two gold maces in a high-status A-Group tomb at Sayala (Trigger 1976). The most probable explanation for this is that A-Group society interacted economically and politically with the developing Upper Egyptian kingdoms. The A-Group acquired elite Egyptian objects and, like the Egyptians, employed them as symbols of power (H. Smith 1991). The Qustul evidence led Williams, however, to propound a rather different theory concerning the nature of A-Group kingship and its relationship to the emergence of pharaonic institutions in Egypt. Based on the Egyptian-style iconography and royal serekh on the Qustul incense burner, Williams concluded that the early definition of pharaonic kingship occurred in Lower Nubia and was later superimposed upon Egypt by politically powerful A-Group kings who, he speculates, were the true unifiers of Egypt (Williams 1980; 1987; 1991; see article in this section).

When the iconography of the Qustul incense burner was recognized, its Nagada IIIA date appeared to give it chronological primacy over evidence for pharaonic institutions in Egypt. However, as Williams himself has more recently demonstrated, there is considerable evidence for the development of the central features and institutions of pharaonic kingship in predynastic Egypt (Williams and Logan 1987). Moreover, recent archaeological research in Egypt has added considerable time depth to our understanding of the indigenous Egyptian elaboration of pharaonic kingship and its accompanying state institutions.

In the royal cemetery of Umm el-Gaab at Abydos (the ancestral burial place of the kings of the Egyptian 1st Dynasty), recent work has revealed a series of royal tombs extending back in time from the Early Dynastic Period (Egyptian Dynasty 1 and 2) into the Nagada II Period. One large, well-preserved tomb of the Nagada IIIA Period has provided considerable new evidence for the early development of state institutions in Egypt (Tomb U-J: Dreyer 1993b; Kaiser 1990). Early hieroglyphic records in that tomb are the result of record-keeping activities of an already quite complex administrative and bureaucratic system with activities reaching as far as the Egyptian Delta (Dreyer 1993a). Clearly, the hieroglyphic writing system was already developing in Egypt in the late Nagada II Period. The evidence from Umm el-Gaab demonstrates that not only pharaonic kingship, but also the primary elements of a centralized state system, including writing and a complex administrative and governmental apparatus, were evolving in Egypt for several centuries prior to the 1st

Dynasty. Although Classic/Terminal A-Group society has recently been shown to be more complex and politically organized than previously thought (O'Connor 1991; 1993: 20-23), there is no comparable evidence for the long-term development of such institutions in the A-Group (also, Adams 1985). The A-Group utilization and adaptation of pharaonic imagery and use of Egyptian-style royal titulary, and, possibly, hieroglyphic symbols in connection with that kingship emerged full-blown in the Classic/Terminal period. The development of pharaonic iconography and symbols and the hieroglyphic writing system is firmly rooted in indigenous cultural and social processes in Egypt. There is thus no evidence to support the contention that the A-Group culture was the fount of the institutions of pharaonic kingship.

Williams's A-Group monarchy hypothesis is the latest in a long history of models that have sought to place the impetus for the development of the pharaonic Egyptian state outside of Egypt itself. A considerable body of archaeological evidence exists showing that during the late Predynastic Period Egypt was involved in dynamic cultural, social, and economic interaction with its neighbors in northeastern Africa and the Near East. This interaction included shared and borrowed iconography—especially visible between Mesopotamia (Elam and Sumer) and Egypt in the late Predynastic Period (Trigger 1982). The Qustul incense burner, and other material from the Cemetery L royal tombs, has demonstrated that the A-Group was also an integral part of these dynamic cultural developments. The Lower Nubian A-Group was closely tied to the emerging Predynastic kingdoms of Southern Egypt, probably competitively as well as through trade and other modes of interaction. That culture appears to have adopted and used aspects of the pharaonic Egyptian royal iconography in a way similar to the later Napatan and Meroitic adoption and transformation of pharaonic iconography.

This participation and political emergence of the A-Group does not, however, indicate either the Nubian development of the iconography and institutions of pharaonic kingship or the A-Group conquest and unification of Egypt. On the contrary, the Classic/Terminal A-Group period in Lower Nubia is the final phase of a long-lived culture that had evolved over the course of nearly a thousand years. Contemporary with the final unification of Egypt at the beginning of the 1st Dynasty, the A-Group culture disappeared completely— erased in the prime of its development. Lower Nubia was depopulated for over 500 years, until the emergence of the C-Group culture. This evidence strongly indicates that in the last stages of the state-formation in Egypt, the A-Group culture was either destroyed or driven out of Lower Nubia (S. Smith 1991). Such a development could have resulted if the A-Group constituted a powerful kingdom or kingdoms in competition with the Upper Egyptian kingdoms. This eradication of the A-Group culture becomes extremely difficult to explain if the A-Group kings themselves were the cultural progenitors of the pharaonic civilization.

REFERENCES CITED

Adams, W. Y.
1985 Doubts about the Lost Pharaohs. *Journal of Near Eastern Studies* 44:185-192.

Dreyer, G.
1993a A Hundred Years at Abydos. *Egyptian Archaeology, The Bulletin of Egypt Exploration Society* 3:10-12.

1993b Umm el-Gaab, Nachuntersuchungen im frühzeitlichen Königsfriedhof 5./6. Vorbericht. *Mitteilungen des Deutschen Archäologischen Instituts, Abteilung Kairo* 49:23-62.

Kaiser, W.
1990 Zur Entstehung des gesamtägyptischen Staates. In *Mitteilungen des Deutschen Archäologischen Instituts, Abteilung Kairo* 46:287-299.

Nordström, H-Å
1972 *Neolithic and A-Group Sites.* Scandinavian Joint Expedition to Sudanese Nubia, Publication 3, Stockholm.

O'Connor, D.
1991 Early States along the Nubian Nile. In *Egypt and Africa, Nubia from Prehistory to Islam.* W. V. Davies, ed. pp. 92-111. London: British Museum Press.

1993 *Ancient Nubia, Egypt's Rival in Africa.* Philadelphia: University Museum, University of Pennsylvania.

Smith, H. S.
1991 The Development of the 'A-Group' Culture in Northern Lower Nubia. In *Egypt and Africa, Nubia from Prehistory to Islam.* W. V. Davies, ed. pp. 92-111. London: British Museum Press.

Smith, S. T.
1991 A Model for Egyptian Imperialism in Nubia. *Gottinger Mizsellen 122.*

Trigger, B.
1976 *Nubia under the Pharaohs.* London: Thames and Hudson.

1982 The Rise of Civilization in Egypt. In *The Cambridge History of Africa,* Vol.1, *From the Earliest Times to c. 500 B.C.* J.D. Clark, ed. Cambridge: Cambridge University Press.

Williams, B.
1980 The Lost Pharaohs of Nubia. *Archaeology* 33(5):14-21.

1986 *Excavations between Abu Simbel and the Sudan Frontier. Part 1, The A-Group Royal Cemetery at Qustul: Cemetery L. The University of Chicago Oriental Institute Nubian Expedition,* Vol. III. Chicago: The Oriental Institute.

1987 Forebears of Menes in Nubia, Myth or Reality. *Journal of Near Eastern Studies* 46:15-26.

1991 A Prospectus for Exploring the Historical Essence of Ancient Nubia. In *Egypt and Africa, Nubia from Prehistory to Islam.* W. V. Davies, ed. London: British Museum Press.

Williams, B., and T. J. Logan
1987 The Metropolitan Museum Knife Handle and Aspects of Pharaonic Imagery before Narmer. *Journal of Near Eastern Studies* 46:245-285.

King Taharqa of Kush

Peggy Brooks-Bertram
Adjunct Professor
Center for Applied Policy Studies
State University of New York at Buffalo

Of the many Kushite (Napatan) kings, perhaps the most outstanding is King Taharqa (ills. 86-87), a Napatan king whose ancestors and descendants had 1,200 uninterrupted years of rule in ancient Nubia, including 100 years in Egypt. Taharqa is known as a king in the Egyptian 25th Dynasty (Kitchen 1973) and as a Kushite or Nubian king (Adams 1984). Van Sertima described these Napatans as "the black princes of the 25th dynasty who from circa 712 to 654 B.C., threw their shadow across the length and breadth of the Egyptian empire, from the shores of the Mediterranean to the borders of modern Ethiopia, almost a quarter of the African continent. They were among the last great sun kings of the ancient world" (Van Sertima 1976). We have learned about the kings of Kush from early Greek travelers (Herodotus), the historical records of their neighbors across the Mediterranean (Ibn-l-Khattib al-Makkary 1964), their North African neighbors and sometimes enemies in Egypt (Kitchen 1973) and from Asia (Luckenbill 1927) and the Old Testament in 2 Kings xix 35.2, Kings vxiii, m. xix; Isaiah xxxvi, xxxvii.

The information about Kushite kings from their contemporaries largely emanates from warfare and international intrigue (Budge 1988). Taharqa spent half of his reign in Egypt and Kush in warfare with the Assyrian giant in the East (Adams 1984) in order to maintain the unity of Upper and Lower Egypt and to support allies at the mouth of the Mediterranean, namely the ancient Hebrews. The Moslem scholar Ibn-l-Khattib al-Makkary wrote an account in 1534 of the establishment of a garrison in the south of Spain by Taharqa in approximately 702 B.C. Other exploits are cited in the Old Testament, where Taharqa is identified both by name and land of rulership and where ancient Hebrews are warned not to consider him as an ally.

King Taharqa is believed to have been born in February in 722 or 721 B.C. (Kitchen 1973). As a royal child he might have spent his days in a royal nursery, gone about nude during the first years of his childhood, and worn a short plaited lock on the right side of his head (Lepsius 1898). His education would have been provided by his father, with whom he often traveled north. His stela at Kawa (known

ill. 86
ancient Nubian people
Kawa
Sudan (Northeastern Africa)

sphinx of King Taharqa
stone
Late Period, 25th Dynasty
690-664 B.C.

Photograph courtesy of the Trustees of the British Museum
EA1770

also as Gematen) describes him as leaving home early and says that he had not seen his mother in many years (MacAdam 1949). He was adorned with body ornaments consisting of a seal ring as a symbol of royalty, arm bracelets, and ram ornaments of Amun of Napata (MacAdam 1949) as well as a special covering for his head (Leclant 1976; Plumley 1975). Most importantly, he would have worn the tight-fitting skull cap, which had enormous religious significance, so significant that it is shown being handed by the god Amun to Peye (Pianhki) on a stela. This is the only known representation showing the royal insignia's connection to the god Amun. A uraeus, or royal cobra, on the front of a crown as proof of kingship was worn over this skull cap. The cobra, both admired and feared, was also a powerful amulet and believed to be the manifestation of divine power (Kendall 1990).

Taharqa was devoted to the god Amun and felt a great obligation to build anew, restore, and protect the temples. Thus, he is credited with erecting numerous temples at various locations in both Egypt and Nubia, and all were dedicated to Amun. The best-known of the temples are those at Kawa and Gebel Barkal, and both became the great religious centers of the Napatan kings. On his stela at Kawa he expressed sorrow about the ruinous condition of these temples and vowed to care for them. He restored those temples, which later provided a trove of Napatan royal inscriptions second only to Gebel Barkal (MacAdam 1949). The temples reflected a return to the iconography of Egypt under the Old and Middle Kingdoms, no doubt recalling a time when Kush gave birth to Egypt (Williams 1980). Generations later Taharqa's descendants also promised to restore the temples at Kawa and did so in his name, a clear indication of Napatan efforts at both cultural unity and continuity (Brooks-Bertram 1988). While little is known of his family life, a family tree indicates a large family (Reisner 1918).

King Taharqa did have some success in battle with the Assyrians. For instance, in 674 B.C. he repulsed an invasion of Essarhaddon of Assyria. However, in a second clash with Essarhaddon in 671 B.C., it is reported that Taharqa lost that part of his family residing at Memphis. Losses included his queen, his harem, his heir, other sons and daughters, and horses, cattle, and sheep in countless numbers (Luckenbill 1927). This loss was commemorated by Essarhaddon on several stelae strategically located throughout Assyria. They include the Sinjirli stela depicting the son of Taharqa as a captive to Essarhaddon (Luckenbill 1927), the Dog River stela (Luckenbill 1927), and at least two other stelae with similar messages of triumph (Thureau-Dangin 1936). It is believed that the loss of his family accounted for his later return to Memphis and the massacre of the Assyrian garrison left by Essarhaddon (Brunton 1930).

Taharqa is a king of many faces. However, the images that have received the greatest attention and praise are those that do not reflect the characteristic Kushite features: the bulbous nose, the prominent folds around the nose, the large lips, round head, and short neck. In fact, some cite these characteristics as unflattering (Leclant 1976). Of the many carvings of Taharqa, perhaps the best known is the Taharqa sphinx in the British Museum (ill. 86) It is hoped that more research will be generated on the personal life and times of this extraordinary king who figured so prominently in the development of ancient Egypt.

ill. 87
ancient Nubian people
Nuri
Sudan (Northeastern Africa)

tomb figure (shabti) of King Taharqa
granite; h. 12 ½ in.
3rd Intermediate Period, 25th Dynasty
690-664 B.C.

Lent by the Museum of Fine Arts, Boston
Harvard University-Museum of Fine Arts Expedition
21.2975

REFERENCES CITED

Adams, William
1984 *Nubia: Corridor to Africa.* London: Allen Lane & Unwin; Princeton, New Jersey: Princeton University Press.

Brooks-Bertram, P.
1988 The Battles of Taharka. Chapter in unpublished manuscript, "Back to Kawa."

Brunton, Winifred
1930 *Great Ones of Ancient Egypt.* New York: Charles Scribner's Sons.

Budge, E. A.
1988 *The History of Essarhaddon, Sons of Sennacherib, King of Assyria B.C. 681-668.* London: Trubner and Co., Ludgate Hill.

Ibn-l-Khattib al-Makkary
1964 *The Mohammedan Dynasties in Spain.* Translated by Pascual de Gayangos. London: W. H. Allen and Company 1884, and reprinted New York: Johnson Reprint.

Kendall, Timothy
1990 Discoveries at Sudan's Sacred Mountain of Jebel Barkal. pp. 90-125. November 1990 *National Geographic,* November 1990: 90-125.

Kitchen, Kenneth
1973 *The Third Intermediate Period in Egypt (1100-653 B. C.).* Warminster, England: Aris & Phillips Ltd.

Leclant, Jean
1976 The Image of The Black in Western Art. In Vol. 1, *Kushites and Meroïtes: Iconography of the African Rulers in the Ancient Upper Nile.* Ladislas Bugner, ed. pp. 89-132. New York: William Morrow and Company, Inc.

Lepsius, C. R.
1898 *Denkmaeler, Aus Aegypten and Aethiopien. Abt. V, Aetiopische Denkmaeler.* Berlin: Nicolaische Buchhandlung.

Luckenbill, Daniel
1927 *Ancient Records of Assyria and Babylonia: From Sargon to the End.* Vol. 11. New York: Greenwood Press.

MacAdam, M. F. Laming
1949 *The Temple of Kawa.* Vol. 1, *The Inscriptions.* London: Oxford University Excavations in Nubia.

Old Testament
2 Kings xix, 35.2, Kings xviii, m, xix; Isaiah xxxvi, xxxvii.

Plumley, J. Martin
1975 Qasr Ibrim. *Journal of Egyptian Archaeology* 61: 5-26.

Reisner, G.
1918 Known and Unknown Kings of Ethiopia. *Bulletin of the Museum of Fine Arts* 16(97).

Thureau-Dangin, F., and Maurice Dunand
1936 *Til-Barsib.* pp. 151-155, plates XII and XIII. Paris: P. Geuthner.

Van Sertima, Ivan
1976 *They Came Before Columbus.* pp. 122-141. New York: Random House.

Williams, Bruce
1980 The Lost Pharaohs of Nubia. *Archaeology* 33: 12-21.

The Diversity of Indigenous Africans

S. O. Y. Keita
Department of Biological Anthropology
Oxford University

The living peoples of the African continent are diverse in facial characteristics, stature, skin color, hair form, genetics, and other characteristics. No one set of characteristics is more African than another. Variability is also found in "sub-Saharan" Africa, to which the word "Africa" is sometimes erroneously restricted. There is a problem with definitions. Sometimes Africa is defined using cultural factors, like language, that exclude developments that clearly arose in Africa. For example, sometimes even the Horn of Africa (Somalia, Ethiopia, Eritrea) is excluded because of geography and language and the fact that some of its peoples have narrow noses and faces. However, the Horn is at the same latitude as Nigeria, and its languages are African. The latitude of 15° passes through Timbuktu, surely in "sub-Saharan Africa," as well as Khartoum in Sudan; both are north of the Horn. Another false idea is that supra-Saharan and Saharan Africa were peopled after the emergence of "Europeans" or Near Easterners by populations coming from outside Africa. Hence, the ancient Egyptians in some writings have been de-Africanized. These ideas, which limit the definition of Africa and Africans, are rooted in racism and earlier, erroneous "scientific" approaches. Classical European writers ("eyewitnesses") are not very helpful either, since they were not working within modern science. Ancient Greeks made a distinction between Egyptians and "Ethiopians," but such a distinction does not mean that the ancient Egyptians were not Africans. Also, it is not clear whether the distinction was actually sometimes more cultural than biological. Curiously, some Greeks reported that Egypt was an Ethiopian colony.

There is a stereotyped image in the minds of many people about what a "real" African looks like, or what characteristics can be "authentically" African. This stereotype also affects scientists, as noted with candor by Professor Jean Hiernaux (1975:54).

Stereotyped concepts of African human biology seem to persist because of a failure to integrate the facts of paleontology, genetics, and ecology into an interpretive framework based on evolutionary principles. This failure has led some scholars erroneously to explain that diversity in Africa is mainly the result of "true Africans" intermarrying with invaders or colonists from Europe and Asia. Hence, the eye fold, yellow skin, and hair form of most Khoisan speakers were once explained as the result of a very ancient mixing of "Mongoloids" with "true Africans." The narrow noses and faces of many Tutsi were seen as the result of "Caucasian," and ultimately European, admixture. What is wrong with these explanations, given that "intermarriage" does take place, producing people with "variable" features? The answer is straightforward, although multifaceted. First, the explanations are mainly the result of erroneous theories that postulated that humans had evolved into distinct non-overlapping types at some point in the past. This required explaining *all* variation as a product of the blending of these types. This perspective largely predates modern understanding, yet it persists to some degree! Secondly, there are no adequate data supporting the massive invasions of Africa required by these explanations, especially those that imply that some groups resident in Africa are not African in origin.

The diversity of Africans, which includes ancient Egyptians and Berber speakers, is real and largely indigenous. An evolutionary perspective helps us understand why. Modern *Homo sapiens* have lived in Africa longer than anywhere else, according to most scholars. This length of time means that more random genetic mutations, the ultimate source of genetic variation, have accumulated in Africa. Furthermore, Africa is climatically and ecologically diverse. This favors diversification by Darwinian selection. The continent is large, which allows great movements and fissioning of populations. This promotes random genetic variation, since small portions of larger populations rarely accurately represent the range of genetic variation in a larger group, whether it is ancestral or exists at the same time.

Molecular data suggest that the early modern human population began to divide between 150,000 to 115,000 years ago. This fissioning would have taken place in Africa. Modern human fossils dated to about 90,000 years ago are found outside Africa, but the next genetic fissioning is believed to have occurred after this, perhaps about 70,000 years ago (Bowcock et al. 1991). Modern human remains in Asia, including Australia, are dated after this period, and in Europe, to around 35,000 years ago. Why are these data important? Because they indicate that the background genetic variation of Europeans, Oceanians, and Asians originated in Africa and *precedes* in time the presence of modern humans in these areas. Europeans and Asian-Australians did develop more unique genetic profiles over time, but had a common background before their average "uniqueness" emerged. This background is African in a bio-historical sense. *Therefore, it should not be surprising that some Africans share similarities with non-Africans.*

The alternative to this explanation would be that a population of genetically uniform individuals left Africa before or between 100,000 and 90,000 years ago, evolved into ancestral Europeans, Oceanians, and Asians, and then returned at some point to Africa. This would then account for certain resident Africans having genetic characteristics only found in Africa, and others being similar to non-Africans. The various kinds of data do not support this scenario. No part of Africa was initially populated from Eurasia-Australia in the time frames given, nor to any great degree in the last 15,000 years, in the sense of different populations replacing each other. This does not mean that the relatively recent historic movements of Europeans and Near Easterners did not probably have some impact on northern African gene pools. However, it may be difficult to determine which genetic variants are not indigenous to northern Africa.

It is important to note that a small amount (one to five percent) of sustained migration, generation after generation, into a population can alter its genetic character in a few thousand years, assuming that the migrants freely intermarry. This is not the same as a new population coming in and displacing, exterminating, or reproducing in greater numbers than the locals. However, both can have the same genetic results. Historical genetic analyses and hypotheses are made more difficult when newcomers may be only slightly different genetically.

"Hamitic hypothesis" is the name given to the migration theory developed by Seligman (Sanders 1969). This theory postulated that "Hamites" migrated to Africa from the Near East bringing new languages, superior genes, and culture and influencing the indigenous people. Hamites were seen as lost Europeans. Hamites allegedly peopled Northern Africa and influenced other regions. Narrow noses and faces, lighter skin, straighter hair, certain lifestyles, and political systems were attributed to Hamites, such that wherever these were found, "Hamitic blood" was alleged to be the source. This is all now known to be untrue. The so-called Hamitic languages are part of a family called Afroasiatic or Afrasian (formerly Hamito-Semitic)), which originated in Africa (see Ehret, Early American Cultures section). Only one branch, called Semitic, is spoken outside of Africa.

Admixture with non-Africans probably does not explain the bulk of the variation from Algeria to South Africa, although northern Africa was more affected in this regard. At the DNA level great African continent-wide diversity preceded the minor European and Near Eastern migrations of later Holocene times. There may have been some migration during the Neolithic Period, although Neolithic Northern African sites do not, in the main, look like the work of European or Near Eastern settler colonists.[1] Even "new" "non-African" genes would be subject to the human and physical environment of Africa and hence would be reworked, thereby becoming a part of African biohistory, just as recent tropical African genes have been processed in Greece, Sicily and Portugal. In any case, it is important to reiterate that Africa equals diversity. Evolutionary theory predicts and extrapolations from molecular analyses and skeletal remains all indicate an early and ongoing diversity in the indigenous populations of Africa. The implication of this is that terms like "Negro," "Caucasian," "Hamite," etc., are misleading and non-scientific as applied to Africa.

1. The Neolithic in Morocco north of the Atlas Mountains is similar to that of Spain. There is evidence suggesting European Copper Age movements into Algeria. However, it is likely that the migrations were minor as neither of these seem to represent large movements of people. Cultural items were probably exchanged.

REFERENCES CITED

Bowcock, A., J. Kidd, J. Mountain, J. Herbert, and L. Cavalli-Sforza
1991 *Drift, admixture, and selection in human evolution: a study with DNA polymorphisms.* Proceedings of the National Academy of Science (USA) 88:839-843.

Hiernaux, Jean
1975 *The People of Africa.* New York: Charles Scribner's Sons.

Sanders, E.
1969 The Hamitic hypothesis: Its function and origins in time perspective. *Journal of African History.* 10:521-532.

The Physical Characteristics of Egyptians and Their Southern Neighbors: The Classical Evidence

Frank M. Snowden, Jr.
Professor of Classics, Emeritus
Howard University

African inhabitants of the Nile Valley south of Egypt between Aswan and Meroe, an area also referred to as Nubia, were usually called Ethiopians in Greco-Roman documents. I refer to these Africans as Ethiopians because the most frequent term describing them in classical sources is *Aithiopes (Aethiopes)*, literally "burnt-faced persons." Since the word "Ethiopian" emphasized the color and physical features of these Africans, the only people in classical texts corresponding roughly to the concept of Negroes or blacks in modern usage, I sometimes refer to them as "Negroes" or "blacks."

Egypt's written documents rarely mention the color of her southern neighbors, refer only occasionally to their woolly or tightly-coiled hair, and never provide detailed descriptions of their other well-known physical features, which are familiar in Egyptian art (see for example the "Nubian" reserve head, ill. 89).[1] Reaction to the Ethiopians' color and other physical characteristics, however, was quite different in the Greco-Roman world, where blacks had not been a familiar part of the daily scene. As the first Europeans to record their impressions of physical traits new in their experience, Greeks and Romans were struck by the novel features of a "newly discovered" people. Greco-Roman written and iconographic documents (see, for example, ill. 90), therefore, are important but often overlooked sources of firsthand anthropological information[2] regarding the physical characteristics of inhabitants of the Nile Valley, and differences between Egyptians and Ethiopians (Snowden 1970; 1976; 1983 passim).

1. I have designated her as *Nubian* because I am one of the many scholars who have considered her features clearly Nubian, i.e., Negroid, not Egyptian. See my *Before Color Prejudice: The Ancient View of Blacks*, figures 1-2, page 11, and page 115, note 42, on the question of her non-Egyptian features.

2. See Kluckhohn 1961:27-28 on the importance of Greek descriptive anthropology and Brace et al., 1993:30, on the significance of ancient iconography and the reports of Herodotus for information on the color of the inhabitants of the Nile Valley.

Ethiopians were the yardstick by which Greeks and Romans measured the color of peoples darker than themselves. Some Ethiopians were described as the blackest people on earth ([Aristotle], *Problemata* 66:898b). Others in the vicinity of Meroe were perceived as exceedingly dark and pure Ethiopians (Ptolemy, *Geographica* 1.9); and those near the Egyptian-Ethiopian boundary, as half-breeds in color, not so black as Ethiopians, but darker than Egyptians (Philostratus, *Vita Apolloni* 6.2). Ethiopians were also the blackest of the dark-skinned peoples appearing in a classical "color-scheme" succinctly stated by Manilius (*Astronomica* 4.723-730): Ethiopians, the blackest; Indians, less sunburnt; Egyptians, mildly dark; and Moors, the lightest (cf. Arrian, *Anabasis* 5.4.4).

Ethiopians also served as the standard for classifying other physical traits of mankind. Ethiopians were the most woolly-haired of all peoples (Herodotus, 7.70). Xenophanes (Fragment 16, Diels) mentions their flat noses and black skin. The majority of Ethiopians, but especially those along the Nile River, were black, flat-nosed, and woolly-haired (Diodorus, 3.8.2). Southern Indians resembled Ethiopians in color, but they resembled other Indians in their countenances and non-woolly hair, while northern Indians resembled Egyptians (Strabo, 15.1.13). Southern Indians resembled Ethiopians in blackness, but were not so flat-nosed or woolly-haired, while the appearance of northern Indians was similar to that of Egyptians (Arrian, *Indica* 6.9; Pliny, *Naturalis Historia* 6.22.70). Both Egyptians and Ethiopians were described as black, but only Ethiopians were described as having exceedingly woolly hair ([Aristotle], *Physiognomonica* 812,a,b).

In short, Greco-Roman textual sources clearly document differences perceived in the physical characteristics of Ethiopians and Egyptians. These sources also show that (1)

ill. 88
ancient Nubian or Egyptian people
Giza
Egypt (Northeastern Africa)

head of Nubian or Egyptian woman from royal tomb
limestone
Old Kingdom, 4th Dynasty
2640-2535 B.C.

Photograph courtesy of Museum of Fine Arts, Boston 14.719

all peoples described as dark-skinned were not Ethiopians in the full sense of the classical word and (2) adjectives for dark and black—*melas* and *niger*, for example—were relative terms embracing gradations in skin-color such as Greeks and Romans noted in their comparisons of Ethiopians, Egyptians, and Indians. Realistic portrayals of diverse physical Ethiopian types by classical artists (Snowden 1970:33-75; 1976:132-245; 1983:6, figures 14-62) illustrate textual descriptions. All Ethiopians did not appear to Greeks and Romans to have been cast from a single mold. Differences between northern Ethiopians and

ill. 89
ancient Egyptian people
Egypt (Northeastern Africa)

relief with profile head
sculptor's model
limestone; h. 4 ⅛ in.
Ptolemaic (Greek) Period
about 332-30 B.C.

Indianapolis Museum of Art
E. Hardey Adriance Fine Arts Acquisition Fund
1995.68

their southern compatriots, for example, were attributed to an environment theory applied uniformly to all mankind. Other physical types are attested by realistically portrayed mulattoes and by references to Ethiopian admixture in the Greco-Roman world, such as Aristotle's mention of transmission of physical characteristics in descendants of families from Sicily and Elis (*Historia animalium* 7.6.585b, *De generatione animalium* 1.18.722a; cf. Plutarch, *De sere numinis vindicta* 21 (563); Juvenal 6.595-601; Pliny, *Naturalis historia* 7.12.51).

In support of the view that Egyptians were black or Negroid, a frequently cited passage (Herodotus, 2,104) has been glaringly misread (e.g., Bernal 1987:52-53). Arguing that Colchians[3] were of Egyptian origin, Herodotus writes that Colchians were dark-skinned and woolly-haired, but emphasizes in the very next sentence that this observation amounts to nothing since it applies to several other peoples also. Therefore, rejecting color and hair as criteria, Herodotus argues that Colchian-Egyptian kinship was based on similarities in languages and customs, i.e., *cultural, not physical criteria* (Snowden 1989:83-93; 1990:543-557 for examples of other misreadings of classical sources).

3. Colchians were ancient Asiatics living at the east end of the Black Sea south of Caucasus.

In short, the totality of classical evidence highlights the fact that physical characteristics of Egyptians were not considered Ethiopian in the Greco-Roman sense. The physical traits of both the blacks of classical art and the Ethiopians of Greco-Roman texts—i.e., color, hair texture, and nose type—have been appropriately described as "Negroid" or "black" in later anthropological and historical usage. And regarding differences between Egyptians and Ethiopians, an observation of D. O'Connor (1971,2) is relevant:

> *"Thousands of sculpted and painted representations from Egypt as well as hundreds of well preserved bodies from the cemeteries show that the typical physical type was neither Negroid nor Negro."*

And classical descriptions of the physical traits of Nile Valley inhabitants are strikingly similar to characterization by later anthropological observers.[4]

4. See, for example, Trigger 1978,27: "On an average, between the Delta in northern Egypt and the Sudd of the Upper Nile, skin color tends to darken from light brown to what appears to the eye as bluish black, hair changes from wavy-straight to curly or kinky, noses become flatter and broader, lips become thicker...."

In conclusion, the color and other traits of Ethiopians were prominently noted in classical descriptions of Egypt's southern neighbors. Color, however, never acquired the importance it has often assumed in either the self-image of many peoples or in the denial of equality to blacks. By contrast, the image of Ethiopians was highly positive from the time of Homer's "blameless Ethiopians" until late in the Roman Empire, favorable impressions persisting generation after generation. Ethiopia was also regarded as an independent state of great military, political,[5] and cultural importance.

5. Echoes of the 25th Ethiopian Dynasty in Egypt (c. 760-663 B.C.) were still heard in the early Roman Empire, Strabo (1.3.21; 16.1.67), for example, including Tearco (Taharqa, 690-664 B.C.) among the world's great conquerors. See Ushabtis of King Taharqa (Museum of Fine Arts, Boston) numbers 4 and 5 in case M-3.

Ethiopians were not excluded from opportunities—occupational, economic, cultural, social, or religious—available to others of alien extraction. Blacks with special qualifications found places for their talent or industry. Some Ethiopians were culturally assimilated, and others physically assimilated. In classic science, philosophy, and religion, color was never the basis of a theory proclaiming the inferiority of blacks. When the Alexandrian theologian Origin (*De principiis* 2,9.5-6) declared that all whom God created he created equal and alike, whether Greek, Hebrew, Ethiopian, Scythian, or Taurian, this declaration recalled the unbiased attitude of the classical world toward Ethiopians (Snowden 1983:37-108).

REFERENCES CITED

Bernal, M.

1987 *Black Athena: the Afro-Asiatic Roots of Classical Civilization Volume 1 The Fabrication of Ancient Greece 1785-1985*. New Brunswick: Rutgers University Press.

Brace, C.L, et al.

1993 Climes and Clusters versus 'Race': A Test in Ancient Egypt and the Case of a Death on the Nile, 1-31. In *Yearbook of Physical Anthropology* 36.

Kluckhohn, C.

1961 *Anthropology and the Classics*. Providence: Brown University Press.

O'Connor, D.

1971 Ancient Egypt and Black Africa—Early Contact. *Expedition: The Magazine of Archaeology/ Anthropology* 14 (1): 2.

Snowden, F M., Jr.

1970 *Blacks in Antiquity: Ethiopians in the Greco-Roman Experience*. Cambridge, Massachusetts: The Belknap Press of Harvard University Press.

1976 *The Image of the Black in Western Art I: From the Pharaohs to the Fall of the Roman Empire*. J. Vercoutter et al. New York: William Morrow and Company, now distributed by Harvard University Press.

1983 *Before Color Prejudice: The Ancient View of Blacks*. Cambridge, Massachusetts, and London: Harvard University Press.

1989 Bernal's 'Blacks.' Herodotus, and Other Classical Evidence. *Arethusa* (Special Fall Issue) 83-95.

1990 Romans and Blacks: A Review Essay. *American Journal of Philology* 3 (4).

Trigger, B. G.

1978 Nubian, Negro, Black, or Nilotic? In *Africa in Antiquity I. The Arts of Ancient Nubia and the Sudan*. S. Hochfield and E. Riefstahl, eds. Brooklyn, New York: The Brooklyn Museum.

Two Tomb-Wall Painted Reliefs of Ramesses III and Sety I and Ancient Nile Valley Population Diversity

Frank J. Yurco
Research Associate
Field Museum of Natural History

ill. 90
ancient Egyptian people
Thebes-Luxor
Egypt (Northeastern Africa)

drawing of painted wall relief in the tomb of Ramesses III
New Kingdom
1181-1150 B.C.

Drawing from Kurt Sethe, *Denkmaler aus Aegypten und Aethiopen, Eganzungband,* 1913, pl. 48c

Two ancient Egyptian royal tomb reliefs of New Kingdom date have often been cited in discussions about the physical appearance of ancient Egyptians. One, the often-depicted Ramesses III tomb relief (ills. 90-91) is from a copy made by Lepsius in the 1840s, but not published until 1913 by a later group of scholars (Sethe 1913, pl. 48c). This was a typical nineteenth-century copy of an ancient painted wall relief. This copied relief scene is a subject found originally in both Ramesses III's tomb and in the earlier tomb of Sety I (ills. 92-93). It depicts humans as offspring of the solar deity. Such ideas in Egypt date back to the Coffin Texts of the First Intermediate Period-Middle Kingdom, 2134-1786 B.C. (Lichtheim 1973:131-132); they later were elaborated in Akhenaten's solar hymn (Lichtheim 1976:98). The Aten, the solar disk deity, was described as fashioning humans: "You made the earth as you wished, you alone, all people, herds, and flocks, all upon earth that walk on legs, all on high that fly on wings. The lands of Khor and Kush, the land of Egypt, you set every man in his place, you supply their needs; everyone has his food, his lifetime is counted. Their tongues differ in speech, their characters likewise; their skins are distinct, for you distinguished the peoples." The Ramesside pharaohs of the 19th and 20th dynasties in depicting the varieties of humankind as creations of Re continued this Egyptian idea.

Erik Hornung's recent publication of Ramesses III's tomb scene of this relief demonstrates that, just as in the tomb relief of Sety I, four depictions each—of Egyptians, *Rmṯ*; Kushites, *Nḥsyw*; Libyans, *Tjḥnw*; and Syro-Palestinians, *ʿAamw*, are shown, with one hieroglyph of each ethnic name written between every two figures. Each ethnic type was depicted with a distinctive complexion and in representative dress. Egyptians regularly were depicted as red-brown, distinctly lighter than the black *Nḥsy* (Kushites). Accordingly, the copy by Sethe-Lepsius, *Erganzungsband,* 1913, pl. 48c, is indeed a pastiche and not at all what actually is on the wall in Ramesses III's tomb reliefs (Hornung 1990:figs. 107-109). These Ramesses III reliefs are exactly like the Sety I wall reliefs (Hornung 1991:pls. 58-59).

ill. 91
ancient Egyptian people
Thebes-Luxor
Egypt (Northeastern Africa)

photograph of painted wall relief in the tomb of Ramesses III
New Kingdom
1181-1150 B.C.

from Erik Hornung, *The Valley of the Kings: Horizon of Eternity,* 1990, pls. 107-109, p. 148

ill. 92
ancient Egyptian people
Thebes-Luxor
Egypt (Northeastern Africa)

drawing of painted wall relief in tomb of Sety I
New Kingdom, 19th Dynasty
1291-1279 B.C.

from Ippolito Rosellini *Monumenti dell' Egitto e della Nubia, Monumenti istorici,* 1834, plates CLV and CLVI

Accordingly, all claims based upon the 1913 pastiche, that demonstrably is not at all like the wall in Ramesses III's tomb, and which posits that Egyptians and Kushites were shown alike with dark complexions and similar costumes, rest upon a nineteenth to early twentieth century copy that is not correct! The original scene, as shown by the photographs of the tomb relief of Sety I, was long, occupying a whole wall section of Hall E and bending around a corner onto the adjacent wall. The same also is true of Ramesses III's scene. This was hard to copy and even photograph, so most copies show only one figure of each type with the hieroglyphs rearranged, full name written between each figure. All such copies are pastiches. Hornung's photographs of the actual walls of Ramesses III's tomb are accurate representations of what Ramesses III had depicted, and those Ramesses III reliefs match the Sety I reliefs, also in Hornung's publications. Egyptians are depicted separately from Nubians in their own traditional dress and red coloration.

When Egyptian statuary, wall reliefs, and painted scenes are viewed without selectivity, they show a population with various complexions, from light to dark brown, mirroring the diversity of the modern Egyptian population. That this was also so in antiquity is indicated by a statement in Sinuhe's autobiography: "as when a Delta man sees himself in Elephantine, a marsh man in Nubia," metaphors describing the broad ethnic and cultural differences within the country (Lichtheim 1973:225). This agrees with anthropological studies (Keita 1990; 1993) that demonstrate that African population is diverse. (See ills. 88, 94, 96.) The Arab conquest of 639-642 A.D. did not alter significantly Egypt's population, which still remains very diverse (Batrawi 1945; 1946). The Islamization of the population came largely through religious conversion from Christianity, although some ten percent of Egyptians remain Christian. This modern population still echoes Nile Valley diversity, where people of the lightest and darkest complexions within Africa are found (Trigger 1978; Yurco 1989). Nonetheless, these Nilotic populations are all Africans, and so was the population, religion, culture, and other aspects of pharaonic Egypt (Frankfort 1948). It is quite correct that many early Egyptologists tried to detach Egypt from its African context, as Asante posits in this section, and that this partly reflects racist thinking of earlier eras. Yet, some of the effort to see foreign influence on late Predynastic Egypt was based upon archaeological finds and the early interpretation of them. Current scholarship in Egyptology, not acknowledged often by Afrocentrists, has demonstrated that Egyptians were most closely related to Saharan Africans, culturally and linguistically (Hoffman 1991), and that such Mesopotamian influence as can be inferred, came

ill. 93
ancient Egyptian people
Thebes-Luxor
Egypt (Northeastern Africa)

photograph of painted wall relief in tomb of Sety I
New Kingdom, 19th Dynasty
1291-1279 B.C.

from Erik Hornung *The Tomb of Pharaoh Seti I*,1991, plates 58-59, p. 122-123

through the Nile Delta town of Buto, as part of long-distance trade. Whatever foreign ideas and cultural items were adopted, they were speedily Egyptianized, and they probably did not include writing or its concept (see Yurco essay in the African Origins of Egyptian Writing section). Egypt made early contact with its Nubian neighbors on its southern boundary. After the unification in about 3100 B.C., a distinct Egyptian state emerged (Hoffman 1991). Thenceforth, Egyptians called their country Kemet and themselves *Rmṯ*. All foreigners were called by distinctive names and portrayed with distinctive dress. Nubians, first called *Nhsy* (Fischer 1961), were depicted darker, with frizzy hair, and wore a distinctive dress. Later, other groups were encountered in Nubia, for example, *Mdja,* and viewed as distinct from the *Nhsy.*

REFERENCES CITED

Batrawi, Ahmed

1945 The Racial History of Egypt and Nubia, Part I. *Journal of the Royal Anthropological Society of Great Britain and Ireland* 75 (1945): 81-101.

1946 The Racial History of Egypt and Nubia, Part II. *Journal of the Royal Anthropological Society of Great Britain and Ireland* (1946): 131-156.

Fischer, Henry George

1961 The Nubian Mercenaries of Gebelein during the First Intermediate Period. *KUSH* 9 (1961): 44-80.

Frankfort, Henri

1948 *Kingship and the Gods.* Chicago: University of Chicago Press.

Hoffman, Michael A.

1991 *Egypt Before the Pharaohs,* 2nd ed. Austin: University of Texas.

Hornung, Erik

1990 *The Valley of the Kings: Horizon of Eternity.* Translated by David Warburton. New York: Timken Publishers.

1991 *Das Grab Sethos' I.* Zurich and Munich: Artemis Verlag.

Keita, Shomarka

1990 Studies of Ancient Crania from Northern Africa. *American Journal of Physical Anthropology* 83:35-48.

1993 Studies and Comments on Ancient Egyptian biological relationship. *History in Africa* 20:129-154.

Lichtheim, Miriam

1973 *Ancient Egyptian Literature,* vol. I. Berkeley, Los Angeles: University of California.

1976 *Ancient Egyptian Literature,* vol. 2. Berkeley, Los Angeles: University of California.

Sethe, Kurt

1913 *Denkmaler aus Aegypten und Aethiopen, Erganzungsband.* Leipzig: J. C. Hinrichs'sche Buchandlungen.

Trigger, Bruce G.

1978 Nubian, Negro, Black, Nilotic? In *Africa in Antiquity:* The Arts of Nubia and the Sudan. 2 vols. Sylvia Hochfield and Elizabeth Riefstahl, eds. vol. I. pp. 27-35. New York: Brooklyn Museum.

Yurco, Frank J.

1989 Were the Ancient Egyptians Black or White? *Biblical Archaeology Review*15(5) (September-October, 1989): 24-29, 58.

Are Africans African?
Scholarship Over Rhetoric and Propaganda,
Valid Discourse on Kemetic Origins

Asa G. Hilliard III
Fuller E. Callaway Professor of Education
Georgia State University

Scholarly dialogue on the biological (phenotypical or "racial") and ethnic or cultural makeup of KMT(Egypt) must feature the major open scientific meeting on these subjects, the 1974 Cairo Symposium (Diop 1981b:27-83; UNESCO 1978). Twenty world-class Egyptologists and observers met under the sponsorship of the United Nations to bring state-of-the art evidence to the question "Who were the Ancient Egyptians?"

Two African Egyptologists, Dr. Cheikh Anta Diop (Senegal) and Dr. Theophile Obenga (Congo), dominated the debate, arguing that KMT was an indigenous African civilization, phenotypically black and ethnically and culturally African. They presented evidence in eleven categories, including physical anthropology, blood type, melanin tests of royal mummies, linguistic and cultural unity with the rest of Africa, historical comment by Greek and Kemetic writers, and ancient paintings and carvings. By contrast, undocumented arguments for a "white" or European origin for the Kemites were tortured or assumed. Sorbonne professor Jean Devisse, reporter for the Cairo Symposium, was definitive in his summary of the meeting.

ill. 94
ancient Egyptian people
Egypt (Northeastern Africa)

head fragment, possibly of Pharaoh Narmer
limestone; h. 4 13/16 in.
possibly Early Dynastic Period
about 3100 B.C.

Lent by the Petrie Museum of Egyptian Archaeology, University College London UC 15989

> *Although the preparatory working paper sent out by UNESCO gave particulars of what was desired, not all participants had prepared communications comparable with the painstakingly researched contributions of Professor Cheikh Anta Diop and Obenga. There was consequently a real lack of balance in the discussion.*
> (UNESCO 1978:102)

This meeting revealed not only the powerful documented and comprehensive arguments of Diop and Obenga, it established a model for an academic approach to the question, as opposed to the "sound bite" journalism that typifies the debate today.

Few Egyptologists have written scientific papers on the "race" or ethnicity of the Kemites, though many have expressed opinions "authoritatively" about these matters. Simply pronouncing that the popular images of *foreign* family queens Nefertiti (Vandenberg 1978) and Cleopatra VII are "black" or "white," implying that they were typical of KMT, based on subjective judgment, without explicit criteria derived from scientific consensus, is not scholarship. What is a scientific definition of "race" or ethnicity?

The rules for investigation must be explicit and universal. For example, we also must determine the origin of the ancient Greeks, culturally and phenotypically. While I might not go as far as one historian, who said, "It is easier to prove that Ancient Egypt is African than to prove that Ancient Greece was European," we do find that there were many Africans in Europe from ancient times to the present, even in the royal families of Europe (MacRitchie 1884; Rogers 1952; Van Sertima 1987; 1992). Will we therefore also call European nations a "mixed" cultural and phenotypic population, as some Egyptologists describe KMT? Since this exhibition seeks to present some of the diversity among African phenotypes (ills. 88-89, 94-96), we must also note a similar range of diversity among European or "white" phenotypes. It is a gross scientific error to assume homogeneity of phenotype in Europe and diversity of phenotype in Africa. Prejudice and stereotyping established a single popular model of African phenotype, thereby eliminating northern Nile Valley Africans from African populations!

The question of the origin of the Kemites is not an issue of "Afrocentrism" versus Egyptology, or any "ism." The challenge is scientific study versus casual and unsupported opinion, by lay persons or professionals. For years, many scholars have argued that KMT was African, phenotypically and culturally. (ben-Jochanan 1988; Van Sertima 1994; Finch 1991; Browder 1992; Hilliard 1994:127-147; Massey 1974; Jackson 1974; Williams 1974). Valid rebuttal cannot be by innuendo, by appeals to "authorities" who have never published systematically researched papers on the subject, by editorial writers in popular media, or by propagandists from think tanks with a political agenda.

Reputable scholars actually argued once that Egypt was in Asia, not Africa! The modern-day equivalent of that geographic absurdity is the argument that the phenotype of Egyptians is "white." James Breasted, of the University of Chicago, argued both ways in two different editions of *Ancient Times*. Kemetic people were "brown" in 1916 and "white"in 1935 (Browder 1992:146). We never knew the evidentiary basis of Breasted's conclusions in either case. He just declared it to be so.

On the other hand, among Egyptologists and other scholars who have studied the topic of origins, Cheikh Anta Diop alone was master of a broad diversity of relevant scientific disciplines that must be applied to this work (physics, chemistry, biology, mathematics, linguistics, history, anthropology, in addition to formal training in traditional Egyptology, with fluency in several European and African languages). He alone applied these talents for decades to study the question of Kemetic origins (Diop 1978; 1981a; 1981b).

So far, evidence from the Cairo Symposium and from subsequent work by scholars who specialize in research on Kemetic origins yields the following: Kemetic language is African, not Indo-European, Semitic or "Afroasiatic" (Obenga 1995; UNESCO 1978). The MDW NTR (hieroglyphic) *images* and *symbols* are native African Nile Valley in origin, not Mesopotamian (Ankh Mi Ra 1995; Churchward 1978; Massey 1974). The royal *mummies* are mostly black and have melanin levels consistent with black people, as far as research reports reveal (Diop 1981b; Partridge 1994). The *blood type* and *physical remains* are consistent with other Nile Valley Africans (Diop 1981b; Keita 1990). The *general culture* of KMT(religion, family structure, etc.) is African. There is no ancient *historical* record in Europe, Asia, or Africa in which the population of KMT is described as white; and there is no evidence of large scale *migrations* of Asians or Europeans into KMT until long after the pharaonic or dynastic periods (Viorst 1995:45-58).

ill. 95
ancient Egyptian people
Egypt (Northeastern Africa)

face of Pharaoh Senwosret III (fragment)
stone (quartzite); h. 3 11/16 in.
Middle Kingdom, 12th Dynasty
1878-1843 B.C.

Lent by the Petrie Museum of Egyptian Archaeology, University College London UC 13249

Chronology and *context* are critical in the study of Kemetic origins. KMT evolved through 10,000 years or more of cultural development and 3,000 years of self-governance as a nation. KMT was old and gray when Europeans came to know it. Its greatest development as a civilization and nation occured long before the founding of the Greek city states. Therefore, the very late Greco-Roman mummies and images tell us virtually nothing about the origin of the Kemites. Even pharaohs of the 19th and 20th dynasties such as Ramesses II and III are very late in Kemetic history. When and in what numbers did European and Arabic-speaking people come to KMT? Was the ancient phenotype and culture of KMT the same then as now? We must view clusters of family portraits in chronological order rather than as decontextualized single items.

This exhibit is one of the first to select items that show more typical African phenotypes (ills. 88, 94-95) rather than the atypical and sometimes foreign images that most Europeans like to see, e.g., Nefertiti (Vandenberg 1978), the Sheik el Bilad, or Kai the scribe, those ambiguous enough to be regarded as "white." Evidence must be in *context and in chronological order.* Let the Africans say and manifest who they were.

ill. 96
ancient Egyptian people
Egypt (Northeastern Africa)

male-female couple (fragment)
limestone, pigment; h. 5 15/16 in.
New Kingdom,
Early 18th Dynasty
1550-1389 B.C.

Lent by the Petrie Museum of Egyptian Archaeology, University College London UC 15513

REFERENCES CITED

Ankh Mi Ra
1995 *Let the Ancestors Speak: Removing the Veil of Mysticism from Medu Netcher, A Guide to the Grammar of the Language of Kemet.* Temple Hills, Maryland: JOM International Inc.

ben Jochanan, Yosef
1988 *Africa Mother of Western Civilization.* Baltimore: Black Classic Press.

Browder, Anthony T.
1992 *Nile Valley Contributions to Civilization: Exploding the Myths,* Vol. I. Washington D.C.: The Institute of Karmic Guidance.

Churchward, Albert
1978 *The Signs and Symbols of Primordial Man: Evolution of religioius doctrines from the Eschatology of the Ancient Egyptians.* Westport Connecticut: Greenwood Press.

Diop, Cheikh A.
1978 *The Cultural Unity of Black Africa: The Domains of Patriarchy and of Matriarcy in Classical Antiquity.* Chicago: Third World Press.

1981a *Civilization or Barbarism: An Authentic Anthropology.* Chicago: Lawrence Hill.

1981b Origin of the ancient Egyptians and Annex to Chapter I: Report of the symposium on "The Peopling of Ancient Egypt and the Deciphering of the Meroitic Script." In *General History of Africa II: Ancient Civilizations of Africa.* G. Mokhtar, ed. pp. 27-83. Berkeley: University of California Press.

Finch, Charles
1991 *Echoes of the Old Dark Land: Themes from African Eden.* Decatur, Georgia: Khenti, Inc.

Hilliard, Asa G. III
1994 Bringing MAAT, Destroying Isfet: The African and African Diasporan Presence in the Study of Ancient KMT 12:127-147. *Journal of African Civilizations: Egypt Child of Africa.* New Brunswick, New Jersey: Transaction Publishers.

Jackson, John
1974 *Introduction to African Civilization.* Secaucus, New Jersey: Citadel Press.

Keita, Shomarka O.Y.
1990 Studies of Ancient Crania From Northern Africa. *American Journal of Physical Anthropology* 83:35-48.

MacRitchie, David
1884 *Ancient and Modern Britons:* Volumes I and II. London:Kegan Paul, Trench and Company (1991 reprint by Freeman, South Dakota: Pine Hill Press).

Massey, Gerald
1974 *A Book of the Beginnings: Containing an attempt to recover and reconstitute the lost origins of the myths and mysteries, types, and symbols, religion and language, with Egypt as the Mouthpiece and Africa as the birthplace,* Volumes I and II. Secaucus, New Jersey: University Books (first published 1881).

Obenga, Theophile
1995 *A Lost Tradition: African Philosophy in World History.* Philadelphia: The Source Editions.

Partridge, Robert B.
1994 *Faces of Pharaohs: Royal Mummies and Coffins from Ancient Thebes.* London: The Rubicon Press.

Rogers, Joel A.
1952 *Nature Knows No Color-Line: Research into the Negro Ancestry in the White Race.* New York: Helga M. Rogers.

UNESCO
1978 The Peopling of Ancient Egypt and the Deciphering of Meroitic Script: Proceedings of the symposium held in Cairo from 28 January to 3 February 1974. Paris: United Nations Educational, Scientific and Cultural Organization (UNESCO).

Van Sertima, Ivan, ed.
1987 *The African Presence in Early Europe.* New Brunswick: Transaction Publishers.

1992 *The Golden Age of the Moor.* New Brunswick: Transaction Publishers.

1994 *Egypt Child of Africa.* New Brunswick: Transaction Publishers.

Vandenberg, Philip
1978 *Nefertiti: An Archaeological Biography.* London: Hodder and Staughton.

Viorst, Milton
1995 Sudan's Islamic Experiment: Fundamentalism in Power. *Foreign Affairs* 74: 45-58.

Williams, Chancellor
1974 *The Destruction of Black Civilization.* Chicago: Third World Press.

European Racism Regarding Ancient Egypt

Molefi Kete Asante
Chair and Professor
Department of African American Studies
Temple University

Perhaps no ancient people have had the question of their ethnicity so corrupted by literature as the ancient Egyptians. One does not read that the ancient Greeks may have been Asians or that the ancient Chinese may have been European, but in the case of the ancient Egyptians (Kemites), the possibility has often been raised by European scholars since the fifteenth century that they may have been other than what they themselves claimed.

Count Constantin de Volney (1757-1820) probably posed the issue most succinctly when he wrote after travels to Egypt:

> *I remembered the remarkable passage where Herodotus says, "As for me, I judge the Colchians to be a colony of the Egyptians because, like them, they are black with wooly hair. In other words, the ancient Egyptians were true Negroes of the same type as all native-born Africans."*

The beginning of what Cheikh Anta Diop calls "the most monstrous falsification in the history of humanity by modern historians" followed closely upon the European colonization of Africa and the enslavement of African people. Volney wrote, "Just think that this race of black men, today our slave and the object of our scorn, is the very race to which we owe our arts, sciences, and even the use of speech!" He was attacked almost immediately by the purveyors of a white supremacist doctrine regarding this civilization so strong in its perfection and monumentality. Imperialism and racism produced an anti-African bias that made the evidence of the race of the ancient Egyptians inadmissible.

In quite a curious manner, the birth of modern Egyptology was marked by an intense antagonism toward the race of the ancient Egyptians. The aim of many of the leading Egyptologists was to endorse a white origin of Egypt in the face of all evidence. By automatic reflex, almost every Egyptologist had to deny the African origin of the Egyptian civilization. They insisted that the grandeur and wonder that was Egypt could not be the result of black intelligence. In the view of these early Egyptologists, if Egypt did not have a European base, then there had to be an Asian base, but certainly not an African one. The ancient Egyptians had provided such a diversity of evidence in their texts and paintings that these modern historians had to invent novel interpretations of this African civilization, even going so far as to define away the blackness of the Egyptians by speaking of "a dark red race," creating the Hamitic theory, conveniently introducing the idea of the Orient into the discussion, and claiming that having "black skin and wooly hair" still did not make the ancient Egyptians black.

In the end the evidence itself was overpowering. There was no "dark red race" as there is no black race or white race, scientifically speaking. However, introduction of the idea of a "dark red race" was meant to create confusion about the Africanness of the ancient Egyptians. Neither the Orient nor the Occident can be credited with originating the ancient Egyptian civilization. The contemporary social and political realities of Egypt are the result of the Arab conquest in 639 A.D.

Eyewitnesses of the ancient period affirm that the Egyptians were blacks. Herodotus uses several examples, which he assumes to be valid, to show the blackness of the Egyptians, as when he wrote of the fact that the Nile flooding could not be caused by snow because the "natives of the country are black with the heat...." Demonstrating that the oracle is of Egyptian origin he writes, "by calling the dove black, they [the Dodonaeans] indicated that the woman was Egyptian...." Finally, Herodotus says that the Colchians must be Egyptians because, like them, "they are black-skinned and have wooly hair." The word Herodotus used for black-skinned, *melanchroes,* in the Greek, cannot be confused with white-, red-, or even brown-skinned. It means black-skinned. Other Greek sources include Aristotle's statement in *Physiognomonica* that "the Egyptians and Ethiopians are very black." Diodorus of Sicily insists that the Egyptians are the colony of the Ethiopians and that the Ethiopians (Nubians) are the ancestors of the Egyptians.

But the most important evidence comes from the Egyptians themselves. In the first ethnologies painted on the walls of temples and tombs, they showed their color to be exactly that of the blackness of their neighbors, the Ethiopians. Bas reliefs depicting various nationalities, such as the one from the tomb of Ramesses III showing Egyptian, Ethiopian, Asian, and Indo-European types, have further demonstrated the attempted falsification of the ancient Egyptians' history.

The effort to dispute the clear evidence of the blackness

of the ancient Egyptians is clearly rooted in the last five hundred years of white cultural imperialism. However, there have been many Europeans who have challenged the racist character of the writing on Egypt. Even Dominique Denon, leader of the French Expedition when the Grand Army conquered Egypt, exclaimed when he saw the Sphinx, "The character is African—the lips are thick—art must have been at high pitch when this monument was executed." Another observer, Gustave Flaubert, said of the Sphinx "It is certainly Ethiopian. The lips are thick." Egyptologist Emile Amelineau (1850-1916), discoverer of the tomb of Ausar at Abydos, wrote: "From various Egyptian legends, I have been able to conclude that the populations settled in the Nile Valley were Negroes, since the goddess Isis was said to have been a reddish-black woman."

False beliefs die hard. They are like the microscopic dust that inhabits clean rooms; the more you try to eliminate them the more they seek to insinuate themselves into the narrowest of cleavages. But with the work of Theophile Obenga, Miriam Maat Ka Re Monges, Maulana Karenga, and a host of other young Kemetologists, the hiding places of anti-African ideas about the continent's most majestic ancient culture are being discovered and eradicated in a flourish of original scholarship.

SUGGESTED READING

Amelineau, Emile
1899 *Nouvelles fouilles d'Abydos*. Paris: Editions Leroux.

Asante, Molefi, and Abu Abarry, eds.
1990 *Kemet, Afrocentricity and Knowledge*. Trenton: Africa World Press.
1996 The *African Intellectual Heritage*. Philadelphia: Temple University Press.

Diodorus Siculus.
1758 *Histoire universelle*. Translated by Abbe Terrason. Paris.

Diop, Cheikh Anta
1974 *The African Origin of Civilization: Myth or Reality*. Edited and translated by Mercer Cook. New York: Lawrence Hill.

Karenga, Maulana
1994 The Moral Ideal in Ancient Egypt: A Study in Classical African Ethics. Unpublished dissertation, University of Southern California.

Miriam Maat Ka Re Monges
1995 Kush: An Afrocentric Perspective. Unpublished dissertation. Temple University.

Obenga, Theophile
1994 *A Lost Tradition: Africa in World History*. Philadelphia: Source Edition.

LENDERS

Lenders to the *Egypt in Africa* exhibition

Museums

The Brooklyn Museum
CRAFT Research Center, Indiana University
Field Museum of Natural History
Indiana University Art Museum
Indianapolis Museum of Art
The Metropolitan Museum of Art
Museum of Fine Arts, Boston
Petrie Museum of Egyptian Archaeology, University College London
Pelizaeus Museum, Hildesheim, Germany
The Seattle Art Museum
University of Pennsylvania Museum of Archaeology and Anthropology
Walters Art Gallery

Private Collections

Anonymous collection
Martha Ehrlich
Mr. and Mrs. Harrison Eiteljorg
Marc Felix
Charles D. Miller III
Wilford Morris
Roy and Sophia Sieber
Dr. and Mrs. Wally Zollman

Exhibition Components

EARLY AFRICAN CULTURES

1
time line

human development
4,000,000 years ago to present

2 (ill. 2)
map

human evolution in Africa
4,000,000 years ago to modern man

3 (ill. 3)
genus Homo (early ancestral humans)
Olduvai Gorge
Tanzania (Eastern Africa)

chopping tool or tool core
stone; l. 3 $\frac{3}{8}$ in.
the time of early Homo and of Australopithecines
about 1,700,000 years ago

Lent by the CRAFT Research Center
Indiana University
TR 8481

4 (ill. 4)
Homo erectus (human ancestor)
Thebes-Luxor
Nile Valley (Northeastern Africa)

hand axe
stone; h. 5 $\frac{1}{8}$ in.
Paleolithic Period
300,000-100,000 years ago

Lent by The Metropolitan Museum of Art
Gift of C. T. Currelly, 1906
06.322.2

5
line drawing

unidentified people
Ishango
Zaire (Central Africa)

bone harpoon point
Mesolithic Period
about 25,000 B.C.

from Sonia Mary Cole, *The Prehistory of East Africa,*
1963, fig. 40b, p. 263

6
line drawing

ancient Sudanese people
Nile Valley
Sudan (Northeastern Africa)

bone harpoon point
Khartoum Neolithic Period
7000-3000 B.C.

from Anthony John Arkell, *A History of the Sudan,* 1961, fig. 2

7
line drawing

ancient Egyptian people
Nile Valley
Egypt (Northeastern Africa)

harpoon point
bone
early Predynastic Period
6100-4000 B.C.

from Anthony John Arkell, *A History of the Sudan*, 1961, fig. 2

8
ancient Egyptian people
Nile Valley
Egypt (Northeastern Africa)

sickle blade
stone; l. 3 $\frac{5}{16}$ in.
Predynastic Period
6100-3100 B.C.

Lent by The Metropolitan Museum of Art
Rogers Fund, 1948
48.105.41L

9 (ill. 5)
ancient Egyptian people
Fayum
Egypt (Northeastern Africa)

hollow-based arrowhead
flint; l. 4 $\frac{1}{16}$ in.
early Predynastic Period, Fayum A
6100-4000 B.C.

Lent by The Metropolitan Museum of Art
Gift of Herbert E. Winlock, 1926
26.10.68

10
unidentified Saharan people
Niger (Northern and Western Africa)

hollow-based arrowhead
flint; l. 2 $\frac{3}{16}$ in.
Neolithic Period
8000-4000 B.C.

Indianapolis Museum of Art
James V. Sweetser Fund
1995.112

11 (ill. 6)
map

African language families
3000-1000 B.C.

Courtesy of Christopher Ehret

12 (ill. 7)
photograph

unidentified people
Tassili Plateau
Algeria (Northern Africa)

rock art pastoral scene with humans
Neolithic Period
7000-2000 B.C.

from Michel Leiris and Jacqueline Delange, *African Art,* 1968, ill. 292

13
video

Saharan rock art
Neolithic Period
7000-2000 B.C.

from *Sahara Before the Desert,* Films for the Humanities and Sciences, 1989

14 (ill. 50)
photograph

unidentified people
Tassili Plateau
Algeria (Northern Africa)

pastoral scene of cattle with deformed horns
rock art
Neolithic Period
7000-2000 B.C.

from Jean-Dominique Lajoux, *The Rock Paintings of Tassili,* 1963, p. 108

15 (ill. 51)
photograph

ancient Egyptian people
Saqqara
Egypt (Northeastern Africa)

cattle with deformed horns
tomb relief
Old Kingdom, 5th Dynasty
2535-2410 B.C.

from C. G. Seligman, *Pagan Tribes of the Nilotic Sudan,* 1935, fig. 8

16 (ill. 52)
photograph

Dinka people
Sudan (Northeastern Africa)

pastoral scene of cattle with deformed horns
20th century

from Henri Frankfort, *Kingship and The Gods,* 1948, fig. 38b

17 (ill. 8)
photograph

unidentified people
Libya (Northern Africa)

rock art scene with tailed garment similar to that of Egyptian kings
Neolithic Period
5000-1000 B.C.

from Palazzo Di Venezia, *Arte Preistorica del Sahara Libico,* 1960, ill 9.

18 (ill. 9)
photograph

ancient Egyptian people
Hierakonpolis (Nekhen)
Egypt (Northeastern Africa)

detail of King Narmer with tailed garment
(from Palette of Narmer)
Early Dynastic Period
about 3100 B.C.

Cairo Museum, Cairo, Egypt
Photograph courtesy of The Metropolitan Museum of Art
CG 14716

AFRICAN ORIGINS OF EGYPTIAN WRITING

19 (ill. 6)
map

African language families
3000-1000 B.C.

Courtesy of Christopher Ehret

20 (ill. 10)
chart

Predynastic graphic images and hieroglyphs

Predynastic-Protodynastic Periods
3650-3100 B.C.

21 (ill. 11)
ancient Egyptian people
Thebes-Luxor or Coptos
Egypt (Northeastern Africa)

vessel
ceramic; h. 8 in.
Predynastic Period, Naqada II
3650-3300 B.C.

Lent by the Indiana University Art Museum
Gift of Frederick Stafford
59.45

22 (ill. 12)
ancient Egyptian people
Hierakonpolis (Nekhen)
Egypt (Northeastern Africa)

tusk fragment with rows of animals in relief
elephant ivory; h. 7 11/16 in.
Protodynastic Period, Naqada III
3300-3100 B.C.

Lent by The University of Pennsylvania Museum of Archaeology and Anthropology
E4903

23 (ill. 14)
ancient Nubian-Meroitic people
Meroe
Sudan (Northeastern Africa)

offering table
sandstone; h. 18 5/16 in.
Meroitic Period
593 B.C.-330 A.D.

Lent by the Museum of Fine Arts, Boston
Harvard University-Museum of Fine Arts Expedition
23.1480

24
photograph

probably Ejagham people
Cross River area
Nigeria or Cameroon (Western Africa)

Janus-faced helmet mask with Nsibidi markings
wood, skin, pigment, metal, fiber; h. 19 3/4 in.
20th century

Indianapolis Museum of Art
Gift of Mr. and Mrs. Harrison Eiteljorg, 1989.884

25
chart

Cross River area

Nigeria or Cameroon (Western Africa)
graphic signs and symbols (Nsibidi)

from Reverend J. K. MacGregor, Some Notes on Nsibidi, *Journal of the Royal Anthropological Institute,* 1909, pp. 215, 217

AFRICA IN MAPS

26 (ill. 1)
map

some peoples, traditional states, and sites of Africa

27
map

present-day nations of Africa

28
map

Mercator projection of Africa

29
map

Peters projection of Africa

MOTHER AND CHILD FIGURES

30 (ill. 21)
photograph

Nubian people
Faras
Sudan (Northeastern Africa)

Virgin, Christ Child, and bishop
wall painting from cathedral at Faras
plaster, pigment
10th century

from K. Michalowski, *Faras: Wall Paintings in the Collection of the National Museum in Warsaw,* 1974, pl. 45

31
photograph

unidentified people
Ethiopia (Northeastern Africa)

Virgin, Christ Child, and angels
page from gospel manuscript (Gunda Gundie monastery)
parchment, pigment
15th century

from Jules Leroy, *Ethiopian Painting,* 1967, pl. VI

32 (cover and ill. 15)
ancient Egyptian people
Saqqara
Egypt (Northeastern Africa)

Pharaoh Pepy II and mother figure
alabaster; h. 15 7/16 in.
Old Kingdom, 6th Dynasty
about 2350-2250 B.C.

Lent by The Brooklyn Museum
Charles Edwin Wilbour Fund
39.119

33 (cover and ill. 16)
Nana Osei Bonsu (carver)
Asante people
Ghana (Western Africa)

royal mother and child figure
wood, pigment, gold leaf; h. 17 11/16 in.
1930s

Lent by The Seattle Art Museum
Gift of Katherine White and The Boeing Company
81.17.323

34 (ill. 17)
ancient Egyptian people
Saqqara
Egypt (Northeastern Africa)

mother figure with two children
limestone; h. 4 1/16 in.
Old Kingdom, 6th Dynasty
2410-2250 B.C.

Lent by The Metropolitan Museum of Art
Edward S. Harkness Gift, 1926
26.7.1405

EXHIBITION COMPONENTS

35 (ill. 18)
probably Fante people
Ghana (Western Africa)

mother figure with two children
counterweight for measuring gold
bronze; h. 2 1/4 in.
late 19th century

Lent anonymously
TR 8538/1

36 (ill. 19)
Soso people
Zaire (Central Africa)

mother and child figure
wood; h. 13 3/8 in.
20th century

Lent by Marc Felix
TR 8545/1

37 (ill. 20)
ancient Egyptian people
possibly Saqqara
Egypt (Northeastern Africa)

Isis and Horus figure
bronze; h. 10 11/16 in.
Late Period, 25th-26th Dynasties
712-525 B.C.

Lent by The University of Pennsylvania Museum of Archaeology and Anthropology
E14293

HEADRESTS

38
map of origin of headrests in this exhibition
2700 B.C. - present

39 (ill. 22)
photograph

ancient Egyptian people
Saqqara, Tomb of Mehu
Egypt (Northeastern Africa)

wall painting with headrest
stone, pigment
Old Kingdom, 5th Dynasty
2535-2410 B.C.

from Ahmed Moussa and Fritz Junge, *Two Tombs of Craftsmen,* 1975, pl. 2

40 (ill. 27)
photograph

Turkana people
Kenya (Eastern Africa)

man resting on headrest
20th century

from David Keith Jones, *Shepherds of the Desert,* 1984, p. 53

41 (ill. 26)
ancient Egyptian people
Giza
Egypt (Northeastern Africa)

headrest
alabaster; h. 8 1/4 in.
Old Kingdom, 3rd-8th Dynasties
2735-2230 B.C.

Lent by the Museum of Fine Arts, Boston
Harvard University-Museum of Fine Arts Expedition
21.2790

42
ancient Egyptian people
Thebes-Luxor
Egypt (Northeastern Africa)

headrest
wood; h. 7 7/8 in.
Middle-New Kingdoms, 12th-18th Dynasties
1991-1550 B.C.

Lent by The Metropolitan Museum of Art
Rogers Fund, 1919
19.3.152

43 (ill. 31)
Beja people
Sudan (Northeastern Africa)

headrest
wood, hide; h. 7 1/2 in.
20th century

Indianapolis Museum of Art
Emma Harter Sweetser Fund
1994.37

44 (ill. 29)

ancient Egyptian people
Thebes-Luxor
Egypt (Northeastern Africa)

headrest
wood; h. 5 1/16 in.
Middle-New Kingdoms, 12th-18th Dynasties
1991-1550 B.C.

Lent by the Metropolitan Museum of Art
Rogers Fund, 1927
27.3.160

45 (ill. 30)
probably Sidamo people
Ethiopia (Eastern Africa)

headrest
wood; h. 7 1/16 in.
20th century

Indianapolis Museum of Art
Emma Harter Sweetser Fund
1994.122

EXHIBITION COMPONENTS

46 (ill. 28)
unidentified people
Chad (Western Africa)

headrest
ceramic; h. 5 $\frac{1}{8}$ in.
probably 12th century

Lent by Wilford H. Morris
TR 8546

47 (ill. 23)
Tellem people
Mali (Western Africa)

headrest
wood; h. 6 $\frac{1}{2}$ in.
11th-17th centuries

Lent by Roy and Sophia Sieber
TR 8283

48 (ill. 25)
Shona people
Zimbabwe (Southern Africa)

headrest
wood; h. 4 $\frac{15}{16}$ in.
20th century

Indianapolis Museum of Art
Gift of Mr. and Mrs. Harrison Eiteljorg
1989.1278

49
Turkana people
Kenya (Eastern Africa)

headrest
wood, brass; h. 6 in.
20th century

Indianapolis Museum of Art
Gift of Mr. and Mrs. Harrison Eiteljorg
1989.1241

50 (ill. 24)
Kuba people
Zaire (Central Africa)
headrest
wood; h. 4 $\frac{7}{8}$ in.
20th century

Indianapolis Museum of Art
Gift of Carole and Richard Darst
1991.68

DEPICTION OF HUMANS IN AFRICAN ART

51
photograph

unidentified people
Tassili Plateau
Algeria (Northern Africa)

rock art scene
Neolithic Period
7000-2000 B.C.

from Michel Leiris and Jacqueline Delange, *African Art*, 1968, ill. 292

52 (ill. 32)
ancient Egyptian people
Egypt (Northeastern Africa)

seated male noble figure flanked by two small females
stone (quartzite); h. 14 in.
Middle Kingdom, late 12th Dynasty
1848-1786 B.C.

Lent by The Field Museum, Chicago
105188

53 (ill. 33)
Yoruba people
Meko
Nigeria (Western Africa)

Sango staff with multi-figured group
wood, glass, fiber; h. 18 $\frac{3}{4}$ in.
20th century

Indianapolis Museum of Art
Gift of Mr. and Mrs. Harrison Eiteljorg
1989.736

54 (ill. 34)
ancient Egyptian people
Egypt (Northeastern Africa)

female figure flanked by son and husband
stone (steatite); h. 4 $\frac{3}{4}$: in.
Middle Kingdom, 11th-12th Dynasties
2020-1786 B.C.

Lent by the Petrie Museum of Egyptian Archaeology, University College London
UC 16650

55 (ill. 35)
Edo people
Benin Kingdom
Nigeria (Western Africa)

commemorative plaque
brass; h. 18 $\frac{3}{4}$ in.
16th-17th centuries

Lent by The University of Pennsylvania Museum of Archaeology and Anthropology
AF2066

56 (ills. 13,36)
ancient Egyptian people
Egypt (Northeastern Africa)

funerary relief
limestone; 16 $\frac{5}{16}$ in.
New Kingdom, early 18th Dynasty
1550-1389 B.C.

Lent by The Metropolitan Museum of Art
Gift of Mrs. S. W. Straus, 1925
25.184.3

57 (ill. 37)
Pende people
Zaire (Central Africa)

mask with symbolic coloring
wood, pigment, cloth, fiber; h. 8 $\frac{1}{2}$ in.
20th century

Lent by Dr. and Mrs. Wally Zollman
TR 8536/1

EXHIBITION COMPONENTS

58 (ill. 38)
ancient Egyptian people
Saqqara
Egypt (Northeastern Africa)

male figure
limestone; h. 21 ¼ in.
Old Kingdom, 5th Dynasty
2535-2410 B.C.

Indianapolis Museum of Art
Gift of Dr. George A. Reisner, through Alex R. Holliday
28.222

59 (ill. 39)
ancient Egyptian people
Egypt (Northeastern Africa)

male figure
stone; h. 23 3/16 in.
Late Period, 30th Dynasty
about 360 B.C.

Lent by The Metropolitan Museum of Art
Rogers Fund, 1908
08.202.1

60 (ill. 40)
Yoruba people
Nigeria (Western Africa)

male twin figure (ibeji)
wood, pigment; h. 12 ½ in.
20th century

Indianapolis Museum of Art
Gift of Mr. and Mrs. Harrison Eiteljorg
1989.714

61 (ill. 41)
Chokwe people
Angola (Central Africa)

royal male figure
wood; h. 19 in.
19th century

Indianapolis Museum of Art
Gift of Mr. and Mrs. Harrison Eiteljorg
1989.1213

62
ancient Nubian or Egyptian people
Egypt (Northeastern Africa)

female figure
wood; h. 7 3/16 in.
Late Period, 25th Dynasty
712-664 B.C.

Lent by the Museum of Fine Arts, Boston
Gift of William G. Weld
78.158

63
Kaonde people
Zambia (Southern Africa)

female figure
wood; h. 13 in.
20th century

Lent by Marc Felix
TR 8545/2

ANCESTOR WORSHIP AND DIVINE KINGSHIP

64 (see photograph of original, ill. 42)
replica

ancient Egyptian people
Hierakonpolis (Nekhen)
Egypt (Northeastern Africa)

replica of Palette of Narmer
stone; h. 25 9/16 in.
Early Dynastic Period
about 3100 B.C.

Lent by the Petrie Museum of Egyptian Archaeology, University College, London

65 (ill. 43)
ancient Egyptian people
Egypt (Northeastern Africa)

head fragment from figure of Pharaoh Senwosret II
diorite; h. 8 ½ in.
Middle Kingdom, 12th Dynasty
1897-1878 B.C.

Lent by the Walters Art Gallery, Baltimore, Maryland
22.351

66 (ill. 44)
ancient Egyptian people
Egypt (Northeastern Africa)

male ancestor bust of Scribe Ahmose
granite; h. 16 in.
3rd Intermediate Period, 22nd Dynasty
945-712 B.C.

Lent by The Field Museum, Chicago
105172

67 (ill. 45)
photograph

Edo people
Benin Kingdom
Nigeria (Western Africa)

royal procession leaving the city of Benin
17th century

from Armand Duchâteau, *Benin Tresor Royal*, 1990, p. 15

68 (ill. 46)
Edo people
Benin Kingdom
Nigeria (Western Africa)

commemorative head of king
brass, iron inlays; h. 18 in.
19th century

Lent by The University of Pennsylvania Museum of Archaeology and Anthropology
AF5081 BT

69 (ill. 47)
Kota people
Gabon (Central Africa)

reliquary figure
wood, copper, brass; h. 16 ¼ in.
19th-20th centuries

Indianapolis Museum of Art
Gift from the Joseph Cantor Collection
1991.292

70
ancient Egyptian people
Egypt (Northeastern Africa)

female tomb figure (shabti)
glazed ceramic (faience); h. 4 in.
3rd Intermediate Period, 22nd Dynasty
945-712 B.C.

Indianapolis Museum of Art
U422

71
ancient Egyptian people
Egypt (Northeastern Africa)

ba figure
wood, pigment; h. 4 5/16 in.
Ptolemaic (Greek)-Roman Periods
332 B.C.-330 A.D.

Indianapolis Museum of Art
Gift of Mrs. Chauncey Murch
283.14

72
Yoruba people
Igbomina subgroup
area of Ila-orangun
Nigeria (Western Africa)

female twin figure (ibeji)
wood, pigment, glass, fiber; h. 10 15/16 in.
20th century

Indianapolis Museum of Art
Gift of Mr. and Mrs. Harrison Eiteljorg
1989.703

ANIMAL DEITIES AND SYMBOLS

73
photograph

ancient Egyptian people
Abu Simbel
Egypt (Northeastern Africa)

Ramesses II with lion
New Kingdom, 19th Dynasty
1279-1212 B.C.

from Silvio Curto, *Nubien,* 1965, ill. 213

74
photograph

Maasai people
Kenya (Eastern Africa)

Maasai warrior with lion mane headdress
20th century

from Leni Riefenstahl, *Vanishing Africa,* 1982, p. 64

75
photograph

Zulu people
South Africa (Southern Africa)

Zulu warrior with multiple animal regalia (leopard, ostrich, and cattle elements)
19th-century painting

from Aubrey Elliott, *Sons of Zulu,* 1978, p. 61

76
Amhara people
Ethiopia (Northeastern Africa)

warrior's hat
lion mane, cloth, metallic thread; h. 10 in.
19th century

Indianapolis Museum of Art
Mary Black Fund
1995.102 b

77 (ill. 55)
ancient Egyptian people
Saqqara
Egypt (Northeastern Africa)

lion head
alabaster; h. 7 in.
Old Kingdom, 3rd Dynasty
2735-2640 B.C.

Lent by The Brooklyn Museum
Charles Edwin Wilbour Fund
68.152

78 (ill. 56)
ancient Nubian-Meroitic people
Sudan (Northeastern Africa)

double-sided plaque with king and the lion deity Apedemek
slate; h. 7 in.
Meroitic Period
593 B.C.-330 A.D.

Lent by the Walters Art Gallery,
Baltimore, Maryland
22.258

79
ancient Egyptian people
Egypt (Northeastern Africa)

Bes figure
ceramic, pigment; h. 3 in.
Late-Ptolemaic (Greek) Periods
712-30 B.C.

Indianapolis Museum of Art
Mrs. Chauncey Murch
287.14

80 (ill. 48)
Edo people
Benin Kingdom
Nigeria (Western Africa)

leopard head vessel lid
brass; h. 7 ¾ in.
15th-16th centuries

Indianapolis Museum of Art
Alliance Income Fund
1992.61

81
ancient Egyptian people
Egypt (Northeastern Africa)

Taweret goddess figure with hippopotamus, lion, and crocodile features
limestone; h. 2 $\frac{9}{16}$ in.
Late Period, 27th Dynasty
525-405 B.C.

Lent by the Museum of Fine Arts, Boston
Morris and Louise Rosenthal Fund
1973.656

82
probably Akan people
Ghana (Western Africa)

animal-human composite figure
bronze; h. 3 in.
19th-20th century

Lent by Roy and Sophia Sieber
TR 8569

83
Baule people
Côte d'Ivoire (Western Africa)

crocodile figure
counterweight for measuring gold
bronze; h. 2 ¼ in.
20th century

Lent by Martha J. Ehrlich
TR 8538/2

84 (ill. 53)
ancient Egyptian people
Saqqara
Egypt (Northeastern Africa)

Apis bull figure
bronze; h. 4 ⅞ in.
Late Period, 26th Dynasty-Ptolemaic (Greek) Periods
663-30 B.C.

Lent by the Walters Art Gallery,
Baltimore, Maryland
54.538

85 (ill. 49)
Karagwe people
Tanzania (Eastern Africa)

cattle figure
iron; h. 16 ⅛ in.
19th-20th centuries

Lent anonymously
TR 8545/3

86
ancient Egyptian people
Egypt (Northeastern Africa)

vessel with cattle imagery
glazed ceramic (faience); h. 5 in.
New Kingdom, 18-20th Dynasties
1550-1070 B.C.

Lent by The Field Museum, Chicago
31555

87 (ill. 54)
Bidjogo people
Guinea-Bissau (Western Africa)

mask
wood, horn, pigment, glass, iron; h. 18 in.
19th-20th centuries

Indianapolis Museum of Art
Gift of Mr. and Mrs. Harrison Eiteljorg
1989.375

MASKING

88
photograph

unidentified people
Tassili Plateau
Algeria (Northern Africa)

rock art masker
Neolithic Period
7000-2000 B.C.

from Michel Leiris and Jacqueline Delange, *African Art,* 1968, ill. 288

89 (ill. 59)
photograph

unidentified people
Tassili Plateau
Algeria (Northern Africa)

rock art masker outline
Neolithic Period
7000-4000 B.C.

from Henri Lhote, *The Search for the Tassili Frescoes,* 1959, pl. 37

90 (ill. 60)
Bobo people
Burkina Faso (Western Africa)

mask
wood, pigment, fiber; h. 58 ½ in.
20th century

Indianapolis Museum of Art
Mr. and Mrs. Harrison Eiteljorg
1989.249

91 (ill. 62)
ancient Egyptian people
Egypt (Northeastern Africa)

Anubis (jackal) helmet mask
ceramic, pigment; h. 19 5/16 in.
probably Late Period
600-300 B.C. (or later)

Lent by Pelizaeus Museum
Hildesheim, Germany
1585

92 (ill. 63)
photograph

ancient Egyptian people
Dendera
Egypt (Northeastern Africa)

line drawing of wall relief in Temple of Hathor showing Anubis helmet-masked priest
Ptolemaic (Greek)-Roman Periods
332 B.C.-330 A.D.

from Auguste Mariette, *Denderah IV.*, 1873, pl. 31

93 (ill. 64)
photograph

ancient Egyptian people
Egypt (Northeastern Africa)

papyrus painting with masked priest of Anubis
New Kingdom, 19th Dynasty
1300 B.C.

from Stephen Quirke and Jeffrey Spencer, *The British Museum Book of Ancient Egypt,* 1992, ill. 113

94 (ill. 58)
Yoruba people
Nigeria (Western Africa)

Egungun helmet mask
wood, pigment; h. 12 in.
20th century

Indianapolis Museum of Art
Gift of Mr. and Mrs. Harrison Eiteljorg
1989.750

95 (ill. 57)
photograph

Yoruba people
Nigeria (Western Africa)

Egungun masking scene
20th century

Courtesy of John Pemberton III

96
ancient Egyptian people
Egypt (Northeastern Africa)

mummy mask
linen, plaster, papyrus, pigment, gilding; h. 14 3/4: in.
Greek (Ptolemaic) Period
332-30 B.C.

Indianapolis Museum of Art
Emma Harter Sweetser Fund
28.243

97 (ill. 65)
photograph

ancient Egyptian people
Egypt (Northeastern Africa)

detail of stone palette with masked hunter stalking ostriches
Protodynastic Period, Naqada III
3300-3100 B.C.

Courtesy of The Manchester Museum,
University of Manchester, England
5476

98
probably Hausa people
Nigeria (Western Africa)

decoy worn on hunter's head
bird's skull, leather; h. 15 1/2 in.
20th century

Indianapolis Museum of Art
Gift of Butler University
1988.126

BODY ART

99 (ill. 66)
photograph

unidentified people
Algeria (Northern Africa)

body art depicted on rock art
Neolithic Period
7000-2000 B.C.

from Henri Lhote, *The Search for the Tassili Frescoes,* 1959, fig. 39

100 (ill. 70)
photograph

ancient Egyptian people
Egypt (Northeastern Africa)

female ceramic figure with body art
Predynastic Period
Naqada I or II
4500-3300 B.C.

The Metropolitan Museum of Art
07.228.71

101 (ill. 73)
photograph

ancient Egyptian people
Thebes-Luxor
Egypt (Northeastern Africa)

Libyan with body art from tomb of Sety I
New Kingdom
1291-1279 B.C.

from Ippolito Rosellini, *Monumenti dell' Egitto e della Nubia, Monumenti istorici,* 1834, pls. CLV, CIVI

102
ancient Egyptian people
Egypt (Northeastern Africa)

mirror with female figure depicting tattoos or body painting
bronze; h. 9 ⅛ in.
New Kingdom, late 18th Dynasty
1350-1293 B.C.

Lent by The Brooklyn Museum
Charles Edwin Wilbour Fund
60.27.1

103 (ill. 72)
ancient Egyptian people
Egypt (Northeastern Africa)

female figure with tattoos or body painting
glazed ceramic (faience); h. 5 in.
Middle Kingdom, 12th Dynasty
1991-1786 B.C.

Lent by The Metropolitan Museum of Art
Rogers Fund, 1908
08.200.18

104 (ill. 71)
photograph

ancient Egyptian people
Thebes-Luxor
Egypt (Northeastern Africa)

drawing of tattooed woman based on mummy from tomb complex of Nebhepetra Mentuhotep II
Middle Kingdom, 11th Dynasty
2060-2010 B.C.

Courtesy of The Metropolitan Museum of Art

105 (ill. 69)
Kuba people
Zaire (Central Africa)

female figure with scarification or other form of body art
wood, pigment; h. 25 ¾ in.
19th-20th centuries

Lent by Dr. and Mrs. Wally Zollman
TR 8536/2

106
Igbo people
Nigeria (Western Africa)

figurative group with two females depicting body painting and tattooing
wood, pigment, metal; h. 30 in.
20th century

Indianapolis Museum of Art
Gift of Mr. and Mrs. Harrison Eiteljorg
1995.122

107 (ill. 67)
photograph

Makonde people
Mozambique or Kenya (Eastern Africa)

woman with tattoos
20th century

from Michel Leiris and Jacqueline Delange, *African Art*, 1968, ill. 121

108 (ill. 68)
photograph

Berber people
Morocco (Northern Africa)

woman with skin painting and tattoos
20th century

from Angela Fisher, *Africa Adorned*, 1984, p. 226

109 (ill. 74)
photograph

ancient Egyptian people
Egypt (Northeastern Africa)

relief of Nubian man with forehead scarification
stone
New Kingdom, 20th Dynasty
Ramesses III
1181-1150 B.C.

Courtesy of The Oriental Institute Museum, University of Chicago
14648

110 (ill. 75)
photograph

Nuer people
Sudan (Northeastern Africa)

man with forehead scarification
20th century

from C. G. Seligman, *Pagan Tribes of the Nilotic Sudan*, 1932, pl. XX

CIRCUMCISION AND MALE INITIATION

111 (ill. 76)
photograph

ancient Egyptian people
Saqqara
Egypt (Northeastern Africa)

circumcision scene from tomb of Ankh-ma-hor
limestone
Old Kingdom, 6th Dynasty
2410-2250 B.C.

Courtesy of Frank J. Yurco

112 (ill. 77)
photograph

Yaka people
Pasanganga
Zaire (Central Africa)

male initiation scene immediately after circumcision

Courtesy of Arthur P. Bourgeois, 1976

113 (ill. 78)
photograph

ancient Egyptian people
Naga ed-Deir
Egypt (Northeastern Africa)

funerary relief with circumcision text
limestone, pigment
1st Intermediate Period, 9th-11th Dynasties
2230-2020 B.C.

Courtesy of The Oriental Institute Museum, University of Chicago
16956

114
Dan people
Liberia (Western Africa)

circumcision knife
wood, iron; h. 4 $^{11}/_{16}$ in.
20th century

Indianapolis Museum of Art
Gift of Charles D. Miller III
7994.93.2

115
ancient Egyptian people
Egypt (Northeastern Africa)

figure with circumcised penis
limestone, pigment; h. 2 in.
New Kingdom, 18th-20th Dynasties
1550-1070 B.C.

Lent by The Field Museum, Chicago
30389

116
Yoruba people
Nigeria (Western Africa)

Sango staff with penis handle
wood, pigment; h. 19 $^{1}/_{4}$ in.
20th century

Lent by Mr. and Mrs. Harrison Eiteljorg
TR 8411

NUBIA

117 (ill. 79)
map

ancient Nubia and Egypt
4000 B.C.-1000 A.D.

Indianapolis Museum of Art

118
photograph

ancient Egyptian people
Giza
Egypt (Northeastern Africa)

Egyptian pyramids
Old Kingdom, 4th Dynasty
2640-2535 B.C.

Courtesy of Frank J. Yurco

119
photograph

ancient Nubian people
Meroe
Sudan (Northeastern Africa)

Nubian pyramids
Meroitic period
593 B.C.-253 A.D.

Courtesy of William J. Murnane

120 (ill. 84)
photograph

ancient Nubian people
Qustul
Egypt (Northeastern Africa)

incense burner
clay
Protodynastic Period, A-Group
3300-3100 B.C.

Courtesy of The Oriental Institute Museum, University of Chicago
24069

121 (ill. 85)

photograph

roll out drawing of Qustul incense burner

Courtesy of The Oriental Institute Museum, University of Chicago

122
ancient Nubian people
Kerma
Sudan (Northeastern Africa)

vessel
ceramic; diam. 6 $^{9}/_{16}$ in.
Kerma Classic Period
2000-1500 B.C.

Lent by the Museum of Fine Arts, Boston
Harvard University-Museum of Fine Arts Expedition
21.11863

123
ancient Nubian people
Sudan (Northeastern Africa)

vessel with giraffe imagery
ceramic; h. 14 $^{3}/_{8}$ in.
Meroitic Period
593 B.C.-330 A.D.

Lent by The University of Pennsylvania Museum of Archaeology and Anthropology
E8213

124
photograph

ancient Nubian people
Sudan (Northeastern Africa)

Winifred Brunton's 20th-century painting of Taharqa
Late Period, 25th Dynasty
690-664 B.C.
from Winifred Brunton, *Great Ones of Ancient Egypt,* 1929

125 (ill. 86)
photograph

ancient Nubian-Egyptian people
Kawa
Sudan (Northeastern Africa)

sphinx of King Taharqa
stone
Late Period, 25th Dynasty
690-664 B.C.

Courtesy of the Trustees of the British Museum
EA 1770

126 (ill. 87)
ancient Nubian people
Nuri
Sudan (Northeastern Africa)

tomb figure (shabti) of King Taharqa
granite; h. 12 $\frac{1}{2}$ in.
3rd Intermediate Period, 25th Dynasty
690-664 B.C.

Lent by the Museum of Fine Arts, Boston
Harvard University-Museum of Fine Arts Expedition
21.2975

127
ancient Nubian people
Nuri
Sudan (Northeastern Africa)

tomb figure (shabti) of King Taharqa
granite; h. 12 $\frac{1}{8}$ in.
3rd Intermediate Period, 25th Dynasty
690-664 B.C.

Lent by the Museum of Fine Arts, Boston
Harvard University-Museum of Fine Arts Expedition
20.222 (Unreg)

128
ancient Nubian or Egyptian people
Sudan or Egypt (Northeastern Africa)

ram head pendant
glazed ceramic (faience); h. 2 in.
Late Period, 25th Dynasty
712-664 B.C.

Lent by The Metropolitan Museum of Art
Gift of Edward S. Harkness, 1935
35.9.8

129
ancient Egyptian or Nubian people
Egypt (Northeastern Africa)

donation stela of Pa-tjenfi
limestone; h. 12 in.
3rd Intermediate Period, 25th Dynasty
Pharaoh Shebitku
701-690 B.C.

Lent by The Metropolitan Museum of Art
Rogers Fund, 1965
65.45

130
photograph

ancient Egyptian people
Thebes-Luxor
Egypt (Northeastern Africa)

wall painting fragment from tomb of Rekhmire
Nubian tribute scene (ostrich eggs, elephant tusk, tropical wood, baboon, animal pelt)
New Kingdom, 18th Dynasty
1504-1450 B.C.

from Jean Vercoutter, *The Image of the Black in Western Art,* 1976, fig. 15

131
photograph

ancient Egyptian people
Thebes-Luxor
Egypt (Northeastern Africa)

wall painting fragment from tomb of Sebekhotep
Nubian tribute scene (gold rings, tropical wood, feathers, leopard pelt, possibly incense balls)
New Kingdom, 18th Dynasty
1504-1325 B.C.

from Stephen Quirke and Jeffery Spencer, *The British Museum Book of Ancient Egypt,* 1992, ill. 160

132
ancient Egyptian people
Egypt (Northeastern Africa)

throwing stick
wood (ebony); l. 28 $\frac{5}{16}$ in.
1st Intermediate Period, 7th-10th Dynasties
2230-2020 B.C.

Lent by the Museum of Fine Arts, Boston
Harvard University-Museum of Fine Arts Expedition
12.1242

133
Beja people
Sudan (Northeastern Africa)

throwing stick
wood; l. 27 $\frac{9}{16}$ in.
20th century

Lent by the Museum of Fine Arts, Boston
Gift of Timothy Kendall
1991.246

134 (ill. 80)
ancient Egyptian people
Lisht
Egypt (Northeastern Africa)

musical clapper
ivory; l. 7 7/8 in.
Middle Kingdom, 12th Dynasty
1991-1786 B.C.

Lent by the Indiana University Art Museum
William Lowe Bryan Memorial
58.20

135 (ill. 81)
Zulu people
South Africa (Southern Africa)

snuff spoon
ivory; l. 6 1/8 in.
20th century

Lent by Roy and Sophia Sieber
TR 8457

136
probably San people
Namibia or South Africa (Southern Africa)

necklace or waist beads
ostrich egg shell; l. 38 in.
19th-20th centuries

Indianapolis Museum of Art
Gift of Mrs. Boyd (Evelyn Roberts) Burkhardt
3985.81.1L

137
ancient Egyptian people
Egypt (Northeastern Africa)

Bes image
glazed ceramic (faience); h. 1 5/16 in.
Late Period, 26th Dynasty
656-525 B.C.

Indianapolis Museum of Art
Mrs. Chauncey Murch
286.147

138
ancient Egyptian people
Abydos
Egypt (Northeastern Africa)

necklace
amethyst; l. 14 1/2 in.
Middle Kingdom, 11-12th Dynasties
2020-1786 B.C.

Lent by The University of Pennsylvania Museum of Archaeology and Anthropology
E9201

139
ancient Egyptian people
Egypt (Northeastern Africa)

necklace
glazed ceramic (faience), modern stringing; l. 31 in.
3rd Intermediate Period, probably 21st Dynasty
1070-945 B.C.

Indianapolis Museum of Art
Gift of Marie Khayat in memory of her father, Mr. Azeez Khayat
70.118.1

140
ancient Egyptian people
Egypt (Northeastern Africa)

vessel
stone (alabaster); h. 1 1/4 in.
New Kingdom, 18th-20th Dynasties
1550-1070 B.C.

Indianapolis Museum of Art
Emma Harter Sweetser Fund
28.269

141 (ill. 82)
ancient Egyptian people
Lisht
Egypt (Northeastern Africa)

ornament in cowrie shell form
gold; l. 5/8 in.
Middle Kingdom, 12th-13th Dynasties
about 1991-1650 B.C.

Lent by The Metropolitan Museum of Art
Rogers Fund, 1909
09.180.1200

142 (ill. 83)
unidentified people
Western Africa

cowrie shell
l. 3/8 in.
19th-20th centuries

Indianapolis Museum of Art
unaccessioned object

143
ancient Egyptian people
Lisht
Egypt (Northeastern Africa)

ornament in seashell form
gold; l. 1 in.
Middle Kingdom, late 12th Dynasty
about 1850-1800 B.C.

Lent by The Metropolitan Museum of Art
Rogers Fund, 1907
07.227.18

EXHIBITION COMPONENTS

144
probably Asante people
Ghana (Western Africa)

ruler's crown
gold, cotton, wood, paper, mastic; w. $7\frac{1}{2}$ in.
19th-20th centuries

Indianapolis Museum of Art
Gift of Mr. and Mrs. Harrison Eiteljorg
1989.475

145
ancient Nubian people
Sudan (Northeastern Africa)

harpoon or arrow point
iron; l. $3\frac{3}{4}$ in.
Meroitic Period
593 B.C.-330 A.D.

Lent by The University of Pennsylvania Museum of Archaeology and Anthropology
E7263

146
ancient Nubian people
Sudan (Northeastern Africa)

cosmetic applicator
iron; l. $10\frac{1}{4}$ in.
Meroitic Period
593 B.C.-330 A.D.

Lent by The University of Pennsylvania Museum of Archaeology and Anthropology
E7383

147
Dan people
Liberia (Western Africa)

miniature ritual spear
iron; l. $9\frac{1}{4}$ in.
20th century

Lent by Charles D. Miller III
TR 8455

FACES OF EGYPT

148 (ill. 94)
ancient Egyptian people
Egypt (Northeastern Africa)

head fragment, possibly of Pharaoh Narmer
limestone; h. $4\frac{13}{16}$ in.
possibly Early Dynastic Period
about 3100 B.C.

Lent by the Petrie Museum of Egyptian Archaeology, University College London
UC 15989

149
ancient Egyptian people
Egypt (Northeastern Africa)

head of noble (fragment)
granite; h. $8\frac{1}{4}$ in.
New Kingdom, 18th Dynasty, Pharaoh Amenhotep III
1389-1350 B.C.

Lent by the Museum of Fine Arts, Boston
Gift by contribution
07.644

150
ancient Egyptian people
Abydos
Egypt (Northeastern Africa)

head from female figure (fragment)
sandstone; h. $7\frac{3}{8}$ in.
New Kingdom, 19th Dynasty
1293-1184 B.C.

Lent by the Petrie Museum of Egyptian Archaeology, University College London
UC 14641

151 (ill. 88)
photograph

ancient Nubian or Egyptian people
Egypt (Northeastern Africa)

head of Nubian or Egyptian woman from royal tomb
limestone
Old Kingdom, 4th Dynasty
2640-2535 B.C.

Courtesy of Museum of Fine Arts, Boston
14.719

152
photograph

ancient Egyptian people
Egypt (Northeastern Africa)

probably Queen Tiye
wood
New Kingdom, 18th Dynasty
1389-1350 B.C.

Courtesy of Ägyptisches Museum SMPK, Berlin
21834

153 (ill. 95)
ancient Egyptian people
Egypt (Northeastern Africa)

face of Pharaoh Senwosret III (fragment)
stone (quartzite); h. $3\frac{11}{16}$ in.
Middle Kingdom, 12th Dynasty
1878-1843 B.C.

Lent by the Petrie Museum of Egyptian Archaeology, University College London
UC 13249

154
photograph

ancient Egyptian people
Egypt (Northeastern Africa)
20th-century

Winifred Brunton's 20th-century painting of Pharaoh Senwosret III
Middle Kingdom, 12th Dynasty
1878-1843 B.C.

from Winifred Brunton, *Kings and Queens of Ancient Egypt,* 1926

155
ancient Egyptian people
Saqqara
Egypt (Northeastern Africa)

figure of bound male Nubian captive
bronze; h. 5 ¾ in.
New Kingdom, late 18th Dynasty
1389-1321 B.C.

Lent by The Brooklyn Museum
Charles Edwin Wilbour Fund
37.267E

156 (ill. 89)
ancient Egyptian people
Egypt (Northeastern Africa)

relief with profile head
sculptor's model or votive object
limestone; h. 4 ⅛ in.
Ptolemaic (Greek) Period
about 332-30 B.C.

Indianapolis Museum of Art
E. Hardey Adriance Fine Arts Acquisition Fund
1995.68

157 (ill. 96)
ancient Egyptian people
Egypt (Northeastern Africa)

male-female couple (fragment)
limestone; h. 5 15/16 in.
New Kingdom, Early 18th Dynasty
1550-1389 B.C.

Lent by the Petrie Museum of Egyptian Archaeology, University College London
UC 15513

158
ancient Egyptian people
Egypt (Northeastern Africa)

figure of Lady Tuty
wood, paint, gilding; h. 10 ¼ in.
New Kingdom, late 18th Dynasty
Pharaoh Amenhotep III
1389-1350 B.C.

Lent by The Brooklyn Museum
Charles Edwin Wilbour Fund
54.187

159 (ill. 92)
photograph

ancient Egyptian people
Thebes-Luxor
Egypt (Northeastern Africa)

drawing of painted wall relief in tomb of Sety I
New Kingdom, 19th Dynasty
1291-1279 B.C.

from Ippolita Rosellini, *Monumenti dell' Egitto e della Nubia, Monumenti istorici,* 1843, plates CLV, CLVI

160 (ill. 93)
photograph

ancient Egyptian people
Thebes-Luxor
Egypt (Northeastern Africa)

painted wall relief in tomb of Sety I
New Kingdom, 19th Dynasty
1291-1279 B.C.

from Erik Hornung, *The Tomb of Pharaoh Seti I,* 1991, pls. 58-59, p.122-123

161 (ill. 90)
photograph

ancient Egyptian people
Thebes-Luxor
Egypt (Northeastern Africa)

drawing of painted wall relief from the tomb of Ramesses III
New Kingdom
1181-1150 B.C.

from Kurt Sethe, *Denkmaler aus Aegypten und Aethiopen Eganzungband,* 1913

162 (ill. 91)
photograph

ancient Egyptian people
Thebes-Luxor
Egypt (Northeastern Africa)

painted wall in the tomb of Ramesses III
New Kingdom
1181-1150 B.C.

from Erik Hornung, *The Valley of the Kings: Horizon of Eternity,* 1990, pls. 107-109

163
photograph

ancient Egyptian people
Egypt (Northeastern Africa)

Queen Kemsit with attendants
painted tomb wall
Middle Kingdom, 11th Dynasty
2061-2010 B.C.

from Joyce L. Haynes, *Nubia: Ancient Kingdoms of Africa,* 1992, fig. 8

164
photograph

ancient Egyptian people
Egypt (Northeastern Africa)

funerary relief depicting a Nubian and his wife (with supporting text)
First Intermediate Period, 9th-11th Dynasties
2230-2020 B.C.

Phoebe Hearst Museum of Anthropology
University of California, Berkeley
6.19911

165
photograph

ancient Egyptian people
Egypt (Northeastern Africa)

painted wall relief
Ramesses II with heads of non-Egyptian enemies
New Kingdom, 19th Dynasty
1279-1212 B.C.

from Mohamed Saleh and Hourig Sourouzian, *Official Catalogue: The Egyptian Museum, Cairo,* 1987, ill. 206

166
videos

The Ten Commandments, Paramount Pictures Corporation, 1956

The Giant Nile, Egyptian Journey, Blue Bird Films, 1990

167
photograph

Egyptian woman from northern Egypt
Northeastern Africa

Courtesy of Timothy Kendall

168
photograph

Egyptian man from southern Egypt
Northeastern Africa

Courtesy of Theodore Celenko

169
photograph

Egyptian man from southern Egypt
Northeastern Africa

Courtesy of Timothy Kendall

170
photograph

Berber woman from Morocco
Northwestern Africa

from Angela Fischer, *Africa Adorned*, 1984

171
photograph

Mangbetu woman from Zaire
Central Africa

Courtesy of Eliot Elisofon Archives,
National Museum of African Art,
Smithsonian Institution

172
photograph

Amhara woman from Ethiopia
Eastern Africa

Courtesy of Bruktawit Asfaw

173
photograph

Egbira man from Nigeria
Western Africa

Courtesy of Theodore Celenko

174
photograph

Hassaniya girl from Sudan
Northeastern Africa

Courtesy of Timothy Kendall

175
photograph

San woman from South Africa
Southern Africa

Courtesy of the Marshall Family Archives
Documentary Educational Resources